T0394734

.

Metaphor and the Portrayal of the Cause(s) of Sin and Evil in the Gospel of Matthew

Biblical Interpretation Series

Editors-in-Chief

Paul Anderson (*George Fox University*)
Jennifer L. Koosed (*Albright College, Reading*)

Editorial Board

A.K.M. Adam (*University of Oxford*)
Colleen M. Conway (*Seton Hall University*)
Nijay Gupta (*Portland Seminary*)
Amy Kalmanofsky (*Jewish Theological Seminary*)
Vernon Robbins (*Emory University*)
Annette Schellenberg (*Universität Wien*)
Johanna Stiebert (*University of Leeds*)
Duane Watson (*Malone University*)
Christine Roy Yoder (*Columbia Theological Seminary*)
Ruben Zimmermann (*Johannes Gutenberg-Universität Mainz*)

VOLUME 182

The titles published in this series are listed at *brill.com/bins*

Metaphor and the Portrayal of the Cause(s) of Sin and Evil in the Gospel of Matthew

By

Judith V. Stack

BRILL

LEIDEN | BOSTON

Library of Congress Cataloging-in-Publication Data

Names: Stack, Judith V., author.
Title: Metaphor and the portrayal of the cause(s) of sin and evil in the
  Gospel of Matthew / by Judith V. Stack.
Other titles: Metaphorical portrayals of the causes of sin and evil in the
  Gospel of Matthew
Description: Leiden ; Boston : Brill, [2020] | Series: Biblical
  interpretation series, 0928-0731 ; volume 182 | Revision of the author's
  thesis (doctoral)—Princeton Theological Seminary, 2013, under the
  title: The metaphorical portrayals of the causes of sin and evil in the
  Gospel of Matthew. | Includes bibliographical references and index.
Identifiers: LCCN 2019059345 (print) | LCCN 2019059346 (ebook) |
  ISBN 9789004418844 (hardback) | ISBN 9789004419506 (ebook)
Subjects: LCSH: Bible. Matthew—Criticisim, interpretation, etc. |
  Sin—Biblical teaching. | Good and evil—Biblical teaching. | Metaphor
  in the Bible.
Classification: LCC BS2575.6.S45 S83 2020 (print) | LCC BS2575.6.S45
  (ebook) | DDC 226.2/06—dc23
LC record available at https://lccn.loc.gov/2019059345
LC ebook record available at https://lccn.loc.gov/2019059346

Typeface for the Latin, Greek, and Cyrillic scripts: "Brill". See and download: brill.com/brill-typeface.

ISSN 0928-0731
ISBN 978-90-04-41884-4 (hardback)
ISBN 978-90-04-41950-6 (e-book)

Copyright 2020 by Koninklijke Brill NV, Leiden, The Netherlands.
Koninklijke Brill NV incorporates the imprints Brill, Brill Hes & De Graaf, Brill Nijhoff, Brill Rodopi,
Brill Sense, Hotei Publishing, mentis Verlag, Verlag Ferdinand Schöningh and Wilhelm Fink Verlag.
All rights reserved. No part of this publication may be reproduced, translated, stored in a retrieval system,
or transmitted in any form or by any means, electronic, mechanical, photocopying, recording or otherwise,
without prior written permission from the publisher.
Authorization to photocopy items for internal or personal use is granted by Koninklijke Brill NV provided
that the appropriate fees are paid directly to The Copyright Clearance Center, 222 Rosewood Drive,
Suite 910, Danvers, MA 01923, USA. Fees are subject to change.

This book is printed on acid-free paper and produced in a sustainable manner.

Contents

Acknowledgements   VII
Abbreviations   VIII

Introduction   1
1   Why a Study of Sin Metaphors?   1
2   Metaphor: What Does It Do and How Does It Do It?   2

PART 1
The Question of Whence Sin and Evil in the Texts of Matthew's Milieu

1   **Diversity and Consistency in the Texts of Matthew's Milieu**   27
   1   Dualism and Dualisms: A Brief Taxonomy   31

2   **Enochic Literature**   35
   1   1 Enoch   35
   2   Jubilees   44

3   **4 Ezra**   60

4   **2 Baruch**   66

5   **Sirach**   71

6   **Qumran Texts**   84
   1   War Scroll (1QM)   84
   2   The Hodayot (1QH)   87
   3   Damascus Document (CD)   94
   4   The Rule of the Community (1QS)   97
   5   Summary of Qumran Literature   101

7   **Conclusion on Texts of Matthew's Milieu**   103

VI
                                                                CONTENTS

PART 2
The Portrayal of the Causes of Sin and Evil in the Gospel of Matthew

8 Review of Previous Scholarship 107
  1 *Righteousness in Matthew and His World of Thought* by Benno Przybylski 107
  2 *Matthew and Paul: A Comparison of Ethical Perspectives* by Roger Mohrlang 110

9 Exegesis of the Portrayal of the Causes of Sin and Evil in Matthew 113
  1 The Use of ἁμαρτ- in Matthew 113
  2 Πλανάω, σκανδαλίζω, and σκάνδαλον 123

10 Metaphors for the Cause of Sin 137
  1 Metaphors of Body Parts as the Cause of Sin 137
  2 Metaphors of Illness and Infirmity for the Cause of Sin 147
    Excursus: Sin, Righteousness, the Kingdom, and the Will of God 152
  3 The Metaphor of the Heart as a Cause of Sin 165

11 Genetic and Familial Metaphors for the Cause of Sin 172
  1 Tree and Fruit Metaphors 172
  2 Animal Metaphors 177
  3 Familial Metaphors 183
  4 Summary 189

12 Satanic Activity as a Cause of Sin 190
  1 Summary 198

13 Conclusion on Causes of Sin and Evil in the Gospel of Matthew 199

14 Summary 201

  Conclusion: The Significance of Metaphorical Dynamics in Portraying the Causes of Sin and Evil for the Theology of Matthew's Gospel 202

  Bibliography 207
  Index of Ancient Texts 215
  Index of Subjects and Terms 218

Acknowledgements

No project of this size comes to completion without the help and support of many people, all of whom deserve thanks and only a few of whom can be thanked, however inadequately, on these pages. Thanks must go first and foremost to my family. Their love and their support of my work were beyond what I or anyone deserved. I owe much to my parents, Barrett and Karen Stack, and their enthusiasm and support for my work.

To the good people at Brill, especially series editor Paul Anderson, not only for the opportunity to work with them on this project, but for Paul's encouragement and appreciation of my work for years prior.

All of this would not have been possible without the opportunity to pursue doctoral work given me by Princeton Theological Seminary. The teaching and mentorship in rigorous biblical scholarship that I received from the faculty of the Bible department is a treasure from which I will draw for a lifetime. Among those teachers, special thanks must go to my dissertation advisor, George Parsenios. His unfailing encouragement and enthusiasm for my project were as necessary to its completion as his sage advice, and the collegial independence he allowed me in its pursuit was a rare and true gift.

I would be remiss if I did not mention at least a few of my colleagues who especially deserve my thanks. My PTS colleague Carla Works was an unfailing source of encouragement, kindness, and good advice as well as commiseration. In the dissertation stage and in the process of revision, the friendship and theological conversation of Robin McCall, Kenneth Reynhout, J.R. Daniel Kirk, and A.K.M. Adam helped refine my thinking and gave me strength in the most needed moments.

Finally, thanks are due to those who set my feet upon the path of this journey: my teacher-mentors. To the late Timothy Polk of Hamline University for introducing me to the academic study of the Bible and profound joy that it can be. To Patrick Keifert of Luther Seminary for not only teaching me systematic theology and how it can fruitfully interact with biblical studies, but for being a stalwart champion of my pursuits and source of good advice. And to the late Donald Juel of Luther Seminary and Princeton Theological Seminary who, in his unflinching openness to the disruptive voice of scripture and commitment to teaching and scholarship, stands as my ideal of a professor of the New Testament. It is to his memory that this book is dedicated.

Abbreviations

AB	Anchor Bible
ABD	*Anchor Bible Dictionary*
ABR	*Australian Biblical Review*
ABRL	Anchor Bible Reference Library
Apoph. Lac.	Plutarch, *Apophthegmata laconica*
B.J.	Josephus, *Bellum Judaicum*
BibRev	*Bible Review*
Bsac	*Bibliotheca sacra*
BDB	Brown, Driver, and Briggs, *A Hebrew and English Lexicon of the Old Testament*
BTB	*Biblical Theology Bulletin*
CBQ	*Catholic Biblical Quarterly*
Crat.	Plato, *Cratylus*
CSCO	Corpus Scriptorum Christianorum Orientalium
DBAG	Danker, Bauer, Arndt, and Gingrich, *Greek-English Lexicon of the New Testament and Other Early Christian Literature*
DSS	Dead Sea Scrolls
EDNT	*Exegetical Dictionary of the New Testament*
ESV	English Standard Version
ET	English translation
HBT	*Horizons in Biblical Theology*
HTR	*Harvard Theological Review*
HUCA	*Hebrew Union College Annual*
Hyp.	Philo, *Hypothetica*
ICC	International Critical Commentary
JBL	*Journal of Biblical Literature*
JSJ	*Journal for the Study of Judaism in the Persian, Hellenistic, and Roman Periods*
JSNTSup	Journal for the Study of the New Testament: Supplement Series
JSP	*Journal for the Study of the Pseudepigrapha*
JSPSup	Journal for the Study of the Pseudepigrapha: Supplement Series
JTS	*Journal of Theological Studies*
LCL	Loeb Classic Library
LEC/LNTS	Library of Early Christianity /Library of New Testament Studies
LSJ	Liddell, Scott, and Jones, *Greek-English Lexicon*
LXX	Septuagint
Mek.	Mekilta

ABBREVIATIONS

MT	Masoretic text
NAB	New American Bible
Nat. Hist.	Pliny, *Natural History*
NIDOTTE	*New International Dictionary of Old Testament Theology and Exegesis*
NovT	*Novum Testamentum*
NRSV	New Revised Standard Version
NT	New Testament
NTS	*New Testament Studies*
OT	Old Testament
OTP	*Old Testament Pseudepigrapha*, Charlesworth, ed.
Poet.	Aristotle, *Poetics*
Prob.	Philo, *Quod omnis probus liber sit*
PTSDSSP	Princeton Theological Seminary Dead Sea Scrolls Project
ResQ	*Restoration Quarterly*
Rhet.	Aristotle, *Rhetoric*
SBLDS	Society of Biblical Literature Dissertation Series
SBT^2	Studies in Biblical Theology, second series
SJOT	*Scandinavian Journal of the Old Testament*
SJSJ	Supplements to the Journal for the Study of Judaism
SNTSMS	Society for New Testament Studies Monograph Series
StPB	Studia Post-Biblica
TDNT	*Theological Dictionary of the New Testament*
THKNT	Theologischer Handkommentar zum Neuen Testament

Introduction

1   Why a Study of Sin Metaphors?

This project grows out of an initial interest in a larger question—and one particularly thorny and under-explored—regarding the Gospel of Matthew, namely, Matthew's understanding of the role that Jesus' death and particularly his resurrection play in the accomplishment of Jesus' work as the Messiah of Israel and savior. Pursuing this question, however, requires first an examination of a smaller but foundational question regarding the Gospel: if, in Matthew's view, Jesus' work (considered holistically) has the effect of rectifying a human/world situation that was not what God desires ("sin"), what were the features of that situation? Put somewhat colloquially, if Jesus' life, death, and resurrection fixes what was wrong with humanity (and perhaps the world), what is the problem that it fixes? What is wrong with humans (and again, perhaps the world) such that Jesus' death and resurrection is integral to the solution? Thus, I took on a project of looking at the source or cause of sin and evil (not merely the definition of it) in the Gospel of Matthew.

In looking at passages in Matthew that indicate a source or cause of sin, it soon became apparent that a dichotomous paradigm that tried to sort the relevant passages into "human agency" (free will in some sense) vs. "spiritual agency" (the work of the devil or some version of "original sin") was too simplistic to represent Matthew's portrayal. In fact, Matthew's ways of talking about this question were more complex in two ways. First, even a cursory glance at Matthew's passages on the topic showed that Matthew rarely addressed the topic forthrightly. Unlike a number of Second Temple Jewish writers, Matthew offers no explicit reflection on the source of sin and evil. Instead, we find in Matthew a consistent use of metaphorical or parabolic language for the cause or source of sin. The use of metaphors introduces complex dynamics that need to be addressed in interpreting the passages. Secondly, the metaphors themselves are diverse in their imagery, spanning a range from sources highly external to humans to others that are highly internal. The overall picture portrayed through Matthew's use of these metaphors—and ultimately the significance of this portrayal as a prolegomenon for exploring Matthean soteriology—is the focus of this study.

While a number of authors have explored in the significance of metaphor and metaphorical dynamics in New Testament texts, especially with regard

---

© KONINKLIJKE BRILL NV, LEIDEN, 2020 | DOI:10.1163/9789004419506_002

to the parables and the kingdom of God/heaven,[1] there is currently no major study of this with respect to Matthew's Gospel. Drawing from this previous work and crucial for the present study, however, is the fundamental perspective agreed upon by many biblical scholars and most modern metaphor theorists that metaphors are not merely poetic ways of expressing an idea that can be translated into plain language but are "tensive" speech—that which embodies a tension, a profound "yes and no," an "is and is not"—the very tension of which imparts a new vision of reality to the hearer or reader.[2] Much of this work grows out of the insights of Paul Ricoeur, particularly those found in his *Rule of Metaphor*, a work that will be the focus of sustained attention in the discussion of the nature and functioning of metaphor in the rest of the introduction.

Thus, this study will explore the portrayal of the causes of sin and evil found in the Gospel of Matthew by first developing a contextual framework through examination of a variety of Second Temple Jewish texts that are also concerned with the cause or source of sin and/or evil (Part 1). Following that, I will examine various passages from the Gospel itself, focusing particularly on the metaphorical images used to portray the cause of sin and evil and their relation to Matthew's most explicit depiction of the cause, the person of the devil in the Parable of the Wheat and the Tares (Part 2). In the conclusion, I will briefly propose some ways in which the use of metaphor and the impact of metaphorical dynamics are significant in the understanding and articulation of the causes of sin and evil, proposals that have significance for other theological topics (soteriology, ecclesiology, etc.) in Matthew and even for religious discourse more generally.

2 Metaphor: What Does It Do and How Does It Do It?

The task of defining what metaphors are and establishing their function and how they carry out that function is a prime example of Bertrand Russell's maxim that "Everything is vague to a degree you do not realize until you have

---

1 Two of the most important for the present work are Norman Perrin (*Jesus and the Language of the Kingdom: Symbol and Metaphor in New Testament Interpretation* [Philadelphia: Fortress Press, 1976]) and Werner Kelber (*The Oral and the Written Gospel: the Hermeneutics of Speaking and Writing in the Synoptic Tradition, Mark, Paul, and Q* [Bloomington and Indianapolis: Indiana University Press, 1997]).

2 Other works on biblical use of metaphor not directly related to Matthew also provided background to the present study, particularly Günter Röhser, *Metaphorik und Personifikation der Sünde: Antike Sündevorstellungen und Paulinische Hamartia* (Tübingen: J.C.B. Mohr, 1987).

INTRODUCTION   3

tried to make it precise."[3] Philosophical and literary-theoretical investigations
of these questions have resulted in myriad arguments and counter-arguments
and a mushrooming of publications since the 1950s.[4] Of these, two that have
been particularly influential also are especially pertinent to our topic: *The
Rule of Metaphor* by Paul Ricoeur[5] and *Metaphor and Religious Language* by
Janet Martin Soskice.[6] These will guide our reflections in the conclusion as
well as serve as main conversation partners here in our introductory remarks,
although we will also examine contributions to the discussion by other important scholars.

2.1   *Defining and Describing Metaphor*
While there has been no lack of discussion regarding what metaphors do and
how they do it, there has been less interest is clarifying how a person might
recognize a metaphor if she saw one. The task is more difficult than it might at
first seem.[7] Still, a useful definition has been proposed by Soskice: "Metaphor
is that figure of speech whereby we speak of one thing in terms which are seen
to be suggestive of another."[8] The language here is quite carefully considered,
as will become clear.

---

3   *The Philosophy of Logical Atomism*, David Pears, ed. (La Salle, IL.: Open Court, 1985), 38. First
     published 1918. The quote continues: "... and everything precise is so remote from everything
     that we normally think, that you cannot for a moment suppose that is what we really mean
     when we say what we think."

4   Monroe Beardsley, "The Metaphorical Twist," *Philosophy and Phenomenological Research*
     22 (Mr 1962): 293–307; Max Black, *Models and Metaphors* (Ithaca: Cornell University Press,
     1962); Jacques Derrida, "White Mythology," trans. F.C.T. Moore, *New Literary History* 6.1 (1974):
     5–74; Colinn Murray Turbayne *The Myth of Metaphor* (New Haven: Yale University Press,
     1962); Philip Wheelwright, *Metaphor and Reality* (Bloomington: Indiana University Press,
     1962) and *The Burning Fountain* (Bloomington: Indiana University Press, 1968); W.K. Wimsatt
     and M. Beardsley, *The Verbal Icon: Studies in the Meaning of Poetry* (Lexington, Ky.: University
     of Kentucky Press, 1954). The importance of metaphor for theology has also received atten-
     tion. See especially Sallie McFague, *Speaking in Parables: a Study in Metaphor and Theology*
     (London: SCM, 2002) and *Metaphorical Theology: Models of God in Religious Language*
     (Philadelphia: Fortress Press, 1982).

5   *The Rule of Metaphor: Multi-disciplinary Studies of the Creation and Meaning in Language*,
     trans. by R. Czerny (Toronto: University of Toronto Press, 1975).

6   Oxford: Clarendon, 1985.

7   Thus, David West in a review of *Introducing Metaphor* by Murray Knowles and Rosamund
     Moon (London: Routledge, 2006) says, "To criticize Knowles and Moon for not defining meta-
     phor adequately is perhaps a little unfair—after all, the problem of definition is one that
     confronts and confounds all who step into the world of metaphor" (*Language and Literature*
     17.2 [2008]: 167–169).

8   Soskice, *Metaphor and Religious Language*, 15.

As a guide for identifying metaphors formally, however, it is somewhat unsatisfactory. The identification of formal verbal structures in the definition and recognition of simile, a figure of speech so close to metaphor at a basic level, is more patent and widely recognized: the use of "like" or "as" indicates a simile. The same phrase or sentence with the *like* or *as* removed yields a metaphor. While some metaphor theorists have developed schemas for identifying metaphors on formal grounds,[9] the lack of an easily recognizable verbal cue (as we have with similes) compels these scholars to develop quite complex structures for identification. One may instead, however, utilize a more operation- or function-based definition, such as Soskice's, above. While this approach avoids the need for overly intricate systems of identification, it carries with it its own necessary explanations and caveats. Let us look briefly at Soskice's own explication and then explore a number of other factors.

The first element of the definition—"metaphor is a figure of speech"—has a number of important implications. First, Soskice points out, this means that when we talk about metaphor, we are talking about a particular type of verbal communication, and not a mental event.[10] While certain mental activities such as "a process of imagination" or a type of "perception" or "synthesis" may precede the making of a metaphor, it is the expression of that perception or synthesis in language that defines metaphor.[11]

---

9   See for example, "The Signaling of Metaphor," Chapter 6 in *The Language of Metaphors* by Andrew Goatly (London and New York: Routledge, 1997), 168–197.

10 Soskice, *Metaphor and Religious Language*, 16.

11 This does not preclude the idea that "making metaphors" is an action, and indeed a mental one, as long it is understood that "metaphor" refers to the particular verbal communication that is a result of that action and not the mental action itself. (See particularly paragraph 2 on p. 16.) While this may not be a necessary limitation philosophically, it is helpful in delimiting the scope of her study. This stipulation also does not preclude the discussion of what we do mentally with this particular use of words, as the discussion of how metaphors work has always necessitated. Soskice is not suggesting that this aspect of the study, difficult as it is to grapple with, should be off limits. Soskice says, "the tendency to speak of metaphor as though it were a special kind of mental act is by no means without significance for our study. It is an important feature of metaphor that, if the metaphor is a good one, in appreciating it one goes well beyond the bare formulation of the utterance.... Perhaps this is why some philosophers speak of metaphor as a special fusion of 'sense' and 'sensa' which produces a mixture of thought and experience unavailable from more prosaic expression.... We are not, then, rejecting psychological terminology completely, but rejecting the suggestion that metaphor is fundamentally a sort of mental event. A metaphor may prompt us into non-linguistic recognitions or comparisons, but of equal if not greater importance are the linguistic associations to which it gives rise" (pp. 17–18).

This naturally introduces the question of the role of cognitive linguistics related to metaphor, an important and potentially very fruitful trajectory for exploring the questions

INTRODUCTION
5

Second, a metaphor is not a physical object.[12] This does not mean that one cannot use a physical object in a verbal metaphor, but simply that the *object itself* is not a metaphor. Soskice argues that

> he who points to the daffodils in the garden and says that they are metaphors for rebirth speaks carelessly ... Daffodils are not themselves and could not be metaphors, for they are not linguistic at all.... one *can* reasonably say that the daffodil is a *symbol* of rebirth or that it provides an *analogy* for rebirth, since neither the category of symbol nor that of analogy is strictly linguistic. However, although we can construct a metaphor in which we speak of daffodils in order to describe rebirth, the daffodils themselves are not metaphors.[13]

The distinction between metaphors and symbols (at least physical objects as symbols) is, however, somewhat trickier than Soskice's page-and-a-half treatment indicates. On the far end, one can see her point that, for example, the color blue can be *symbolic* (purity, heavenliness, or on the other hand, sadness) but "blue" as a color cannot very well be metaphorical.[14] The ability, however, of a symbol (daffodils, for example) to carry meanings or connotations that can be transferred to something else (carried over, *metapherein*) sounds a good deal like Soskice's "one thing in terms which are seen to be suggestive of another." So, for example, if we say, "If your right hand should ensnare you, cut it off," is "right hand" symbolic or metaphorical? Following Soskice, it seems that one might say that the words "right hand" in this sentence are metaphorical (since it is portrayed as an agent that can act to ensnare or trip one up, thus "terms which are seen to be suggestive of another"), but an actual right hand would be symbolic (perhaps of ability to act or of strength or of something else).[15] This is perhaps to introduce an over-nice distinction, however. Such a distinction is necessitated, though, by Soskice's insistence that "metaphorizing" is not

---

of this study, but not the trajectory we have chosen to pursue. Hopefully others will do so and expand the conversation in various ways.

12 Soskice, *Metaphor and Religious Language*, 17–18.

13 Soskice, *Metaphor and Religious Language*, 17, italics mine.

14 See also Ricoeur's discussion of color symbolization in art in relation to metaphor (pp. 237–238).

15 In fact, the whole statement could be literal—a literal hand that literally trips up or traps you should literally be cut off—except that in the context the whole statement becomes metaphorical for moral "stumbling" and thus each element within the statement becomes symbolic or metaphorical. See discussion below regarding the necessity of context for determining whether statements are metaphorical.

6 INTRODUCTION

a mental act but a linguistic one.[16] All metaphors must be *"speaking* of one thing terms of another."* In so doing, Soskice shows that, unlike most metaphor theorists, Aristotle is not significantly foundational for her reflection except as a historical starting point. Although one section of her first chapter deals with Aristotle's treatment of metaphor in the *Poetics* and *Rhetoric*, her main point is to show why Aristotle has been seen by many as advocating a substitution theory of metaphor,[17] a reading that she is not quite willing to deem unjustified, though she admits that "in other places Aristotle shows his sensitivity towards the capacity of metaphor to name the unnamed, that is to fill what linguists now call lexical gaps."[18] She goes on to quote—but then hurry past—the passage in which she sees this:

> It is a great thing to make a proper use of each of the elements mentioned, and of double words and colloquial words,[19] but to be metaphorical is by far the greatest. For only that cannot come from someone else; it is given as a sign of good natural ability.[20] For to metaphorize well is to observe resemblances.[21]

As W.H. Fyfe says in his footnote to his LCL translation of this passage, the ability to "observe resemblances" (τὸ ὅμοιον θεωρεῖν) is "the power of detecting 'identity in difference' which distinguishes also both the philosopher and the scientist."[22] Thus, in this comment, Aristotle connects "metaphorizing well" with abilities of observation and perception—seeing similarities. More than simply filling lexical gaps[23] or saying in a decorative way things that could be said plainly,[24] "to be metaphorical is by far the greatest" because it recognizes

---

16 Soskice does not pause to refute the now commonly held idea that all thought (apart from simple sense perception and recollection) is linguistic in form, a proposition that if correct would mean that it is impossible to have a metaphorical thought that was non-linguistic, and thus her distinction is spurious.

17 The substitution theory says that metaphors are decorative, figurative ways of saying what could be said in "literal language." Ricoeur, however, problematizes the idea that is such a thing as "literal language" exists, arguing rather that all natural language in imbued with and based upon metaphor, figuration, and analogy.

18 Soskice, *Metaphor and Religious Language*, 9.

19 γλώτταις, here perhaps with the connotation of a "dialect," or perhaps "unusual" or "rare."

20 εὐφυΐας.

21 Arist. *Poet.* 1459a, my translation.

22 Aristotle, Vol. 23, *Poetics*, LCL 199 (Cambridge: Harvard University Press, 1932); the same idea is articulated by Ricoeur, *The Rule of Metaphor*, 26.

23 *Poet.* 1457b.

24 *Poet.* 1458a and *Rhet.* 1410b.

INTRODUCTION

and communicates connections among attributes of things despite dissimilarity, or perhaps more powerfully because of it.

2.2 *Metaphor as Transference*

This passage has proved fertile for many reflecting on metaphor, particularly for Ricoeur.[25] Ricoeur's first chapter, "Between Rhetoric and Poetics: Aristotle," engages this passage at length, as well as another: "A metaphor (μεταφορὰ) is a word belonging to something else—a 'bringing-upon' (ἐπιφορὰ) either from the genus to the species or from the species to the genus, or from one species to another, or else by analogy."[26] The idea of metaphor as a kind of transference is one that is picked up by many interpreters and one that deserves some extended consideration as it will lead us to consider some of the core questions regarding the functioning of metaphors. Ricoeur spends a good deal of time working with the idea of transference, though he begins by noting that "this notion of *epiphora* enlightens at the same time as it puzzles us."[27] The idea of transference is particularly problematic for Soskice:

> The difficulty with any mention of transference is that it immediately begs the question 'transference of what to what?' Inability to answer this question casts doubt upon the value of speaking in terms of transference at all. In Aristotle's use of the notion there is a further ambiguity over whether he intends us to regard metaphor as the process of transference, or as the product of it. He seems to mean both, yet his account of any process of transference is scarcely filled out.[28]

Soskice is right to point out that "while the notion that it is words which are transferred is difficult to make sense of, the notion that it is the meanings of words which are transferred, with its suggestion that means are detachable things that words have, is no easier."[29] Ricoeur, however, in his discussion of Aristotle's use of *epiphor*, points out that in the key passage, Aristotle shifts

---

25   In the balance of *Rule of Metaphor*, Ricoeur also repeatedly returns to this and other passages from Aristotle as a touchstone. In fact, while it may not be that Aristotle sets the limits of the discussion for Ricoeur, he certainly sets the playing field, and *Rule of Metaphor* could arguably be construed as an extended exegesis of Aristotle's remarks and an exposition of their implications.

26   μεταφορὰ δέ ἐστιν ὀνόματος ἀλλοτρίου ἐπιφορὰ ἢ ἀπὸ τοῦ γένους ἐπὶ εἶδοςἢ ἀπὸ τοῦ εἴδους ἐπὶ τὸ γένος ἢ ἀπὸ τοῦ εἴδους ἐπὶ εἶδος ἢ κατὰ τὸἀνάλογον. *Poet.* 1457b, my translation.

27   Ricoeur, *The Rule of Metaphor*, 17.

28   Soskice, *Metaphor and Religious Language*, 6.

29   Soskice, *Metaphor and Religious Language*, 6.

from talking about "metaphor," the noun, to talking about "metaphorize," the verb. In commenting on *Poetics* 1459 a 3–8, he says, "Several things are notable in this text. [First] metaphor becomes a verb, 'metaphorize'; this brings to light the problem of usage—process prevails over result."[30] As Ricoeur goes on to explain, a metaphor is less a thing that *is* than a thing that *happens*: "metaphor is a semantic event that takes place at the point where several semantic fields intersect."[31] Thus, "metaphorical attribution is essentially the construction of the network of interactions."[32]

Several aspects are significant here. First, Ricoeur is not claiming that the terms constitutive of the metaphor "have" meanings that are transferred. Rather linguistic communities share a network of associations ascribed to a term, and when two terms are put in conjunction, the networks interact. If the networks that are brought together contain attributes that are not usually assumed to be compatible within the linguistic community, the resulting discontinuity will result in a metaphor that is "living." Ricoeur's idea of metaphor as a combination of discordant networks of attributes is consistent with Soskice's phrase "one thing in terms which are seen to be suggestive of another."

2.3　*Living and Dead Metaphors*

Ricoeur, however, is insistent that this is not the case for all combinations of words where an exchange of attributes would be untenable on a literal level. His distinction here is that polysemy is not the same as metaphor. When a word has come to have more than one literal meaning[33] (that is, a commonly agreed upon lexical meaning and usage or "dictionary definition"), it no longer functions as a metaphor, though it may have originally done so. It is a "dead metaphor":

> In the metaphorical statement ... a contextual action creates a new meaning, which truly has the status of event since it exists only in the present context.... In this way, the innovation of an emergent meaning can be taken as a linguistic creation. And if it is adopted by a significant part of a linguistic community, it in turn can become a common meaning and add to the polysemy of the old lexical entities, thus contributing to the history of the language as code system. But at this final stage, where the meaning-effect we called metaphor has become this shift of meaning

---

30　Ricoeur, *The Rule of Metaphor*, 23.
31　Ricoeur, *The Rule of Metaphor*, 98.
32　Ricoeur, *The Rule of Metaphor*, 98.
33　On the problems of "literal meaning," see below.

INTRODUCTION 9

that increases polysemy, the metaphor is then no longer living but a dead metaphor. Only authentic metaphors, that is, living metaphors, are at once meaning and event.[34]

Because words themselves are more or less arbitrary placeholders for communally attributed meanings, those attributed meanings can change or multiply. When the same word has multiple agreed upon meanings ("literal" or lexical definitions), polysemy is the result, and this can engender a variety of types of word play (for example, a pun), but these are not necessarily metaphors.[35] So, Ricoeur would say, an "electrical current" and a candidate "running for office" are no longer metaphors. "Current" now *means* the thing that electricity does. The original metaphor that communicated the observation that electricity behaves in ways comparable to water is no longer a living metaphor. Once the community comes to a point that a term or phrase is commonly understood to *mean* a certain thing, the term or phrase becomes "literal," regardless of the metaphorical genesis of the term or phrase, and the polysemy is lexicalized.

In this, both Ricoeur and Soskice seem agreed in their rejection of what Soskice calls the metaphor-as-myth theory which understands the use of metaphors—especially those that go unrecognized—to structure our corporate and individual thought-life. Though the theory has many notable proponents,[36] as general approach to metaphor function, it is lacking precisely because it does not sufficiently take account of dead metaphors. As Soskice explains:

---

34   Ricoeur, *The Rule of Metaphor*, 99.
35   Along these same lines, Soskice notes, "The same word can have a number of senses. We are not speaking here of homonymy, instances of several words which have the same shape (for example, the 'mail' which is armor and the 'mail' which is post), but of polysemy, cases where the same word has a number of related yet different senses." Soskice then cites the various polysemic and literal senses of flight including: passing through the air, power of flying, air journey, digression, series of steps, the process of fleeing away. When a word is polysemic, "At a given time, it may be difficult to determine whether a particular usage is properly regarded as embodying one of the lexicalized and literal senses of the term in question or whether it is a figurative usage" (Soskice, *Metaphor and Religious Language*, 83–84).
36   Soskice mentions Antole France and Jacques Derrida (*The White Mythology*), although with the caveat that these are coming "from different philosophical traditions and tending to different ends," apparently granting that they are discussing particularly the normative and structuring role of metaphors in philosophical discourse rather than the general functioning of metaphor in common language.

One of the most interesting things about the metaphor-as-myth thesis is that, despite its actual antiquity, it is invariably presented as a new and startling theory concerning the victimization of thought by language. One of the most recent books to present it in this way is George Lakoff's and Mark Johnson's *Metaphors We Live By*, which argues that metaphor forms the implicit and unrecognized structure of most human life.... Carried to an extreme, it is in danger of falling into the fallacy, criticized by James Barr in the *Semantics of Biblical Language*, of confusing word derivation with word meaning. Word meaning, modern linguistics stresses, is properly understood synchronically; few present-day speakers of English know that 'ancillary' derives from the Latin term for a serving maiden, yet they may nonetheless understand perfectly the current meaning of the term. Similarly, it is absurd to think that one misunderstands the true meaning of dandelion if one does not know all of its origins in '*dent-de-lion*', or of 'malaria' because one fails to associate it with '*mal aria*', bad air. Etymologizing such as that of Anatole France is spurious if it puts itself forward as the 'true' meaning of the terms, for, as Barr has pointed out, 'the etymology of a word is not a statement about its meaning but about its history'.

In a dead metaphor, people cease to see "one thing in terms which are suggestive of another." Thus, to pick up our previous example, regardless of what might be posited by Lakoff and Johnson, when someone "runs for office," no one is put in mind of politicians moving their legs quickly to get elected, and unless one pauses to reflect upon it, it does not likely affect their understanding of the election process. Yet, Soskice also claims, and I think rightly, that metaphor, unlike simile,[37]

---

37 Although, just a few pages prior to this, in discussing the difference between metaphors and similes, Soskice says, that "Simile may be the means of making comparisons of two kinds, the comparison of similars and of dissimilar, and in the latter case, simile shares much of the imaginative life o and cognitive function of its metaphorical counterparts. For this reason we can say that metaphor and simile share the same function and differ primarily in their grammatical form." Thus, "Our contention here is that the presence of a 'like' [in some cases] is an aspect of superficial grammar, and in no real way impedes meaning. In such cases, metaphor and simile, while textually different, are functionally the same" (Soskice, *Metaphor and Religious Language*, 59). Soskice's method for culling those similes which are essentially decorative (or that she calls illustrative from those which truly have the cognitive power of metaphors is, on the one hand fairly simple: if you can remove the "like" or "as" and still have a sensible sentence, the simile will have the power of a metaphor. Thus, "She's as lovely as a flower" is not as powerful as "The kingdom of God is like a grain of mustard seed." We might say that similes that are essentially

INTRODUCTION   11

... has the added capacity to expand our lexicon, and in so doing, it expands the conceptual apparatus with which we work.... Metaphors become not only part of our language, but also part of the way in which
we interpret our world.... [thus] metaphor is not a neutral or ornamental
aspect of speech. Rather in almost all areas of abstract thought, the very
frames within which we work are given by metaphors which function in
structuring not only what sort of answers we get, but what kind of questions we ask.[38]

Soskice's later discussion of how the use of metaphors and models in the field
of scientific inquiry might illumine their role in religious reflection is helpful
in navigating this seeming inconsistency.

2.4   *Metaphors versus Models*

Soskice finds that it is important first to distinguish between metaphors and
models. While both metaphors and models function heuristically to help us
grasp a concept or to open up understandings of something abstract, they
have characteristic differences. While metaphors consist in "speaking about
one thing in terms which are seen to be suggestive of another," models represent a thing via a one-to-one correspondence of aspects. If a metaphor is "one
thing in terms of another," in a model there is no "another." Thus, a model of
the solar system is not a metaphor of the real solar system, nor is a model airplane a metaphor of the real airplane or an architect's drawing a metaphor of
the finished building. Each element—though it is made of different material
and perhaps not exactly proportional to the thing represented—represents
one aspect and all the aspects together give a picture of the thing itself. In this
sense, models are analogical. Metaphors, however, help one grasp the nature of
something by giving a picture of something else, and in so doing, some (though
not all) propose a model, and those that do are called "theory-constitutive
metaphors."[39] For example, one such metaphor that is common and functions
as a fruitful illustration for Soskice is the metaphor of the mind as a computer.
The notable feature of a theory-constitutive metaphor is that, once it is taken
up, it gives rise to many other metaphors, such as, in this example, experiences

adjectival or adverbial ("he works like a horse") are not as close to metaphors as those
that are predicative. Thus, at points in our study below we will consider similes as well as
metaphors since they will also shed light on our topic and to exclude them seems to en-
force an unwarranted distinction on purely grammatical grounds that modern metaphor
theory rejects as artificial.

38   Soskice, *Metaphor and Religious Language*, 62.
39   Or "conceptual metaphors."

as "input," what the mind does them as "processing," certain aspects of the mind being "hard wired" and others being "programmed," etc. Such metaphors generated by the governing metaphor are called "metaphorically constituted theory terms."[40]

Soskice further distinguishes between homeomorphic models (such as the architect's drawing or the model airplane) and paramorphic models (such as a model of a molecule built using balls and sticks). Paramorphic models are an intermediate area between homeomorphic models and theory-constitutive metaphors. Thus,

> The models used by the sciences for theoretical purposes are primarily paramorphic models [since] ... the task of theory construction itself is customarily the task of constructing models to explain better what we do not fully understand, rather than that of building models of states of affairs whose nature is clear to us. Rather than demonstrating clear parallels, the paramorphic model suggests candidates for similarity and gives form to deliberation on unfamiliar subject matters.... In science, social science, ethics, theology, indeed the whole realm of abstract theorising, it is the paramorphic models which are used in attempts to speak about the 'mysterious overplus.'[41]

Thus, theory-constitutive metaphors are also analogical, although not in as strict and direct a sense as models, per se. With theory-constitutive metaphors (as opposed to non-metaphorical models) and with paramorphic models, as with all metaphors, there is always a tension between the ways the metaphor works as a model and the ways it does not.[42]

---

40 Soskice, *Metaphor and Religious Language*, 101–103. More will be said in the conclusion about this with respect to our topic.

41 Soskice, *Metaphor and Religious Language*, 103.

42 One of Lakoff and Johnson's favorite examples of the power of metaphor to shaping thinking (or at least its potential power) is the difference it makes if we talk about a nation as a "body politic" or as "the ship of state," both of which are "theory-constitutive metaphors." Since neither of these metaphors, however, are prominently used today, they may seem a moot example for the point Lakoff and Johnson are trying to make—rather than be unconsciously carried along by either of these metaphors, most hearers would find them so uncommon as be somewhat arresting and they would provoke the hearer to reflect on the aptness of the metaphor rather than to have her unconscious ideas about nationhood formed by it. In this sense, it is only dead or nearly-dead model metaphors that function as Lakoff and Johnson propose. Lively metaphors open up new possibilities to be considered.

INTRODUCTION

2.5   *The Tension of Metaphors*

This leads us to examine one of the most important and universally recognized of the attributes of metaphor, that is, "tension." Among Soskice's "rough guidelines" for distinguishing living from dead metaphors, "The first is that one recognizes a dissonance or tension in a living metaphor whereby the terms of the utterance used seem not strictly appropriate to the topic at hand.... This tension varies with the strength of the metaphor. A hackneyed or dead metaphor generates no tension."[43]

Ricoeur also sees tension as a fundamental element in living metaphor, and this tension (or "tensive" quality) is between the "is not" of the literal sense of the metaphor and the "is" of the metaphorical sense: as readers or hearers, we recognize that on a literal level, the metaphor is untrue, yet we feel compelled to affirm that the statement expresses truth about its subject. Since "'It was and it was not' ... contains *in nuce* all that can be said about metaphorical truth,"[44] each metaphor embodies for the hearer a "yes and no" tension between the literal sense and the metaphorical aptness of the expression, and "the metaphorical statement captures its sense as metaphorical midst the ruins of the literal sense."[45] The more acute the tension, the livelier the metaphor, as noted above. The incongruity (or "impertinence") of the literal gives way before the congruence of the metaphorical attribution (its "pertinence"):

> In its literal sense, the expression constitutes an enigma to which the metaphorical meaning offers the solution. Now, the tension and contradiction point only to the form of the problem within the enigma, what one could call the semantic challenge or, in Jean Cohen's terms, the 'semantic impertinence'. The metaphorical meaning as such is not the semantic clash [the "no" to the literal] but the new pertinence that answers its challenge [the "yes"]. In the language of Beardsley, the metaphor is what forms a meaningful self-contradictory statement from a self-destructive self-contradictory statement.... tension, contradiction, and controversion are nothing but the opposite side of the reconciliation in which metaphor 'makes sense.'[46]

---

43   Soskice, *Metaphor and Religious Language*, 73. The other two guidelines are "the relative ease of paraphrase" (live metaphors resist simple translation into non-metaphorical language) and whether or not the metaphor has become so commonplace that "its initial web of implications becomes, if not entirely lost, then difficult to recall," this final criterion echoing, obviously, Ricoeur's distinction between metaphor and lexicalized polysemy.

44   Ricoeur, *The Rule of Metaphor*, 224.

45   Ricoeur, *The Rule of Metaphor*, 221.

46   Ricoeur, *The Rule of Metaphor*, 194–195.

Or as he says earlier in the same chapter:

> It is the 'clash' on the literal level that leads one to seek out a meaning beyond the lexical meaning; while context allows one to maintain the sense of certain terms, it prevents one from doing so for others. However, the metaphor is not quite the clash itself, but rather its resolution. One must decide, on the basis of various 'clues' provided by the context, which terms can be taken figuratively, and which cannot. One must therefore 'work out' the parallelism between situations that will guide the iconic transposition of one to the other. This activity has become useless in the case of conventional [that is, "dead"] metaphors, where cultural usage decides on the figurative sense of certain expressions. It is only in living metaphors that one sees this activity at work.[47]

Soskice, for her part, is at pains to emphasize that what is unique about metaphors is their ability to "disclose for the first time" rather than simply "redescribe"[48] and that "a strong metaphor compels new possibilities of vision."[49] In this, Soskice's and Ricoeur's understandings of the functioning of metaphor are quite congruent. Despite some extensive critiques of Ricoeur, Soskice's understanding of the role of "resemblance" in metaphor seems similar to Ricoeur's. She remarks, "the good metaphor does not merely compare two antecedently similar entities but enables one to see similarities in what previously had been regarded as dissimilar."[50] This sounds very much like what Ricoeur says regarding the establishment of resemblance through metaphor:

> In other words, if it serves some purpose in metaphor, a resemblance must be a characteristic of the attribution of predicates and not of the substitution of names.[51] What constitutes the new pertinence is the kind

---

47   Ricoeur, *The Rule of Metaphor*, 190–191.

48   Soskice, *Metaphor and Religious Language*, 89.

49   Soskice, *Metaphor and Religious Language*, 57.

50   Soskice, *Metaphor and Religious Language*, 26.

51   The "substitution theory" of metaphor is that, in a metaphor, the writer or speaker is substituting an improper word (figurative, e.g., fox) for a proper one (literal, e.g., cunning). Soskice says, "Substitution theories argue that the content or meaning of metaphor could equally be expressed in non-metaphorical terms." However, "the Incremental theorists," of which both she and Ricoeur are ones, disagree: "Basic to their position is the view that what is said by way of metaphor can be expressed adequately in no other way, that the combination of parts in a metaphor can produce new and unique agents of meaning" (Soskice, *Metaphor and Religious Language*, 31). The congruence of this with the last portion of the above Ricoeur quote is easily seen.

INTRODUCTION

of a semantic 'proximity' established between the terms despite their 'distance' apart. Things that until that moment were far apart suddenly appear as closely related. Aristotle was aware of this strictly predicative effect of resemblance when he considered, among the 'virtues' of good metaphors, that of being 'appropriate'. On guard against far-fetched metaphors, he recommends that metaphors be derived from material that is 'kindred' and 'of like form', such that one as the expression is produced, it will appear clearly that the names involved are 'near of kin'.... *Epiphora*, we recall, is Aristotle's term. It is transposition, transference as such, that is, the unitive process, the sort of assimilation that occurs between alien ideas, ideas distant from one another. As such, this unitive process arises from an apperception—an insight—that belongs to the order of *seeing*. Aristotle was pointing to this apperception when he said: 'to metaphorize well is to see—to contemplate, to have the right eye for—the similar.' *Epiphora* is this glance and this genius-stroke, unteachable and impregnable. But there is no epiphor without diaphor, no intuition without construction. Indeed, the intuitive process, bringing together what is disparate, contains an irreducibly discursive moment. The same Aristotle who contemplates the similar is also the theoretician of that proportional metaphor in which resemblance is more constructed than seen ... There is no contradiction, therefore, in giving an account of metaphor now in the language of apperception, that is, of vision, and then in the language of construction. It is at once the 'gift of genius' and skill of the geometer, who sees the point in the 'ratio of proportions'.[52]

Thus, as Soskice says, "the particularity of a metaphorical description is not that it translates literal thought, but that the very thinking is undertaken in terms of the metaphor. What interests us in metaphor is precisely that we find in it an increment to understanding."[53] The resemblances perceived in transposition (epiphor) of the two elements of a metaphor results in a new way of seeing, a new vision of the thing(s).[54]

---

52   Ricoeur, *The Rule of Metaphor*, 194–195.
53   Soskice, *Metaphor and Religious Language*, 25.
54   Ricoeur puts this nicely when he discusses the example from the 19th-century poet Jeremy Taylor's *Of Holy Living*, in which Taylor writes, "virginity is a life of angels, the enamel of the soul." Ricoeur says that in penning this metaphor, "something develops in the language. There accrue to the language various properties of enamel that until then had never been clearly established as recognize connotations of the word: 'thus this metaphor does not merely thrust latent connotations into the foreground of meaning,

Thus, in explaining her definition of metaphor (speaking about one thing in terms suggestive of another) in relation to other theories, she says that metaphor cannot be understood as simply a conflict of word meaning (contra Beardsley) nor can it be understood as the interaction of two separate "subjects" (Black), but her definition "retains aspects of both of these theories": "metaphor is properly a linguistic phenomenon—an interanimation of terms." It is "a use of language with a unity of subject-matter and which yet draws upon two (or more) sets of associations,"[55] or as Ricoeur says, "Metaphor is a semantic event that takes place at the point where several semantic fields intersect."[56] It is this idea of "fields" or "networks" or "webs" or "sets" of associations that illumines the similarity of Soskice's and Ricoeur's perspectives. In a metaphor, there are always (at least) two elements. Each element has attributes associated with it. When the elements are brought together (through "transference," *epiphora*), some overlap of attributes—perhaps before unperceived—becomes apparent, but there are other attributes that cannot be seen to overlap. We might think of this, perhaps, in the image of a Venn diagram. It is the existence of non-overlapping characteristics—the "is not" in Ricoeur's parlance—that makes an expression metaphorical rather than literal.[57] It is the "similarity (overlap) within dissimilarity (non-overlap)."

but brings into play if some properties that were not previously meant by it'" (*The Rule of Metaphor*, 97–98, quoting Beardsley, "The Metaphorical Twist," 303).

55　Soskice, *Metaphor and Religious Language*, 49. The aspect of "conflict" is one for which, as we have seen, she critiques Ricoeur, and the other (interaction) affirms the idea of "transposition" or "transference," a notion about which, she said, "immediately begs the question 'transference of what to what?' Inability to answer this question casts doubt upon the value of speaking in terms of transference at all" (Soskice, *Metaphor and Religious Language*, 6). Ricoeur, however, like Aristotle sees a thorough understanding of *epiphora* as key to understanding how metaphors operate, as we have seen.

56　Ricoeur goes on: "It is because of this construction that all the words, taken together, make sense. Then, and only then, the metaphorical *twist* is at once an event *and* a meaning, an event that means or signifies, an emergent meaning created by language" (Ricoeur, *The Rule of Metaphor*, 98–99).

57　Of course, not all instances of two elements with a lack-of-overlap are a metaphor. If I say, "Karen is a librarian," there is more to Karen than being a librarian (aspects of that "element" that do not overlap with "librarian"), and likely there are things associated with being a librarian that Karen does not embody. Still, if the agreed upon (literal, lexical) definition of "librarian" fits what Karen does, the statement is non-metaphorical. Karen is, at least within the context of the statement, a subset of "librarian" or conversely "librarian" is a subset of the many things Karen is. If, however, Karen does not actually work in a library but works, rather, in a car parts store, "Karen is a librarian" would be metaphorical. The statement might point to an overlap (similarity) in the way she goes about doing her job despite the fact that the material with which she works does not overlap (dissimilarity) with that of a librarian.

INTRODUCTION   17

Both are necessary to create a metaphor. Were the networks of associations to overlap completely, were there no dissimilarity, there would be only the substitution of one element for another—the metaphor would be dead and the "metaphorical meaning" would be the literal meaning.[58] Thus, Soskice and Ricoeur are in essential agreement regarding the "tension" of "is/is not," and indeed almost all modern explanations of metaphor point to something like "tension" or "conflict" as the foundational dynamic of metaphor.[59] Soskice's "suggestive of another" seems to express this.

Thus, we will adopt this notion of metaphorical tension, of an "is/is not" or a "yes-and-no" dynamic, as key to the functioning and to the interpretation of metaphor. Yet there is a valid critique to be level against Ricoeur's use of the "is/is not" or "yes-and-no."[60] Soskice's main critique of Ricoeur is that his schema sees metaphor in terms of a two-part experience or a two-level interpretation—a "literal-no" and a "figurative-yes"—whereas, from Soskice's perspective, the metaphorical "seeing one thing in terms of another" is a singular process. She asserts that some metaphors do not have any obvious literal sense to which we are forced to say "no."[61]

To return to our analogy of the networks of associations, to claim that there is a "no" to the literal seems merely to recognize that the two sets of associations do not completely overlap. It is, however, this lack of overlap that causes the tensive dynamic of metaphor. Thus, it is less a conflict of literal sense with metaphoric sense than a tension *within* the metaphorical sense. That is to say, the more acute tension or conflict is not between and obviously untrue literal sense and an easily affirmed figurative sense, but between—or really among— the many possible figurative senses that one might perceive, not so much

---

58 For example, if I say, "Edgar Jones is the head of the company," the term "head" here is no longer metaphorical. The network of meanings in this context fit exactly the idea to which it is applied because one of the literal, lexicalized meanings of head is to be the foremost person within an organization or group.

59 For a summary of those holding this view, see, for example, Andrew Goatly, *The Language of Metaphors* (New York: Routledge, 1997), 118; and Carl R. Hausman, *Metaphor and Art: Interactionism and Reference in the Verbal and Non-Verbal Arts* (Cambridge, U.K.: Cambridge University Press, 1989), 59–66.

60 Ricoeur himself, in one of his most daring claims, posits that, apart from some artificially created technical and scientific languages (what Ricoeur calls "steno-languages"), there is no "literal" language, if by literal we mean "a word in which tenor and vehicle cannot be distinguished can be taken provisionally to be literal" (*The Rule of Metaphor*, 81; see also discussions of technical language on pp. 91, 140–141,). All language (all "natural language," that is) is fundamentally metaphoric. If this is the case, it seems odd to posit that the "no" we speak to a metaphorical statement is a "no" to the literal sense.

61 Soskice, *Metaphor and Religious Language*, 84–85.

between the subject and what is being attributed to it, but among the many possible attributes of both elements and how we are to make sense of them in combination. Thus, I would argue the "yes-and-no" tension of the metaphor exists not between the metaphorical and the literal meanings, but within the statement itself *as a metaphor*. If metaphor is "seeing similarity in the dissimilar," the tensive quality of the metaphor is manifest precisely in the way it compels the reader or hearer both to affirm and to deny the validity or aptness of the metaphor, to sort out the similar from the dissimilar. It forces the reader/hearer to say "yes" to some aspects and "no" to others. In this regard, our approach has some aspects in common with those who have discussed metaphor as "filter" or "lens" by which some attributes are highlighted (similarities) while others are downplayed (differences). Metaphor thus "organizes" our thinking about a thing.[62] In this conception, metaphors function heuristically to impart clarity and insight regarding the thing spoken about, and we will have occasion to draw on this function significantly in our study.[63]

2.6 *Metaphor, Context, and Interpretation*

While semantic units as small as two words can function as metaphors (for example, "writhing smoke"), entire sentences can function metaphorically—but also, potentially, not. If we say, "That is not my cup of tea," the sentence might or might not be metaphorical. Even traditional metaphorical sentences like "That is a cold coal to blow at" or "You would be carrying coal to Newcastle" are not necessarily metaphorical apart from some context, either literary or with regard to the occasion of the remark.[64] Thus, context is not just important for the recognition of a metaphor and for its interpretation, it is at least partially determinative of a statement's status *as* a metaphor.

Consideration of the importance of context brings us to one of the aspects of metaphor that is often unaddressed by theorists: the role of speaker and hearer—and indeed the entire linguistic community—in the formation and

---

62 Ricoeur has certain critiques of this position (*The Rule of Metaphor*, 200–206), but also says, "Metaphor's power of reorganizing our perception of things develops from transposition of an entire 'realm'" (*The Rule of Metaphor*, 236).

63 Such a perspective, however, does come under criticism (by both Soskice and Ricoeur) for focusing on the redescriptive power of metaphor—its ability to point out pre-existing but latent or unobserved similarities—and undervaluing the generative potential of metaphor to actually create new attributes for an element because of its combination with the other, as we have already seen.

64 Soskice, *Metaphor and Religious Language*, 21. Soskice is concerned, based on Ricoeur's work, lest we replace the "tyranny of the word" (semiotic theories of metaphor) with the "tyranny of the sentence," thus her emphasis on the necessity for considering context in understanding something like "That is a cold coal to blow at" as metaphorical.

INTRODUCTION   19

reception of metaphors. Despite the language of most metaphor theorists, it must be noted that that metaphors do not, in fact, *do* anything. Because there is no non-metaphorical way to speak about metaphors,[65] theorists often resort to using personification (itself a type of metaphorical speech) in discussing metaphor. While this may be unavoidable to some extent, continued unreflecting use of language about "how metaphors work" or "what metaphors do" tends to obscure the fact that metaphors themselves are contextual linguistic constructs (locutionary and illocutionary acts done by someone) and not themselves acting agents. Just as words do not inherently *have* meanings but simply bear the meanings ascribed by the community, so too metaphors are only metaphors by virtue of their tensive, non-identical networks of associations within a linguistic community.[66] On the one hand, this may seem almost absurdly obvious. However, not pausing to reflect on this fact leads to underrecognizing the fact that metaphors themselves do nothing. People speaking or writing and hearing or listening within a particular context *do*. This is particularly important to keep in mind when undertaking, as we will be, interpretation of metaphors within texts from another era and culture.

Both Ricoeur and Soskice touch on this in a variety of ways. We have already noted that one of the litmus tests for whether a metaphor is alive or dead is whether, within a linguistic community, the metaphorical meaning has become lexicalized and is now part of the accepted polysemy of the word or whether there still remains tension and a certain level of strangeness (impertinence) about the metaphor. It is the metaphorical tension perceived by the hearers that makes a metaphor "work," and conversely, the hearers becoming inured to the tension that makes the metaphor dead. We should, however, perhaps adjust our terminology somewhat. Carl Hausman has proposed, and I think with good reason, using the term "frozen" or "dormant" for this type of metaphor.[67] This seems a better term for lexicalized metaphors than "dead" since, should the reader or hearer pause to reflect upon a dormant metaphor, the metaphor may again spring to life and be full of tension. In fact, this may be one of the most important functions of interpretation of metaphorical

---

65   "It is impossible to talk about metaphor non-metaphorically ... the definition of metaphor returns on itself.... There is no non-metaphorical standpoint from which one could look upon metaphor, and all the other figures for that matter, as if they were a game and played before one's eyes" (Ricoeur, *The Rule of Metaphor*, 18).

66   Soskice even goes so far as to locate the existence or non-existence of metaphor in the intentions of those involved: "A metaphor is only a metaphor because someone, speaker or hearer and ideally both, regards it as such; the intentional component is essential" (*Metaphor and Religious Language*, 36).

67   *Metaphor and Art*, 3 and 15, *et passim*.

statements: the revitalization of metaphors that have become dormant. This is especially important in the case of religious texts where so many metaphors have become dormant through their great familiarity.[68]

Interpreting metaphors is, however, a tricky business. As already noted, it is the linguistic community that bring to bear the networks of association connected to the twinned elements of a metaphor. Interpreting metaphors outside of their original communities—not to mention across languages—makes it exceptionally likely that the new interpreter will bring different associations to the metaphor. This is perhaps the reason why, in the literature exploring metaphors and the theories about how they operate, writers offer scores of examples of metaphors but seldom venture to put forward an interpretation.

Their reticence is well-founded. One of the aspects of metaphor on which most of the prominent theorists agree is that metaphors are not simply decorative ways of saying something that could be said in literal language, that metaphors cannot be "translated" into literal language without loss of meaning.[69] The moment we being to say, "In using this metaphor, the speaker is trying to communicate that...." we find we are trying to walk on water. We have no solid foundation of specified and agreed upon aspects of our networks of associations, especially when working with metaphors from ancient texts. Even when reading the interpretations of metaphors from those of one's own language and culture, we may find that a writer's interpretation(s) of what a metaphor "means" is surprising or even at odds with what a metaphor evokes for us. For example, at one point Soskice mentions the use of the phrase "ship of the desert" as a metaphor for camel. She says, "The relational irreducibility of the metaphor lies in the potentially limitless suggestions that are evoked."[70] This naturally led me to think of what this metaphor evokes for me. Perhaps this was Soskice's intention. Regardless of that, when she listed her ideas of what this called to mind, all but one was things that had not occurred to me. Her list included, "the implied corollaries of a swaying motion, a heavy and precious cargo, a broad wilderness, a route mapped by stars, distant ports of call, and so on." In contrast, I thought of the desert as a vast, forbidding expanse, dangerous, undulating, with the camel small in the vastness, with the wind whipping the foam of sand around it. It becomes clear then that there are actually two metaphors operating: the camel as a ship and the desert as an ocean.

---

68 Attention to the use of metaphors in texts or in description generally is, however, also a feature of teaching and scholarship in most fields, obviously.

69 Soskice, *Metaphor and Religious Language*, 94–95 *et passim.*

70 Soskice, *Metaphor and Religious Language*, 95.

INTRODUCTION   21

The fact that hardly any of what the metaphor brought to mind for me was the same as what Soskice articulated was perhaps precisely what she expected would happen and would prove her point. It does, however, also demonstrate the reason for some significant tentativeness when offering an interpretation of a metaphor. Though she and I are of relatively the same culture and time-frame, the metaphor evoked a different set of associations. I could see the validity of her associations, but they were not what immediately came to mind for me. Similarly, when Hausman discusses Shakespeare's "Juliet is the sun," his point is the same: "Every summary of sentences intended to give a paraphrase [of this metaphor] is recognized as needing an 'and so on'. In short, the metaphor in its initial formulation is indispensable." Again, in this instance, what came to mind for me was none of the specific things that Hausman set out, though they were not completely unrelated and certainly were not at odds— themes of warmth, growth, guidance, attraction, etc. were similar. These were the same sorts of associations that Shakespeare might have had coming, as he did, from an island in the North Atlantic where warm sunlight is much appreciated. If, however, this metaphor was read by a person in say, Saudi Arabia, would the metaphor "Juliet is the sun" work in the same way? It is unlikely. Such a person would bring a network of dangerous associations for the sun— something that dehydrates, that scorches, something from which you must protect yourself, something that can kill you as well as bringing light, warmth, and growth. Similarly, if we are going to interpret the metaphors for the causes of sin and evil in Matthew, we will need to be as mindful as possible of the differences between the networks we bring and the networks of associations Matthew and his readers might have had.

But is it necessary to interpret these metaphors at all? Given that metaphorical speech is not fully translatable into a literal statement, should we perhaps simply identify the metaphors without trying to explain what they are trying to express? While a certain amount of interpretive humility will certainly be necessary before the polyvalence of the metaphor, some at least tentative assertions about the meaning of these metaphors are necessary. This is not simply because the nature of such a study demands that the interpreter take a stand on such issues, but it could be argued, the nature of metaphor itself demands that one take up the challenge.

Just such a position has been put forth by Werner Kelber.[71] Kelber argues that parables have the same sort of dynamics as metaphors, that they are, in a sense, metaphors writ large. "What all parables have in common is the

---

71   *The Oral and Written Gospel: the Hermeneutics of Speaking and Writing in the Synoptic Tradition, Mark, Paul, and Q* (Philadelphia: Fortress Press, 1983).

metaphoric quality. 'The parable that has only a literal level of meaning does not exist'. Whether marked by extravagance or not, a parable is never self-explanatory."[72] Thus, parable shares with metaphors both untranslatability and tension: "Owing to the metaphorical quality parables are hermeneutically unfinished products. They encourage but withhold meaning, suggest but conceal understanding."[73] The dynamics at the heart of both metaphors and parables make them both memorable and provocative:

> The metaphoricity of parabolic stories sheds still more light on their mnemonic quality.... The mnemonic attractiveness of parables lies in their hermeneutical inexhaustability and susceptibility to multiple hearings ... they prompt retelling and rehearsing. Simple as they appear to be, they engage and intrigue the mind on account of their concealing and revealing disposition.... Parables, insofar as they are hermeneutically unfinished stories, stimulate a process of interpretation that is never entirely brought to completion or under control.[74]

Thus, to reverse Kelber's logic to *a maiori ad minus*, if "parables cry out for interpretation due to their metaphorical quality,"[75] metaphors also push the reader or hearer to interpret them, to consider their meaning and significance, to probe what might be communicated through them and what insights can be gained. Yet, "in articulating meaning, the interpretation transacts the very operation that the metaphoricity of parables [or the parabolicalness of metaphors] suggests cannot be transacted"[76]—a living metaphor will compel the reader or hearer to try to interpret, to translate, to articulate the meaning of the metaphor. Kelber's analysis coincides in important ways with C.H. Dodd's classic definition of parables: "Parable is a metaphor or simile drawn from nature or common life, arresting the hearer by its vividness or strangeness, and leaving the mind in sufficient doubt about its precise application to tease it into active thought."[77] Metaphors, too, tease our minds into active thought, and despite the uncertainty caused by doubt about their precise application, this study will attempt to offer some reflections on the meaning of the metaphors Matthew uses to portray the causes of sin and evil. This will be especially important if it is to serve the function outlined above: to serve as a prolegomenon

---

72   Kelber, *Oral and Written Gospel*, 61.
73   Kelber, *Oral and Written Gospel*, 61.
74   Kelber, *Oral and Written Gospel*, 62.
75   Kelber, *Oral and Written Gospel*, 63.
76   Kelber, *Oral and Written Gospel*, 63.
77   C.H. Dodd, *The Parables of the Kingdom* (New York: Scribner, 1961), 5.

INTRODUCTION

to the larger question of Matthean soteriology and the role of the resurrection within such a soteriology. If we are going to prepare to explore how Matthew understands Jesus' life, death, and resurrection solving the problem of sin and evil in humans and the world, we will have to make some claims about how he conceives of that problem, even if the claims be preliminary and open to revision.

PART 1

The Question of Whence Sin and Evil in the Texts of Matthew's Milieu

∵

CHAPTER 1

Diversity and Consistency in the Texts of Matthew's Milieu

The Gospel of Matthew, and indeed all of the NT writings, were composed within a milieu in which questions of the origin and continuing locus of the emanation of evil and sin received sustained attention. Much important work has been done on the influence of apocalyptic thinking, especially apocalyptic dualism, on Jewish Second Temple understandings of the source(s) of sin and evil both within the individual and in the cosmos generally. Many of these investigations have focused on the Qumran texts,[1] but other Second Temple texts such as Ben Sira, 2 Baruch, and 4 Ezra have also been the objects of study.[2] The myths used to understand sin and evil and explain its genesis during the Second Temple period, especially those found in the Enochic literature, have also received a good deal of scholarly attention.[3] The preservation of some of these Enochic works among the Qumran texts combined with the attention given the question of evil and its source among the sectarian documents found there indicates that this was a question of interest for at least some in the

---

1 John J. Collins, "The Origin of Evil in Apocalyptic Literature and the Dead Sea Scrolls" in *Seers, Sybils, and Sages*, 288–299; Phillip R. Davies, "Dualism and Eschatology in the Qumran War Scroll," *Vetus Testamentum* 28, no. 1 (Ja 1978): 28–36; Annette Steudel, "God and Belial," in *The Dead Sea Scrolls, Fifty Years After Their Discovery: Proceeding of the Jerusalem Congress, July 20–25, 1997*, edited by Lawrence H. Schiffman, Emanuel Tov, and James VanderKam (Jerusalem: Israel Exploration Society, 2000), 332–340. On the relationship of Qumran understandings of sin and evil to NT perspectives on the topic, see, for example, Karl Georg Kuhn, "New Light on Temptation, Sin, and Flesh in the New Testament" in *The Scrolls and the New Testament*, edited by Krister Stendahl with James H. Charlesworth, Christian Origins Library (New York: Crossroad, 1992), 94–113.
2 Benedikt Otzen, "Old Testament Wisdom Literature and Dualistic Thinking in Late Judaism," in *Congress Volume: Edinburgh 1974*, Supplements to Vetus Testamentum (Leiden: Brill, 1975), 146–157.
3 Phillip R. Davies, "The Origin of Evil in Ancient Judaism," *Australian Biblical Review* 50 (2002): 43–54; Loren T. Stuckenbruck, "Giant Mythology and Demonology: from the Ancient Near East to the Dead Sea Scrolls," in *Die Dämonen/Demons: the Demonology of Israelite-Jewish and Early Christian Literature in Context of their Environment* (Tübingen: Mohr Siebeck, 2003), 318–338; *idem*, "The Origin of Evil in Jewish Apocalyptic Tradition: the Interpretation of Genesis 6:1–4 in the Second and Third Centuries B.C.E.," in *The Fall of Angels*, edited by Christoph Auffarth and Loren T. Stuckenbruck, Themes in Biblical Narrative 6 (Leiden; Boston: Brill, 2004), 87–118; James C. VanderKam, "The Demons in the Book of Jubilees," in *Die Dämonen/Demons*, 339–364.

© KONINKLIJKE BRILL NV, LEIDEN, 2020 | DOI:10.1163/9789004419506_003

Essene movement,[4] and perhaps for Jews more widely in the Second Temple period.[5]

In surveying these perspectives in the literature of the Second Temple period, we find a significant tension regarding the source of sin and evil. In this milieu with strong apocalyptic tendencies, various factors complicate the etiologies of sin. The tension created by the simultaneous affirmation of a dualistic worldview and divine sovereignty is especially acute, and the interaction of this perspective with the perspective and themes of the wisdom tradition further complicates the issue.[6]

Some works proposed ancient etiological answers to the question while other writers were less concerned with primeval legends and more focused on questions of contemporary moral culpability.[7] The result is that the lit-

---

4 While the multiplicity of documents and the perspectives expressed would not allow us to attempt the construction of a comprehensive or definitive "Qumran doctrine of sin and evil," we can surmise that that topic was important to the community and perhaps the focus of some debate since both outside documents preserved by the community and documents seemingly produced with the community display interest in the topic.

5 To what extent the Essenes interacted with and thus influenced or were influenced by other currents in Judaism is unclear. The relative isolation of the Qumranites seems to have been the exception rather than the norm since Josephus notes that the Essenes "settle in large numbers in every town" (*B.J.* II:124–125; in agreement with Philo *Hyp.* 11.1, though in *Prob.* 75 Philo states that they live in villages to avoid the immorality of the larger cities) and only Pliny describes them as living in seclusion near the Dead Sea (*Nat. Hist.* v.xv.73). In such a situation, it seems likely that, despite their internal focus on the brotherhood of the community, some regular and substantive interaction with outsiders must certainly have taken place, especially since the process of induction of new members into the community was a topic covered at length both in their own documents and in Josephus (e.g., *B.J.* II:137–142; Pliny, *ibid.*, also comments).

6 On what is now recognized to be the very fuzzy boundary (if one exists at all) between sapiential and apocalyptic perspectives in the first century, see John J. Collins, "Wisdom, Apocalypticism, and the Dead Sea Scrolls"; and *idem*, "Wisdom, Apocalypticism, and Generic Compatibility," in *Seers, Sybils, and Sages in Hellenistic-Roman Judaism* (Leiden: Brill, 1997), 385–404.

7 Although, in order to give a more balanced picture of the probable complexity of Matthew's milieu, a section surveying relevant Greco-Roman traditions would have been desirable, space hardly allows such an undertaking, and it is not clear that such a survey would add significantly to this study. There are a number of reasons for this. First, Matthew has historically been recognized as the most "Jewish" of the Gospels, and I think with validity. In designating it as such, I do not mean to ignore or minimize the widely-recognized problematic nature of the terms "Jewish" and "Greco-Roman" as labels either for patterns of belief and practice, or for texts. Still, problematic though they may be, these terms do retain a modest usefulness in differentiating what seems to be the dominant, self-conscious religious, ethnic, or philosophical identification of the author(s) of a text, despite widely varying levels of assimilation of influences from the pluralistic culture of the time (see literature listed below). Thus, given that the texts we will be examining as part of Matthew's milieu are already part

DIVERSITY AND CONSISTENCY IN THE TEXTS OF MATTHEW'S MILIEU

erature's attribution of responsibility for sin is sometimes unclear or at least multifaceted.

of this Hellenistically-influenced culture of the 300 or so years prior to and including the time of Matthew's composition, Greco-Roman influences are already present in these "Jewish" texts. Thus, the ways in which Greco-Roman ideas might have come to Matthew was just as likely—perhaps more likely—through Jewish texts as through any other route. Further, in researching this project, it became apparent that the direct and notable connections between Matthew and previous literature were not as obvious with Greco-Roman texts as with the Jewish. This being the case, the texts that seem most relevant to Matthew are those that share some distinguishing characteristics with him, specifically a rooting in the OT narrative and prophetic tradition and a dual emphasis on Torah observance and apocalypticism. These are the texts our study will focus on.

Some similar and some different considerations stand behind the decision not to discuss the early Rabbinic literature. First, because of the significantly later writing, it is difficult to discern which of the sayings and actions attributed to the early Tannaim reflect the actual early to mid-first century teachings and thus would be relevant in Matthew's milieu. Second, the most commonly noted feature of rabbinic reflection on the cause of sin—the conflict of the *yetser ha-ra* with the *yetser ha-tov*—is an idea already available in Second Temple literature and will be discussed with respect to its presence there. (Note, however, the article by Ishay Rosen-Zvi, "Two Rabbinic Inclinations? Rethinking a Scholarly Dogma" [*JSJ* 39 (Nov. 2008): 513–539] wherein he argues that the dominant perspective of the Rabbis was of a single *yetser* and that it was either neutral [R. Akiva] or evil [R. Ishmael].) Third, a serious exploration and assessment of rabbinic portrayals of the causes of sin and evil would prove to be (like the investigation of the Greco-Roman perspectives) a study in and of itself, not to mention a study of them in comparison with Matthew, thus putting such a project beyond the scope of our present work. Finally, since the aim of part 1 of this work is to briefly outline the spectrum of ways of portraying the causes of sin that was available to Matthew, the investigation of the Second Temple Literature should be sufficient to give sense of Matthew's milieu. On rabbinic ideas regarding sin, however, see: W.D. Davies, *Paul and Rabbinic Judaism: Some Rabbinic Elements in Pauline Theology* (London: S. P. C. K., 1958), particularly pp. 20–35; Adolf Büchler, *Studies in Sin and Atonement in the Rabbinic Literature of the First Century* (London, Oxford University Press, 1928); and E.P. Sanders, *Paul and Palestinian Judaism: A Comparison of Patterns of Religion* (Philadelphia: Fortress Press, 1977), 33–238.

On the complexities of religious, and particularly Jewish, identity during this period, and the manifestation of these complexities in a variety of texts, see: John M.G. Barclay, *Jews in the Mediterranean Diaspora: From Alexander to Trajan (323 BCE–117 CE)* (Edinburgh: T&T Clark, 1996); John J. Collins, *Between Athens and Jerusalem: Jewish Identity in the Hellenistic Diaspora*, Biblical Resources Series (Grand Rapids: Eerdmans, 2000); Karl P. Donfried and Peter Richardson, eds., *Judaism and Christianity in Rome in the First Century* (Grand Rapids: Eerdmans, 1998); Erich S. Gruen, *Heritage and Hellenism: The Reinvention of Jewish Tradition* (Berkeley: University of California Press, 1998); Troels Engberg-Pedersen, ed., *Paul Beyond the Judaism/Hellenism Divide* (Louisville: Westminster John Knox Press, 2001); Judith Lieu, John North, and Tessa Rajak, eds., *The Jews among Pagans and Christian in the Roman Empire* (New York: Routledge, 1992); George Nickelsburg and Robert Kraft, eds., *Early Judaism and Its Modern Interpreters*, 2nd ed., The Bible and Its Modern Interpreters (Atlanta: Scholars Press, 1986).

In this section we will focus on Jewish apocrypha and pseudepigrapha and the Dead Sea Scrolls.[8] The texts we will examine include the Enochic literature of *1 Enoch* and *Jubilees*, the revelatory texts 4 Ezra and 2 Baruch, the wisdom-tradition text of Sirach, and the Qumran sectarian documents 1QM, 1QH, CD, and 1QS. All of these texts display an interest in or depiction of the cause or source of sin and evil in the world and in humans. In each of these, we see not only overt reflection on why humans sin but also metaphorical statements that point to the underlying cause, source, or reason for sin. Some of the causes (both those overtly asserted and those metaphorically suggested) are portrayed as external to humans while others are internal to varying degrees. At times the causes or dynamics of sin suggested by the metaphors are in tension with the overt reflections, and when multiple metaphorical statements are present within the same text, they often point in differing directions. The resulting picture is of multifaceted attribution of sin's causation and the source of evil, even in texts attempting to develop a consistent point of view.

As will become apparent, one of the most interesting commonalities among the texts we will explore dealing with sin and evil is an underlying dualistic conception of reality.[9] This is not surprising. Questions about the presence and cause(s) of evil and sin in the world seem to necessitate some sort of dualistic schema that conceives of the evil as over against the good, thus resulting in a

---

8   This section will not survey the voluminous scholarship on conceptions of the causes of sin and evil in the OT. There are several reasons. First, the trend toward textual specialization and away from more general, all-encompassing treatments means that little has been done in recent years in terms of an overview of sin in the OT, and a survey of the many various perspectives of all the texts is clearly beyond the scope of this project. Second, beyond the issue of the sheer size of such a project, the focus here is on Second Temple literature precisely because, on the whole, the literature is interpreting or consciously looking back to the figures and events of the OT texts and reflecting on the causes of sin and evil in conversation with those traditions, such that we may be able to gain some insight into the scope and issues of the apparent conversation about sin and evil in the environment that was most likely to have formed a context for Matthew's own reflections and message. Third, particular points at which Matthew's perspective is notably informed by OT traditions that seem to be un- or under-represented in the Second Temple literature will be addressed in the exegetical portions of part 2. For two helpful though somewhat older overviews of sin and evil in the OT utilizing a lexical approach, see Gottfried Quell, "ἁμαρτάνω, ἁμάρτημα, ἁμαρτία; A. Sin in the OT," *TDNT*, 1:267–286; and Štefan Porúbčan, *Sin in the Old Testament: a Soteriological Study* (Rome: Herder, 1963). More recently, see Robin Cover, "Sin, Sinners (OT)" *ABD* 4:31–40; and articles for the relevant terms (עָוֹל, חטא, אָוֶן and related) in *NIDOTTE*, volumes 1–5 (Grand Rapids, Mich.: Zondervan, 1997). For a treatment which analyzes the various concepts for sin and evil and their likely historical connection and development, see Paul Ricoeur, *The Symbolism of Evil* (New York: Harper & Row, 1967), 25–210.

9   This dualism is essential for an apocalyptic worldview—a trait that Matthew shares with many of the texts we will explore—though, it should be noted, dualism does not necessarily imply apocalypticism.

DIVERSITY AND CONSISTENCY IN THE TEXTS OF MATTHEW'S MILIEU

dualism of some sort, though of what sort precisely is the question to which we will turn next. Since the term "dualism" can be used to designate a variety of concepts, we must first address this issue of definition and establish a working taxonomy of the dualisms we will be encountering in our texts.

1 Dualism and Dualisms: A Brief Taxonomy

In its most basic and general form, dualism is the conception that reality is characterized by a pair (or often pairs) of oppositional forces. It is a philosophical or religious system that explains phenomena in terms of the conflict or interplay between these opposing principles or forces. The tendency in religious studies and the history of religions field, however, has been to use "dualism" in a much more restricted sense. Thus, Ugo Bianchi stresses that:

> As a religio-historical phenomenon, dualism is more specific than either simple duality or polarity. Not every polarity is dualistic, but only those that involve the duality or polarity of *causal* principles. Thus, not every pair of opposites (such as male and female, right and left, darkness and light, good and bad, spirit and matter, sacred and profane) can be labeled as dualistic, even when their opposition is emphasized. They are dualistic only when they are understood as principles or *causes* of the world and its constitutive elements.[10]

In this definition of dualism, neither Judaism nor Christianity (except in highly Platonized or Gnostic forms) is properly dualistic, Bianchi argues, since in these religions God alone is the creator, and the forces that oppose God do not *create* anything nor is their existence necessary for the creation of humans or the cosmos.[11]

The scholarly literature relevant to our study, however, does not utilize this more restricted definition of the term but rather the broader. Thus, following this precedent, we will understand dualism to mean "the contrasting of good and evil, life and death, light and darkness, and so on [that] is in fact coextensive with religion itself," though "it cannot be equated with the much more specific phenomenon of dualism [in the history-of-religions tradition]."[12]

---

10   Ugo Bianchi, "Dualism," *The Encyclopedia of Religion*, ed. Mircea Eliade (New York: Macmillan Publishing, 1987), 4:506; italics mine.
11   Bianchi, "Dualism," 4:506–507.
12   Bianchi, "Dualism," 4:506.

32   CHAPTER 1

Having a broader and more general working definition such as this does have its drawbacks. Thirty years ago, the very broad scope of the term led John Gammie to complain that even reputable scholarship suffered from "a lamentable lack of precision in defining and distinguishing between types of dualism."[13] Such, however, is no longer the case. In fact, the attempts of scholars to define the types of dualism underlying various Second Temple and early Christian texts has led to a multiplication of labels for the various types, a situation which can now cause confusion since the terms used by various authors to identify a dualism have not been consistent: the same dichotomy is identified with different labels by different authors or the same label is applied by different authors to different dualisms.[14] Thus, to avoid confusion as we move forward, I will clarify below how the terms will be used in this study. The types listed below are ordered roughly from the micro to the macro, that is, from those which apply to aspects of an individual person to those that describe more universal, all-encompassing dualities.[15]

Physical—The dichotomy in this dualism is between the body or matter and the mind or spirit.[16] This type is not much present in our Second Temple Literature but is an important concept in the Greco-Roman philosophical tradition.

Psychological—This is the understanding of the human moral capacity (psyche, heart, soul, will, etc.) as bifurcated into a good or positive impulse and a negative or evil impulse. In every situation, humans must choose to follow one or the other impulse.

Anthropological—Related to *physical dualism*, in this duality the human is made up of two parts, usually a body and a soul or spirit or mind. Where these

---

13   John G. Gammie, "Spatial and Ethical Dualism in Jewish Wisdom and Apocalyptic Literature," *JBL* 93 (S 1974): 356.

14   In fact, given that the texts under discussion often manifest multiple, overlapping dualism (or perhaps constellations of dualistic tendencies), the compulsion to develop ever more precise, thorough, and detailed sets of categories may in the end be anti-heuristic rather than helpfully clarifying, the dissection process serving more to cut off pieces that originally were connected in important ways than to highlight their unique qualities vis-à-vis the surrounding structures. Obviously, this section will seek to avoid such over-compartmentalization while attending to the valid need for differentiation.

15   This list of types is based primarily on Gammie, "Spatial and Ethical Dualism," 356–362; James H. Charlesworth, "A Critical Comparison of the Dualism in 1QS 3:13–4:26 and the 'Dualism' Contained in the Gospel of John," *John and Qumran*, ed. James Charlesworth (London: Geoffrey Chapman, 1972), 76–106; Otzen, "Old Testament Wisdom Literature and Dualistic Thinking in Late Judaism," 146–157, esp. 147; and Bianchi, "Dualism," 4:506–512.

16   Cf. Charlesworth, "A Critical Comparison," 77n1. It should be recognized, however, that even the nature of "spirit" might be conceptualized in the ancient world as a type of material, albeit a significantly finer substance than that of which bodies were made.

are seen to be antagonistic forces, the mind/soul/spirit is usually considered superior and ought to rule the body.[17]

Ethical/Moral—Based on one's ethical choices, a person is classified as "good" (godly, righteous, etc.) or "bad" (evil, sinful, wicked, unrighteous, etc.).

Ontological—People (or other beings such as angels, daimons, or spirits) are intrinsically, by nature, good or bad. Good or evil actions are manifestations of the being's ontological status.

Spatial—Heaven (the celestial realm, the realm of goodness, light, and perfection or unchangeability) is opposed to the earth (including Hades, Sheol, or the underworld; places of imperfection, darkness, pain, and evil).[18]

Temporal/eschatological—The present age is evil and (oftentimes) ruled by the devil, in contrast to the age that is to come which will be characterized by the victory of goodness, righteousness, peace, God, and those who have been faithful to God.

Metaphysical/theological—God and the devil (Satan, Beliar/Belial, the Evil One, etc.) are opposing spiritual rulers, gods, or instantiations of the cosmic forces of Good and Evil.

Cosmic—Within the world (the cosmos, all of creation, the universe), there are two opposing (though not necessarily equal) forces, Good and Evil, which are antagonistic to one another and which continually vie for sway over humanity and control of the world.[19]

As we explore selected texts from the Second Temple period,[20] it will become apparent that, while not all the conceptions about the source (or sources) of sin and evil are based in a dualism of some sort, many are. The diversity of conceptions is such, however, that even a paradigm as broad as "dualism"

---

17 This seems to be fairly pervasive in Mt (e.g., contrasting of σομα and ψυχη in 6:25 and 10:28), though a tripartite view of humanity (human as body, soul/mind, and spirit) is also present in some other NT texts (1 Th 5:23, most notably). The tripartite view of the incorporeal part of the human (heart, mind, and soul [Mt 22:37] or reason, will, and desire [Plato's *Republic* IV]) presents an interesting overlap in the Jewish and Greek traditions.

18 On Jewish cosmology as being spatially dualistic rather than tripartite, see Jonathan T. Pennington, "Dualism in Old Testament Cosmology: Weltbild and Weltanschauung," *SJOT* 18 (2004): 260–277.

19 It should be noted that, in the Second Temple texts we will explore, this and the following dualisms are all *moderate dualisms*, that is, the two opposing entities, though antagonistic, are not conceived of as equal opposing forces as in *radical* or *absolute dualism*. Thus, the outcome of the conflict is never in doubt in these texts; God, good, and the heavenly realm are sure to prevail over their opponents.

20 This survey will not attempt to be exhaustive, exploring every relevant text from the period. It will focus on those texts that seem either to have exerted significance influence in the period or that seem to have the most in common with Matthew and thus the most relevance for our study of his perspective.

is not sufficient to encompass all the ideas found in these texts.[21] Further, the connection to and significance of metaphorical dynamics in these conceptions quickly becomes apparent. For example, the use of terms like "sons of light" and "sons of darkness" to express an ontological dualism is fairly apparent, given the symbolic nature of light and darkness and the ambiguity of the genitive. On the other hand, some dualistic language is used in ways that seem less metaphorical. The use in the NT of "the kingdom of God" seems, at least as used within the narratives, to be a non-metaphorical way of referring to some *thing* and refers to something that is dualistic both spatially (it is a place, a kingdom, a realm) and temporally (it is an imminent but future reality distinct from the present age). Only a brief pause of consideration is required, however, to recognize that "Kingdom of God" must be a metaphorical term—this "kingdom" or "reign" both is and is not like any kingdom or reign we have experienced—and the fact that the descriptions or explanations of the character of the Kingdom are generally expressed in parables (extended metaphors) reinforces this. Dualism, as an abstract idea or principle, in some sense must proceed metaphorically, and because of this there will always be the metaphorical yes/no tension at play.

---

21   Thus, it should be clear that our argument is not that all conceptions of the causes of sin have as an underlying principle some form of dualism, although many do.

CHAPTER 2

Enochic Literature

Generally, the authors of the Enochic literature focused on the activity of the Watchers as the cause of the pervasive and persistent sins of humanity.[1] The Watchers are responsible both in that they taught people illicit arts[2] and in that they transgressed the divide between the heavenly and the earthly in their intercourse with human women. Yet, the texts are not univocal on this point. As will be seen below, humans are still held culpable for their transgressions and at some points are portrayed as actively seeking the corrupting teaching of the Watchers, and not merely as victims of their powerful angelic instructors. The perspective of the Enochic literature has some parallels in Matthew's portrayal of the devil as a source of sin, a connection that will be discussed at the end of part 2.

1   1 Enoch

As a composite text, *1 Enoch* presents a variety of problems for interpreters attempting to discern a coherent perspective. Since, however, it seems that all of the constituent parts of *1 Enoch* were written before or during the last half of the first century,[3] and since our task is simply to trace out the variety of

---

1   Though Adam and Eve's primordial sin is mentioned (*1 Enoch* 31:3–5), it is not portrayed as contaminative of the entire race in the same way the activity of the Watchers and their offspring is.

2   E.g., *1 Enoch* 9:6, 64:2. These arts, which include metallurgy, the making of weapons and cosmetics, various fortunetelling and magical arts, writing, and the revelation of various "mysteries" are enumerated in *1 Enoch* 8:1–4, 65:9, and 69:2–12.

3   The possible composition of ch. 108 in the latter part of the first century (see for example Stuckenbruck, *1 Enoch 91–108*, [Berlin; New York: Walter de Gruyter, 2007], pp. 13 and 693–694) notwithstanding, as 108 does not bear on our investigation. Although Milik's dating of the Similitudes/Parables (chs. 37–71) to sometime after 100 was widely held for many years, historical arguments have been advanced leading to a somewhat earlier dating for the composition. See for example James H. Charlesworth, "Can We Discern the Composition Date of the Parables of Enoch?" in *Enoch and the Messiah Son of Man: Revisiting the Book of Parables*, ed. Gabriele Boccaccini (Grand Rapids/Cambridge, U.K.: Eerdmans, 2007), 450–468. Further, arguments for Milik's later dating (third century) based on "Christian" influences in the depiction of the "Son of Man" are shown to be groundless by, for example, the work of Nickelsburg in his essay on the familiarity of the author of the Parables with the Hebrew Bible/OT (George W.E. Nickelsburg, "Enochic Wisdom and Its Relationship

---

© KONINKLIJKE BRILL NV, LEIDEN, 2020 | DOI:10.1163/9789004419506_004

perspectives available in Matthew's milieu rather than to trace the relationships or disjunctions within the text or even to argue for literary dependence of Matthew on any particular Second Temple text, we will consider the entire text as potentially representative of perspectives that may have been informing Matthew, and thus of value for our discussion.

In the early sections of *1 Enoch*, the activity of the Watchers is portrayed as the primary source of sin and evil in the world. Their instruction of people in illicit arts combined with their union with human women and the resulting birth of the Giants is the catalyst of a downward spiral of depravity that is only checked, and then only temporarily, by the Deluge. After the Deluge, the evil fruit of the Watchers' activity continues to produce sin in people since the Giants (the Watchers' offspring) continue to exist in the world as evil spirits although their physical bodies were destroyed in the flood; they tempt people to worship demons as gods (19:1), and so people become idolatrous.

The close connection between the degenerating spread of evil and the transgression of the boundary between the celestial and terrestrial, between spiritual and physical, by the Watchers is apparent in several places. In 9:7–8 Michael and his three angelic colleagues report to the Lord that Shemihazaz and his fellows (the Watchers) "have gone in to the daughters of the men of the earth, and they have lain with them, and have defiled themselves with the women."[4] As a result of this trespass of the boundary between the spiritual and fleshly, "the daughters of men have borne sons from them, giants, half-breeds. <And the blood of men is shed on the earth,> And the whole earth is filled with iniquity" (9:9). Apparently, the Lord finds this a persuasive indictment, for in ch. 15 he commands Enoch to chastise the Watchers for precisely this reason:

---

to the Mosaic Torah," in *The Early Enoch Literature*, eds. Gabriele Boccaccini and John J. Collins, SJSJ 121 [Leiden/Boston: Brill, 2007], 81–94; see esp. 82 and 90). Charlesworth, summarizing research on the issue, concludes: "It became obvious that Milik had not proved his position, as Fitzmyer pointed out as soon as The Book of Enoch had been published. Repeatedly the specialists on I Enoch have come out in favor of the Jewish nature and its first century AD origin, and probable pre-70 date. The list of specialists on I Enoch arguing for this position has become overwhelmingly impressive: Isaac, Nickelsburg, Stone, Knibb, Anderson, Black, VanderKam, Greenfield and Sutter. The consensus communis is unparalleled in almost any other area of research; no specialist now argues that I Enoch 37–71 is Christian and postdates the first century" (*The Old Testament Pseudepigrapha and the New Testament*, SNTSMS 54 [Cambridge; New York: Cambridge University Press, 1985], 89).

4 All quotations are from the translation in George Nickelsburg and James VanderKam, *1 Enoch: a New Translation* (Minneapolis: Fortress Press, 2004). In the following quotations, emendations of corrupted text made by the translators are marked with < > as in the published translation.

'Why have you forsaken the high heaven, the eternal sanctuary; and lain with women, and defiled yourselves with the daughters of men ... and begotten for yourselves sons, giants? You were holy ones and spirits, living forever. With the blood of women you have defiled yourselves, and with the blood of flesh you have begotten.... But you originally existed as spirits, living forever and not dying for all generations of eternity; therefore I did not make women among you.' The spirits of heaven, in heaven is their dwelling; But now the giants who were begotten by the spirits and flesh—they will call them evil spirits on earth, for their dwelling will be on earth.... Evil spirits they will be on the earth, and evil spirits they will be called.[5]

As evil spirits created through an unnatural union of heavenly (the Watchers) and earthly (the women), the Giants' appropriate habitat is not heaven, as was the Watchers', but the earth, where they continue to "<lead astray>, do violence, and attack and wrestle, and hurl upon the earth, and cause illnesses" (15:11). Thus, the issue at the heart of the charge against the Watchers is the transgression of a combined spatial and physical dualism. This lies at the core of their misdeeds. Obviously, for the author of *1 Enoch*, the spatial and physical dualistic divide cannot be transgressed without calamitous and enduring repercussions.

The proper separation of the heavenly from the earthly is also the core issue in the Watchers' unauthorized teaching of heavenly mysteries to humans. In 9:6, Michael's first charge against the Watchers to the Lord is that Asael "has taught all iniquity on earth and revealed the eternal mysteries that were in heaven." The result of Asael's activity is that "there was much godlessness on the earth and they[6] made their ways desolate" (8:2). The same message is reiterated in 64:2 and 69:6–12.

This attribution of guilt, however, is perhaps not so unambiguous as it may seem. To return to 9:6, if we accept the emendation of Nickelsburg and

---

5   15:3–9.

6   It is unclear whether "they" and "their" refers to humans or to the Watchers who were attracted (or perhaps more attracted) to the women after the introduction of cosmetics, as is indicated in the Nickelsburg/VanderKam translation of 8:1: "And the sons of men made them [cosmetics] for themselves and for their daughters, and they transgressed and led the holy ones astray." In this scenario, the initial transgression of the heavenly/earthly divide by the Watchers in teaching the mysteries to humans leads directly to further transgression of the spatial and physical dualistic divides in the Watchers fornication with the women.

VanderKam,[7] the passage reads: "You see what Asael has done, who has taught all iniquity on the earth, and has revealed the eternal mysteries that are in heaven, <which the sons of men were striving to learn.>" If this is correct, the Watchers and humanity are held mutually responsible.

Further, in 65:6–10, the Lord's decision to destroy the earth is initially portrayed as his response to *humanity's* sin of searching out and learning the various forbidden arts, rather than a response to the sins of the Watchers in teaching the secrets of heaven:

> A command has gone forth from the presence of the Lord against the inhabitants of the earth that their end is accomplished, for they have learned all the secrets of the angels, and all the violence of the satans, and all their powers, the hidden secrets, and all the powers of those who practice sorcery, and the powers of spells, and the power of those who cast molten images in all the earth.... Because of their iniquity their judgment has been accomplished and will not be <withheld> in my presence; because of the <sorceries> that they have searched out and learned, the earth will be destroyed, and those who dwell on it.[8]

In 65:11, however, the Lord returns to condemning the Watchers to destruction for the revelation of the mysteries: "And these will have no place of refuge, for they have shown them what was hidden, and they are judged." Thus, in the matter of the teaching and learning of mysteries, both the angels and the humans are culpable.

In stark contrast to this is the imagery of the Animal Apocalypse (chs. 85–90). Here, the graphic depiction of the Watchers as bulls with horse-like genitalia (86:4, 88:3) that mate with human "cattle" (the allegorical descendants of Adam and Eve), portrays the women (and thus humanity) as completely

---

7 So also R.H. Charles' translation (*The Apocrypha and Pseudepigrapha of the Old Testament in English: with Introduction and Critical and Explanatory Notes to the Several Books* [Oxford: Clarendon Press, 1913]). Charlesworth and Isaac, OTP 1:17 (James H. Charlesworth, ed., *Old Testament Pseudepigrapha* [Garden City, N.Y.: Doubleday & Co., 1983–1985]) reads "(and which) man learned."

8 A similar emphasis on the responsibility of humans seems to underlie their condemnation at the Judgment in the Similitudes (38:2–3): "Where will be the dwelling place of the sinners, and where will be the resting place of those who have denied the Lord of Spirits? It would have been better for them if they had not been born. When his hidden things shall be revealed to the righteous, the sinners will be judged, and the wicked driven from the presence of the righteous and chosen."

passive victims, essentially raped by the Watchers (86:3–4).[9] What role the revelation of the heavenly mysteries might have played, if any, in this transgression is left undiscussed.

Despite attributions of guilt to the Watchers in various places, there is a recurring, underlying theme in *1 Enoch* that people are ultimately responsible for their actions, good or evil. Noah was (or remained) righteous in his time, and although he is symbolically depicted as being exceptionally righteous even at birth (106:2–3), the text makes no mention of any special ability that was given to him to remain so (10:1–3 and chs. 106–107) such that the symbolism of 106:2 seems to be the result of the proleptic attribution of Noah's later-achieved righteousness rather than the indication of superhuman ability. The author presumes that while others were culpable for their sins and justly punished, Noah was to be rewarded for his righteousness, a destiny that was known to God (and Enoch) even before Noah's birth, and thus indicated by the baby's unusual appearance.

Further, in some later sections, there is a distinct emphasis on human responsibility for sin. The Epistle of Enoch (chs. 92–107) casts no blame at all upon the Watchers or other spiritual beings.[10] The focus is on human moral responsibility and the judgment that awaits those who mistreat or oppress their fellows. Here the text shows significant influence from the wisdom tradition, particularly in Enoch's highly traditional exhortation to his children regarding the "two ways" of righteousness and iniquity (94:1–5). As Stuckenbruck notes:

> Such language about 'walking' on one of two opposing paths functions as a metaphor for behavior which classifies human beings as either good or bad, righteous or wicked, moral or immoral.... The 'two ways' motif frequently envisions individuals as standing before a parting of the road, having to make a make a choice between two clear alternatives.[11]

---

9   A similar conception may behind the statement in 10:15 that the "spirits of the half-breeds and the sons of the Watchers" must be destroyed "because they ἀδικῆσαι humanity." While the verb ἀδικεω can mean simply "to wrong" or "to injure" someone, it also can mean to "ruin" a young girl (LSJ 23, "ἀδικεω," II).

10   "It is interesting to observe that ... *1 Enoch* 91–105 nowhere co-ordinates language about contrasting ways with angelic beings, especially since angels play such an important role elsewhere in the Enochic tradition.... If anything, the authors of chapters 91–105 steer clear of drawing a link between the different ways and cosmic powers, and instead participate in that stream of tradition that restricts language to ethical dualistic categories" (Stuckenbruck, *1 Enoch 91–108*, 248–249).

11   *1 Enoch 91–108*, 246–249. For general discussion of the "two ways" tradition in Judaism and early Christianity and the relation of *1 Enoch* to it, see Stuckenbruck's discussion and commentary, pp. 246–256, and attendant bibliographic notes.

40 CHAPTER 2

The underlying assumption of the two ways is that humans do have the capacity to choose behaviors which will result in their categorization as "good" or "bad," "righteous" or "wicked."[12] Thus, the dualism invoked here is an ethical dualism contrasting the good or righteous man with the unrighteous or wicked sinner.[13] The perspective of this section is aptly summarized in a brief, but often cited, verse: "Thus, lawlessness was not sent upon the earth; but men created it by themselves, and those who do it will come to a great curse" (98:4).

Thus, the overt reflections on culpability in *1 Enoch* do not attribute the responsibility for the pervasive and enduring sin present in the world solely to humans or to angelic beings or their offspring. Each bears a measure of the blame. The authors see the heart of the problem, however, on all levels as the lack of an appropriate respect for the dualistic divide between heaven and earth.

The ambiguity of responsibility evident in the more overt reflections is reinforced by the more subtle treatments of the issue via the use of particular metaphors for sin throughout the work.

Causes external to human beings underlie the metaphor of sin as sickness or some disability such as blindness or deafness. The solution in this case is obviously healing, and even healing that goes beyond the human sinners to include the whole world which has been infected. In 10:7, God instructs Raphael to "heal the earth which the watchers have desolated;[14] and announce the healing

---

12 Stuckenbruck's caveat that "Though in *1 Enoch* 91–105 this capacity to choose is assumed in the exhortations," it is perhaps only the righteous who have a choice since "it is only the 'righteous' who are thus addressed, while the 'wicked' or 'sinners' are thus designated because they have already taken wrong decisions" (247), seems self-contradictory; affirming that the wicked have already chosen their (wrong) path implies that they had before them at some time in the past the same opportunity that is being presented to the righteous in the "two ways." The comment also seems at odds with the earlier remark that "the notion of being on either one path or the other is logically incompatible with the complexities of experience, which can include the simultaneous negotiation between wrongdoing and righteous behavior" (246–247). Though it is the righteous who are addressed here by Enoch (94:3), the sinners are also repeatedly addressed in the "Woes" and curses that follow; thus the underlying assumption of this section seems to be that each person has sufficient moral agency to choose the right or the wrong. While one could perhaps imagine that the author sees the "wicked" as having eroded that capacity by their previous choices, thus now eliminating the possibility of repentance and ensuring their condemnation and punishment, an assertion of their incorrigibility is not clearly articulated, only the certainty of their punishment.

13 This dualism is not confined to the Epistle, however. It also appears to be invoked in the Similitudes in 50:2, 60:6, 62:13, though it is less clear that there was independent moral agency available on both or either side of the dualistic divide of sinners and righteous.

14 The translation here of ἠφάνισαν as "desolated" (and of ἀφανισθεῖσα in 10:8 as "made desolate") seems to strike the wrong note, though it is consistent with the English translation

ENOCHIC LITERATURE

of the earth, that the plague may be healed, and all the sons of men may not perish because of mystery that the watchers told and taught their sons."[15]

In the Animal Apocalypse, metaphors of blindness and deafness for sin play a significant role in the author's characterization of the Israelites. In retelling the Exodus story, he says that when Moses was on the mountain, "the sheep began to be blinded and to stray from the path ... And the Lord of the sheep was filled with great wrath against them, and that sheep [Moses] discovered it and went down from the summit of that rock and came to the sheep and found most of them blinded and straying" (89:32–33). This motif is reiterated in the description of the Israelites in the time of the Judges: "And sometimes their eyes were opened, and sometimes they were blinded, until another sheep arose and led them and brought them all back, and their eyes were opened" (89:41). In the period after the return from exile, "the eyes of the sheep were blind, and they did not see, and their shepherds likewise" (89:74). And later, "lambs were born of those white sheep, and they began to open their eyes and to see and to cry out to the sheep. But they did not listen to them nor attend to their words, but they were extremely deaf, and their eyes were extremely and excessively blinded" (90:7). And still later, "after this <there will arise a sixth week, and> all who live in it will become blind, and the hearts of all will stray from wisdom" (93:8).

The use of this image emphasizes that "blindness" and "deafness" are not the natural state of these creatures; contrary to the way they were created, this is a disability that inhibits living in the way they were intended. Thus, as a metaphor for the cause of sin, blindness and deafness convey the sense that sin is not an inherent part of what it means to be human; sin is a defect contrary to God's design. It is also something over which the sheep/human would have no control. It is a situation that has become internal to the creature in that it

---

of the word in, for example, the NRSV of Joel 2:20 and Zech 7:14. The sense of ἀφανίζω as to wipe clean, obliterate, or make empty, however, does not fit with the thrust of the charges against the Watchers and Asael elsewhere. R.H. Charles' rendering of ἀφανισθεῖσα as "corrupted" fits better though it risks confusion with φθείρω used elsewhere. Perhaps "mar" or "disfigure" is more apt (as in most English translations of Mt. 6:16, though it is noteworthy that in Mt 6:19–20 the meaning seems to be more or less synonymous with φθείρω, i.e., destructive rot or degenerative consumption, in this case by moths and rust). In any case, the use of the combined ideas of plague and healing within the verse militate against a sense of ἠφάνισαν as obliterating destruction of the land/world and point more in the direction of disfiguring infection.

15 The use of the metaphor of "corruption" may also fall into this category, in as much as φθορά—death and consequent rot—is the ultimate sickness and also its consequence. "And he will cleanse the earth from all the corruption that is on it" (106:17). Cf., *LSJ* 1930, φθορά.

affects a body part, yet it is not an inherent tendency, and it is a situation over which the subject can exercise no freedom of choice; it cannot choose on its own to become un-blind. The use of the passive ("their eyes were blinded") reinforces this. There are occasional indications of willfulness on the part of the sheep ("but they did not listen to them nor attend to their words" 90:7), and while these do potentially complicate the picture, these do not predominate. Thus, in the metaphor of blindness, the cause of sin is some blinding, deafening external force that has become internal to humans through (metaphorically) disfiguring a body part, and this force is something from which the sheep cannot free themselves.[16]

Further, the metaphors of blindness and deafness are combined with the metaphor of straying. In this case (as opposed to others we will examine later), the use of the image of straying portrays more the *character* of the sinning than the cause. Yet the image tends to reinforce the helplessness of the "sheep" in the scenario: sin lies outside the path, yet the sheep cannot help but stray into it because of their blindness and deafness.

Our most recent quotation above also introduced a new metaphor: that of the heart. The passage prophesies that "the hearts of all will stray from wisdom" (93:8). In the Epistle of Enoch, we also see the conjunction of the blindness metaphor with that of the heart when the writer warns that those involved in idolatry "will be led astray by the folly of their hearts, and their eyes will be blinded by the fear of their hearts, and the visions of your dreams will lead you astray" (99:8). The use of this image indicates something internal to the human (not an external force such as the coercion or temptation of the watchers or giants), and when its functioning is defective, it leads to sin.[17] Its conjunction with the blindness metaphor invites the reader to see a connection between the two—either implicitly or, even more so, explicitly in the phrase "their eyes will be blinded by the fear of their hearts": perhaps the force that has caused the blindness was, in fact, internal after all. Perhaps it was the folly and fear of the heart.

An even more internal cause is communicated in the use of the imagery of differentiated species that is integral to the Animal Apocalypse (85:1–90:42). The image that some are sinful and rebellious (or conversely righteous) because of some inherent genetic differentiation is initially articulated in terms

---

16   Matthew also uses (although via quotation from Isaiah) images of blindness and deafness as metaphors of the disposition that sets people in opposition to Jesus and his message and thus in opposition to God (a fundamentally sinful stance). See also part 2, "Metaphors of illness and infirmity for the cause of sin."

17   For further discussion of the heart metaphor and its background in the OT, see the literature cited in ch. 3 and the discussion of its use in *Jubilees*, below.

ENOCHIC LITERATURE

of the color of the animal but soon expands—God's righteous people are depicted as white cattle and later the sheep, and the giants and unrighteous as various other animals.[18] The implication of the use of this imagery is that one's status as righteous or unrighteous is analogous to one's genetic species or "nature." Thus, the cause of any sinful action is utterly internal: these individuals are sinful because it is their nature to be so.

The fact that the imagery of blindness (an external factor internalized, not an inherent trait) is applied to the straying Israelites actually compliments the use of this genetic imagery. As God's people ("sheep"), they are understood to be "genetically" clean and holy but straying because of the debilitating effect of blindness. They do have the hope of healing and recovery of sight (return to righteousness), unlike those who, as other species, will never be "sheep." Whether the author conceives of a possibility of conversion for these other "species" is not addressed. The statement of *1 Enoch* 41:8 that the Lord "made a separation between the light and the darkness, and divided the spirits of men, and strengthened the spirits of the righteous, in the name of his righteousness" utilizes the language of ontological dualism, and so its use is congruent with the use of genetic metaphors in the Animal Apocalypse.

Finally, in 42:2–3 we see yet another angle on the cause of sin. Here, iniquity is personified, but with an interesting twist on the canonical scenario. We read that "Wisdom went forth to dwell among the sons of men, but she did not find a dwelling. Wisdom returned to her place, and sat down among the angels. Iniquity went forth from her chambers, those whom she did not seek she found, and she dwelt among them, like rain in a desert and dew in a thirsty land." Among the several aspects that depart from typical use of the "Dame Wisdom and Dame Folly" trope, there are two that are particular germane to our investigation. First, Iniquity finds those "whom she did not seek." This indicates that iniquity only comes upon one by chance or by one's own seeking of it. It does not seek you out and overcome you. This is supported by the second departure: Iniquity is characterized in terms that are usually reserved for those things which benefit people and are seen as gifts of God: rain in a desert and dew in a thirsty land. The implication is that people desired Iniquity and that they saw her as beneficial and able to satisfy their needs. This depiction of humans as the being actively desirous of sin, if not perhaps quite intentionally pursuing it, paints a different and much more indicting picture than those noted above where humans are essentially victims or helpless before the situation into which they are born (blind or inherently, "genetically" sinful), and

---

18   Esp. 85:9, 86:4, 89:9–27, 89:42–47, 89:54–56, 90:4–16, 90:30–38.

44   CHAPTER 2

different from those uses of personified Folly/Sin in which people are pursued and seduced.

Thus, in *1 Enoch* we see a significant diversity of perspectives on the causes of sin in humans, some explicit and seemingly intentionally put forward and some more subtle and perhaps the result of a less intentional use of the images and metaphors available to the writers from scripture (e.g., blindness, the heart) or the culture.

2   Jubilees

As with *1 Enoch, Jubilees* manifests both explicit reflection on the source of sin and evil as well as more implicit, subtle perspectives embedded in the imagery of the text, particularly its metaphors. Many scholars[19] see explicit reflection in *Jubilees*, as in *1 Enoch*, as focusing heavily on the activity of a variety of evil spirits or entities.[20] *Jubilees* attributes to the activity of the Watchers the "beginning of impurity"[21] that led to the rampant wickedness of the antediluvian

---

19   So, for example, O.S. Wintermute in his introduction to his translation of *Jubilees* (*OTP* 2:47–48). See also, James C. VanderKam, *The Book of Jubilees*, Guides to Apocrypha and Pseudepigrapha (Sheffield: Sheffield Academic Press, 2001), 127–131; Philip Davies, "The Origin of Evil in Ancient Judaism," *ABR* 50 (2002): 45–46; Bruce J. Malina, "Some Observations on the Origin of Sin in Judaism and St. Paul," *CBQ* 31 (Ja 1969): 22–23; and scholars cited below.

20   These include Belial, Mastema/Satan, the Watchers, the Naphidim, the Giants, and "demons." Though there is good reason to investigate the differences—great and subtle—among these characters in *Jubilees*, particularly with regard to the historical development of the idea of Satan or the devil and demonic powers, their general character as external spiritual powers is the key aspect for our investigation and makes exploration of the distinctions among them relatively unnecessary for the present project. It is enough to recognize that in Matthew's milieu there was a conception of spiritual powers under a variety of names and that these powers had influence either by virtue of their perennial activity in the world, or by virtue of their previous activity which had enduring ramifications for human conduct, or both.

21   "For it (was because) of the fornication which the Watchers, apart from the mandate of their authority, fornicated with the daughters of men, and took for themselves wives from all whom they chose and made a beginning of impurity" (7:21). Here and elsewhere, ET used is that of O.S. Wintermute in *OTP* 2:52–142, unless otherwise noted. Differences between Wintermute's translation and R.H. Charles' are generally not significant, mainly consisting of the use of slightly different but essentially synonymous terms, such as Wintermute's use of "impurity" or "pollution" where Charles has "uncleanness," etc. In general, such divergences in translation do not significantly affect the overall message of a passage and thus will only warrant occasional attention in our investigation. Since this study will often focus on particular turns of phrase and metaphors in the text,

ENOCHIC LITERATURE

world. As in *1 Enoch*, it is the transgression of the celestial-terrestrial boundary in the union of the angels with mortal women that serves to introduce the infectious impurity.[22] The breaching of God's order—which includes the separation of the earthly and celestial—is noted regularly in the early chapters of *Jubilees* as a root trait of sin,[23] and this transgression begins with the illicit

---

VanderKam's translation (*The Book of Jubilees: a critical text*, James C. VanderKam, ed. and trans., CSCO 511/*Scriptores Aethiopici* 88 [Lovanii: Peeters, 1989]), though authoritative in many ways, is less helpful since, as he himself notes in his introduction, "an effort has been made to avoid the archaic words and expressions" (xxxi) that more literal translations render (see Wintermute's introduction, *OTP* 2:50) in favor of "a more contemporary idiom." Nevertheless, VanderKam's translation and textual notes have been consulted and compared for all quotations, and notable differences are indicated in brackets.

22 4:22: "[Methuselah] bore witness to the Watchers, the ones who sinned with the daughters of men because they began to mingle themselves with the daughters of men so that they might be polluted [VanderKam: "they became defiled"]." As Michael Segal notes: "The assault on the natural order of the world did not begin with human behavior, but with the fornication of the sons of god with the daughters of men ... The cohabitation of the divine being with women, which produced the giants, represented a callous violation of the clear boundaries between heaven and earth, and led to destructive results" (*The Book of Jubilees: Rewritten Bible, Redaction, Ideology, and Theology*, SJSJ 117 [Leiden, Boston: Brill, 2007], 108). Segal also notes that the same dynamic is implied in 5:1–3. It is interesting to note that Adam and Eve's consumption of the fruit in 3:18–22, though it seems to be an attempt to transgress the earthly-divine divide ("You will become like gods"), does not have the same consequences, perhaps because it is unsuccessful in its attempt to attain to any divinity by the action, thus indicating that the serpent was deceptive in his enticement. His statement was misleading because, while eating the fruit would give them a knowledge of both good and evil, this knowledge would not make them like God.

23 5:2: "And all flesh corrupted its way; man and cattle and beasts and birds and everything which walks on the earth. And they all corrupted their ways and their ordinances [Charles: 'orders'; VanderKam: 'prescribed course'], and they began to eat one another, and injustice [Charles: 'lawlessness'; VanderKam: 'wickedness'] grew upon the earth and every imagination of the thoughts of all mankind was thus continually evil"; 5:13: "And the judgment of all of them has been ordained and written in the heavenly tablets without injustice. And if any of them transgress from their way with respect to what was ordained for them to walk in, or if they do not walk in it, the judgment for every sort of nature and every kind is written"; 5:19: "[Noah's] heart [VanderKam: 'mind'] was righteous in all of his ways, just as it was commanded concerning him. And he did not transgress anything which was ordained for him"; 7:21: "For it (was because) of the fornication which the Watchers, apart from the mandate of their authority [Charles: 'ordinances'], fornicated with the daughters of men, and took for themselves wives from all whom they chose and made a beginning of impurity." In later chapters, there is an emphasis on God's ordering of the world through those things which he "ordains" though "eternal ordinances" which are inscribed forever on the heavenly tablets (e.g., the command to eat the Passover "is an eternal ordinance, and engrave[d] on the heavenly tablets regarding all the children of Israel that they should observe it every year on its day once a year, throughout all their generations; and there is no limit of days, for this is ordained forever" [49:8] and "But if

relationship of the Watchers and the women. Unlike *1 Enoch*, however, there is little mention of the teaching of mysteries or forbidden knowledge by the Watchers as a cause of human sin.[24]

Jubilees asserts, however, that the fornication of the Watchers with the daughters of men not only introduces "uncleanness" but physically introduces their offspring who set in motion a spiral of violence and injustice that eventually involves all the creatures of the earth. After the flood, the activity of the surviving demonic offspring of the Watchers leads to the corruption of Noah's sons.[25] Their nefarious work is particularly focused on leading humans astray,[26] but it is not confined to that. In his prayer to God for the protection of his grandsons, Noah claims that the offspring of the Watchers "are cruel and created in order to destroy" (10:5). Their destructive nature, like the impurity that is tied to both literal and metaphorical fornication and transgression, is apparently also infectious:

> And they [the Watchers] begot sons, the Naphidim, and all of them were dissimilar. And each one ate his fellow. The Giants killed the Naphil, and the Naphil slew the Elyo, and the Elyo mankind, and man his neighbor. And every one sold himself in order that he might do injustice and pour out much blood, and the earth was full of injustice. And afterward, they

---

[the times for the feasts] are transgressed and [the people] do not observe them according to his commandment, then they will corrupt all their (fixed) times and the years will be moved from within this (order), and they will transgress their ordinances [VanderKam: 'prescribed pattern']" [6:33]).

24   The only instance seems to be 8:3: "And [Cainan] found a writing which the ancestors engraved on stone. And he read what was in it. And he transcribed it. And he sinned because of what was in it, since there was in it the teaching of the Watchers by which they used to observe the omens of the sun and moon and stars within all the signs of heaven."

25   7:25–27: "And the Lord destroyed everything from off the face of the earth; because of the wickedness of their deeds, and because of the blood which they had shed in the midst of the earth He destroyed everything. [Noah said,] 'And we were left, I and you, my sons, and everything that entered with us into the ark, and behold I see your works before me that you have not been ones who walked in righteousness because you have begun to walk in the paths of corruption.... For I see, and behold the demons have begun to mislead you and your children. And now I fear for your sakes that after I die you will pour out the blood of men upon the earth.'" So also in 10:1–5: "And in the third week of that jubilee the polluted demons began to lead astray the children of Noah's sons and to lead them to folly and to destroy them. And the sons of Noah came to Noah, their father, and they told him about the demons who were leading astray and blinding and killing his grandchildren. And he prayed before the Lord his God, and said: '.... Let your grace be lift up upon my sons, and do not let the evil spirits rule over them, lest they destroy them from the earth.'"

26   See, for example 7:27 and 10:1 in previous footnote, and also below.

ENOCHIC LITERATURE

sinned against the beasts, and birds, and everything which moves or walks on the earth. And they poured out much blood upon the earth.[27]

It is unclear, however, whether this continuing influence of the spirits of the giants/demons—influence involved both in human erring and in the perpetuation of violence—takes the form of simple temptation and seduction or outright manipulation and coercion. In many places, the main way in which the spirits cause iniquity to increase among humans is through temptation: the language of "leading astray" is particularly prevalent in connection with the activities of the post-diluvian demons. Noah tells his children that "the demons have begun to mislead[28] you and your children" (7:27). Despite Noah's prayers, "in the third week of that jubilee the polluted demons began to lead astray the children of Noah's sons and to lead them to folly" (10:1). According to their leader, Mastema, the ten percent of demons that are not bound "are (intended) to corrupt and lead astray" (10:8). Idolatry grows up in Ur because "cruel spirits assisted [the city's people] and led them astray so that they might commit sin and pollution" (11:4). Abram prays in 12:20, "Save me from the hands of evil spirits which rule over the thoughts of the heart of man, and do not let them lead me astray from following you, O my God." Further, in discussing the election of Israel and circumcision, the angel of the presence reveals to Moses that there are "many nations and many people, and the all belong to [God], but over all of them he caused spirits to rule so that they might lead them astray from following him" (15:32). Thus, the activity of the demons is, if not exclusively then significantly, to lead people astray.

As we see in the quotes above, however, in both the prayer of Abram and the comment on the election of Israel, it is notable that there is both the language of leading astray and rulership.[29] So, at least in some cases, the "leading" is more coercive, and the demons' power is not simply temptation that leads people on toward sin,[30] while the people could, in fact, resist. The demons are, in these two instances and elsewhere as well, depicted as having actual control over the thoughts and perhaps actions of people. In fact, the first mention in *Jubilees* of the malicious spiritual forces includes this idea. After the Lord warns Moses of the people's coming apostasy and repentance, Moses prays,

---

27 7:22–24.

28 Charles: "seduce."

29 12:20: "Save me from the hands of evil spirits which rule over the thoughts of the heart of man"; 15:32: there are "many nations and many people, and the all belong to [God], but over all of them he cause spirits to rule so that they might lead them astray."

30 Or as with the idolatry of Ur, a case of *assisting* the people in their plans to turn away from the Lord.

"O Lord, let your mercy be lifted up upon your people, and create for them an upright spirit. And do not let the spirit of Beliar rule over them to accuse them before you and ensnare them from every path of righteousness so that they might be destroyed from before your face" (1:19; VanderKam 1:20). After the flood, Noah prays:

> Let your grace be lift up upon my sons, and do not let the evil spirits rule over them, lest they destroy them from the earth ... And let [the spirits of the Giants] not rule over the spirits of the living for you alone know their judgment, and do not let them have power over the sons of the righteous from henceforth and for evermore.[31]

In 10:8 Mastema asks the Lord to refrain from allowing the angels to bind all the demons but rather "leave some of them before me ... because if some of them are not left for me, I will not be able to exercise the power of my will among the children of men." God's granting of Mastema's request implies that Mastema's will has continuing power over humans through the work of the demons, at least until the Judgment. Abraham, in his speech to Jacob, prays that Jacob and his descendants would be protected from the power of evil spiritual forces: "And may the spirit of Mastema not rule over you or over your seed in order to remove you from following the Lord, who is your God henceforth forever" (19:28). In the retelling of the Exodus narrative, it appears that the Egyptians are under the control of Mastema and the demons[32] since, while these spirits are bound by the angels, the Egyptians do not hinder the Israelites.[33]

---

31   10:3 and 6.

32   The text does not mention the demons specifically, but their presence seems to be implied. The text shifts in this section from referring to "Prince Mastema" and "he/him" to "they/them," implying that Mastema's demonic "entourage" goes with him even when it is not specifically mentioned; e.g., 48:15–16: "Prince Mastema was bound and shut up from coming after the children of Israel so that he might not accuse them. And on the nineteenth day we released them so that they might help the Egyptians and pursuer after the children of Israel."

33   48:15–19. Mastema also assisted the Egyptians magicians (48:9). Interestingly, the majority of the references to Mastema in the retelling of Exodus narrative do not speak of him acting to lead or coerce humans to do wrong but of him acting independently to commit evil, that is, without using any human as his instrument. So in 48:2–3 the angel says to Moses: "And you know what was related to you on Mount Sinai, and what prince Mastema desired to do with you when you returned to Egypt, on the way when you met him at the shelter. Did he not seek to kill you with all of his might and save the Egyptians from your hand because he saw that you were sent to execute judgment and vengeance on the Egyptians?" Similarly, it is Mastema who slays the first born in Egypt (49:2). Prior to this passage, Mastema's ability to act in the world was also asserted following the discussion of

ENOCHIC LITERATURE

49

Thus, the idea of the spirits having some level of power over humans is a note that is sounded at regular intervals in the first twenty chapters of the text alongside the depiction of their activity of temptation.[34]

It is notable, however, that these spiritual beings are not the only forces at play in engendering sin and evil in the world.[35] Again, as with our investigation of *1 Enoch*, if we examine all of the language the text uses to attribute the cause of sin to something, we see that the message of the explicit reflection that attributes sin to the work of the Watchers, *et al*, is at least tempered if not contradicted by more subtle reflections including the use of images and metaphors for the source of sin.

---

the growth of idolatry in Ur: "And the prince Mastema, acted forcefully to do all this. And he sent other spirits to those who were set under his hand, to practice all error and sin, and all transgression, to destroy, to cause to perish, and to pour out blood upon the earth" (11:5). VanderKam's translation is even more forceful: "Prince Mastema was exerting his power in effecting all these actions and, by means of the spirits, he was sending to those who were under his control (the ability) to commit every (kind of) error and sin and every (kind of) transgression." This is in keeping with the assertion that the giants perpetrated violence first among themselves and then against humans (7:22–24 and 10:1–2, 6).

34   The several references to an idyllic time of peace and prosperity in the latter chapters of *Jubilees* also include references to the evil spirits, but in the negative. In the angel's prophecy of the eschatological future of God's people, Moses is told that "there will be no Satan and no evil (one) who will destroy" (23:29). We see similar language in the closing prophecy of Israel's future: "And jubilees will pass until Israel is purified ... and then [the land] will not have any Satan or any evil one, and the land will be purified from that time and forever" (50:5). Based on the equation of Satan with Mastema in the conjunction of 10:8 and 10:11, I take the use of the name Satan in these and the following verses to refer to an evil spiritual entity and not simply an "adversary" or "opponent," political or military, that will be no more. The fact that it requires mentioning that this future includes the abolition of Satan implies his (and presumably his demons') continuing presence and activity until that time. The only exception seems to be the time of Joseph's rulership of Egypt. The idealization of that time is summed up in language almost identical to the prophecies of eschatological purity: "And the land of Egypt was at peace before Pharaoh on account of Joseph because the Lord was with him ... and the kingdom of Pharaoh was upright. And there was no Satan and there was no evil" (40:9); "And there was no Satan or anything evil all the days of the life of Joseph" (46:2). *Jubilees* thus casts Joseph's reign as essentially proleptic of God's eventual reign. No particular aspect of the spirits' work is mentioned here (either temptation or rulership), but its conjunction with evil more generally points toward understanding their work in its most holistic sense.

35   Michael Segal's *The Book of Jubilees* notes differences in the perspectives on the cause of sin and evil in our text, however, his project is diachronic in its intention to identify the sources and redactional layers and pinpoint the perspective of the final redactor while ours is synchronic. As with *1 Enoch*, it is enough for our project to identify the perspectives present in Matthew's milieu without needing to attribute them to a particular stratum of the tradition leading up the final version that was translated from Hebrew into Greek and thence to Latin and Ethiopic.

A secondary source of sin in *Jubilees* is the gentiles. In 1:18–24 Moses prays "O Lord my God, do not abandon your people and your inheritance, to walk in the error of their heart. And do not deliver them into the hand of their enemy, the gentiles, lest they rule over them and cause them to sin against you." Though it is not clear here how the gentiles might cause God's people to sin, Moses is praying in response to the prediction of the angel in 1:8–9, which makes it clear that the particular danger of the gentiles is their idolatry. The angel says to Moses, "they [the Israelites] will eat and be satisfied, and they will turn to strange gods.... and they will walk after the gentiles, and after their defilement and shame. And they will serve their gods, and they will become a scandal[36] for them and an affliction and a torment and a snare."[37] It is not surprising, however, that this should be the case, since according to *Jubilees* the gentiles are under the power and sovereignty of the demons.[38] Thus, the gentiles themselves are not the ultimate source of the pull towards idolatry or other sins for the Israelites; the ultimate source remains the spiritual powers exerting influence through their human instruments, the gentiles. This fits with way in which the latter part of Moses' prayer (noted above) juxtaposes a petition for preservation from influence of the spiritual powers (in this case Beliar) with the previous petition for Israel to be saved from the dominion of the gentiles. The use of the language of the "ensnaring" with regard to the work of Beliar against the Israelites further strengthens this connection, echoing as it does the language applied elsewhere to the idolatrous influence of the gentiles.

---

36   Charles: "offense"; VanderKam: "obstacle." Cf. our investigation in ch. 3 of the use of σκανδαλ-terms in Matthew.

37   See also 1:13–14. The theme of other gods becoming a "snare" or "trap" (מוֹקֵשׁ) for Israel is common: "They shall not dwell in your land, lest they make you sin against me; for if you serve their gods, it will surely be a snare to you" (Ex 23:33); "And you shall destroy all the peoples that the LORD your God will give over to you, your eye shall not pity them; neither shall you serve their gods, for that would be a snare to you" (Deut 7:16); "So now I say, I will not drive them out before you; but they shall become adversaries to you, and their gods shall be a snare to you" (Jdg 2:3). The gentiles themselves, it seems, can also be a snare: "Know assuredly that the LORD your God will not continue to drive out these nations before you; but they shall be a snare and a trap for you, a scourge on your sides, and thorns in your eyes, till you perish from off this good land which the LORD your God has given you" (Jos 23:13).

38   15:31: "There are many nations and many peoples, and they all belong to him, but over all of them he caused spirits to rule so that they might lead them astray from following him."

ENOCHIC LITERATURE

Still, despite the influence, subtle or tyrannical, of the evil spiritual forces,[39] *Jubilees* does hold humans culpable for their sins,[40] and in various instances locates the cause of the sinning with the person. Sometimes, though the cause lies with the person, the sin may be understood as unintentional. *Jubilees* spends some time exonerating Judah for his unintentional sin with Tamar, while at the same time emphasizing the seriousness of the infraction. According to the angel, "there was forgiveness for him because he turned from his sin and from his ignorance."[41] Judah's ignorance leads him to sin, and while his ignorance does not mitigate the gravity of the transgression, it does contribute to his forgiveness.

Though this is more or less an isolated incident, the motif of forgetting is more common, and similar in that forgetting can be understood as a temporary ignorance. Forgetting is first mentioned as a cause of sin in connection with the lure of the gentiles and their gods:

> And they will eat and be satisfied, and they will turn to strange gods, to those who cannot save them from any of their affliction. And this testimony will be heard as testimony against them, for they will forget all my commandments, everything which I will command them, and they will walk after the gentiles, and after their defilement and shame. And they will serve their gods, and they will become a scandal for them and an affliction and a torment and a snare.[42]

---

39 The fact that "over Israel [God] did not cause any angel or spirit to rule because he alone is their ruler" (15:32) certainly seems to remove from Israel any possibility of shifting the blame for sin to any outside forces. Still, the passages outlined above regarding the coercive power of the demons seem to assert the possibility that God's people can be dominated by other sprits unless God intervenes to preserve them.

40 See Segal's discussion of "YHWH as a Righteous Judge and the Judgment of the World" (*Book of Jubilees*, 137–143). Regarding 5:13–18 he writes: "Each of the groups in this story (angels, giants, and people) received a punishment appropriate to them.... Alongside the punishments for those who sinned in antiquity, the Heavenly Tablets also record the punishments for every creature that will deviate in the future from their [*sic*] assigned path. This approach should not be seen as deterministic: human behavior is not set in advance, but rather the way in which each person should behave [is set], and the sanctions that will be used against them if they fail to act accordingly" (138–139). Thus, at least in this passage, humans are held responsible for their going astray (sin); they are expected to follow the order prescribed, and if they do not, the fault lies with them, not with outside forces.

41 41:25.

42 1:8.

52 CHAPTER 2

This leads to greater and greater transgression and apostasy (vv. 9–12), such that eventually God declares:

> I will remove them from the midst of the land, and I will scatter them among the Gentiles. And they will forget all My law and all My commandments and all My judgments, and will go astray as to new moons, and sabbaths, and festivals, and jubilees, and ordinances. And after this they will turn to Me from amongst the Gentiles with all their heart and with all their soul and with all their strength, and I will gather them from amongst all the Gentiles....[43]

Apparently, forgetting begets sin which begets further forgetting until a time of repentance.[44]

Yet, in other passages human transgressions are portrayed as acts of willful, rebellious disobedience. In these texts, people are intentional perpetrators, not merely victims of the powers of evil around them or their own imperfect abilities to remember and thus obey. In 5:2–3 we find that:

> Injustice increased upon the earth and all flesh corrupted its way; man and cattle and beasts and birds and everything which walks upon the earth. And they all corrupted their way and their ordinances, and they began to eat each other, and injustice grew upon the earth and every imagination of the thoughts of all mankind was thus continually evil. And the Lord saw the earth, and behold it was corrupted, and all flesh had corrupted its order and all who were on the earth had done every sort of evil in His sight.

As noted above, the activities of the Giants here and in the later retelling of this in 7:22–25 are a catalyst or at least a reprehensible model for the behavior that eventually is manifest also in humans. Yet, in both passages, comments on the

---

43   1:13–14. In this quotation, I follow Charles' translation since Wintermute has "nations" in place of "gentiles," thus obscuring the obvious connection to 1:9.

44   Forgetting is also the cause of sin in 6:34–35 and 23:19. Conversely, Joseph is preserved from sin with Potiphar's wife because "he remembered the Lord and the words which Jacob, his father, used to read which were from the words of Abraham ... And Joseph remembered these words and did not want to lie with her" (39:6–9). The relation of remembering and forgetting to obeying and disobeying in the OT is at points so deep that, with regard to the Lord and the Law, remembering becomes nearly synonymous with obeying and forgetting tantamount to disobeying. See, for example, Brevard S. Childs, *Memory and Tradition in Israel*, SBT² 37 (Naperville, IL.: A.R. Allenson /S.C.M. Press, 1962).

active, willful participation of humans and other creatures in "corrupting their orders" are notable. In 5:2, it is not that humans' ways *were* or *became* corrupted, but that "they corrupted their ways" actively. So also in 7:23, the violence and injustice begun by the Naphidim takes hold in humanity precisely because "everyone sold himself in order that he might do injustice." The impetus for the sins of humanity in these passages is rooted far more in the intellectual activities of humanity than in the outward activities of the Giants. In both passages, the articulation of humanity's sins of violence and injustice is followed immediately by comments on their intellectual life. In 7:24, we hear that "all the thoughts and desires of men were always contemplating evil and vanity" and in 5:2 "injustice grew upon the earth and every imagination of the thoughts of all mankind was thus continually evil." All this apparently takes place independently of the activities of the Giants/Naphidim; though the activities of the two groups are juxtaposed in the texts, it is humans who have actively "corrupted their ways" and "done every sort of evil in [God's] sight," thus provoking God to wipe out intentionally-sinful humanity through the flood (5:4, 7:25). After the Flood, despite the assertion that God "made for all his works a new and righteous nature, so that they might not sin in all their nature forever, and so that they might all be righteous, each in his kind, always" (5:12), Noah says to his sons, "Behold, I see your deeds before me that you have not been ones who walked in righteousness because you have begun to walk in the paths of corruption" (7:26). Since Noah's sons are therefore without excuse with regard to any inherited defect, the responsibility for their sin and corruption is solely theirs.[45]

It is, in fact the descendants of Noah, not any evil spiritual force, who are credited prophetically with multiplying the evil in the world:

> And [Noah's sons] all said, 'So be it and so let it be to them and to their sons forever in their generations until the day of judgment, in which the Lord God will judge them with a sword and with fire on account of all the evil of the pollution of their errors which have filled the earth with sin and pollution and fornication and transgression.'[46]

Following this, "the polluted demons began to lead astray the children of Noah's sons and to lead them to folly and to destroy them" (10:1). This situation prompts Noah to pray for the binding of spirits. As noted above, at Mastema's request, one tenth are allowed to remain at liberty "to corrupt and lead astray"

---

45   The seductive temptations of the demons notwithstanding (7:27).
46   9:15.

(10:8). They are allowed to do this, however, "because the evil of the sons of men is great" (10:8). Thus, human wrongdoing is to blame even for the continuing activity of the demons against them.[47]

The narration of the wicked occupations of Noah's descendants up to the time of Abram then continues in 11:2–4, the pinnacle of which is that "they made for themselves molten images, and everyone worshipped the icon which they had made for themselves as a molten image. And they began making graven images and polluted likenesses."[48] The fact that "cruel spirits assisted them and led them astray so that they might commit sin and pollution" simply serves to emphasize the human element: the demons assist the residents of Ur in the unrighteous activities they have already undertaken of their own volition.

Though these reflections are fairly overt in assigning causation or at least blame for sin and evil, some passages that may be less intentionally indicting also locate a source of sin by their use of metaphors. One of the most common of these, just as in *1 Enoch*, is the metaphor of the heart. The metaphor is invoked immediately in the opening prophecy of Israel's apostasy. Though the gentiles are certainly invoked as a snare to God's people, the many idolatrous activities (including the sacrifice of children) are comprehended as "every work of the error of their heart" (1:10). Though there are external factors, the determinative one is the erring condition of the heart. This is emphasized at the end of the prophecy when it is predicted that the remedy for the spiritual and political oppression of Israel by the gentiles is that God's people would "turn to [God] from among the nations with all their heart and with all their soul and with all their might" (1:15). Escape from the sinful influence of the gentiles does not free the Israelites to obey; rather, by a change of heart, God brings about righteousness and gathers his people from the midst of the gentiles (1:15–16). The critical factor in sinning is the condition of the people's heart, not the external environment.

---

47 See Annette Yoshiko Reed, *Fallen Angels and the History of Judaism and Christianity: the Reception of Enochic Literature* (Cambridge, UK; Cambridge University Press, 2005), 94–95.

48 11:2–3: "And the sons of Noah began fighting in order to take captive and to kill each other, to pour the blood of man upon the earth, to eat blood, to build fortified cities and walls and towers, so that one man will be raised up over the people, to set up the first kingdoms to go to war, people against people and nation against nation and city against city, and everyone (began) to do evil and to acquire weapons, and to teach their sons war, and they began to take captive a city to sell male and female slaves. And Ur, the son of Kesed, built the city of Ur of the Chaldees, and called its name after his own name and the name of his father."

Overall, *Jubilees'* use of the heart metaphor displays characteristics similar to its use in the canonical Old Testament,[49] the most notable for our purposes being a certain ambivalence regarding the nature of the heart: when it is corrupt, it is a source of disobedience, but it is not inherently evil.[50] Hearts can err and be misled,[51] but they can also, as in the case of Noah, be righteous (5:19). As we see in Moses' prayer in response to the prophecy and, in turn, in God's response to Moses' prayer, the hearts of God's people are understood to be the source of walking in disobedience,[52] but God can "create a pure heart and a holy spirit for them,"[53] and so that they will not "be ensnared in their sin from henceforth and forever."[54] The only solution for "their contrariness and their thoughts and their stubbornness,"[55] according to the Lord's response, is for him to "cut off the foreskin of their heart and the foreskin of the heart of their descendants."[56] By this he "shall create for them a holy spirit and shall purify them so that they will not turn away from following me from that day and forever."[57] Thus, the heart, while potentially a source of disobedient action when it is corrupt, is not portrayed here as irredeemably bad.

In some respects, the portrayal of issues surrounding Esau's heart supports just such a conception, but other aspects also complicate it. In the passage narrating the imminent reunion of the brothers, Esau "remembered all of the evil which was hidden in his heart against Jacob, his brother, and he did not remember the oath which he swore to his father and his mother that he would not seek any evil against Jacob, his brother, all of his days" (37:13). Here, the heart is analogous to a container—certainly a neutral object—in which Esau

---

49   Given the broad range of English-language concepts comprehended by the term, it is not problematic for this argument that VanderKam chooses to translate this term (לב/לבב in the Hebrew texts) as "mind." As noted above, see the literature cited in part 2 for further on the metaphor of the heart.

50   This seems to be parallel to Paul's use of σάρξ; the organ is neutral but subject to temptation, and when corrupt becomes a source of sin. Also similar is the need for, metaphorically, some kind physically injurious operation to restore the organ once it has become corrupt—in the case of Paul's understanding of the flesh, crucifixion; in the case of the OT and *Jubilees'* use of heart, circumcision.

51   2:29, 12:2–5.

52   "And Moses fell upon his face and he prayed and said, 'O Lord my God, do not abandon your people and your inheritance to walk in the error of their heart'" (1:19).

53   1:21.

54   1:21.

55   1:22. Despite Wintermute's claims of literalness in his translation, Charles' "stiffneckedness" is certainly the more literal, albeit rather awkward, version.

56   1:23.

57   1:23.

has stored his latent malice toward Jacob.[58] After Esau declares to Jacob his intention never to be reconciled, Jacob "saw that he had planned evil against him from his heart and from his whole being[59] so that he might kill him."[60] Here, the heart is not merely a repository for Esau's malice, it is the instrument by which Esau moves that malice from thought to action.[61]

Aside, however, from having a heart that, like those of all people, can be corrupted and plan and will evil as well as be righteous and aim at obedience, we are told that Esau also has a *yetser* (יֵצֶר) that is evil from his youth (35:9). Esau's *yetser hara*, however, is not balanced with the expected *yetser hatov* that would give him the ability to decide either for good or for evil.[62] Rebecca says, on the contrary, that "there is no goodness in him"[63] and that he has "abandoned us with his whole heart."[64] The unalloyed evil of Esau's *yetser* manifests itself in "manifold evil deeds"[65] such that "he has no righteousness in him, because all of his ways are unrighteousness and violence."[66] Esau's corruption is so complete that, as Isaac warns Rebecca, even "if he swears [not to harm Jacob], he will not abide by his oath, and he will not do goodness but only evil."[67] Even attempts at right action by Esau will come to naught because of his nature.

---

58   The *OTP* includes in 37:19 an interruption by Jacob of this speech, the text of which is only found in Syriac text, not in Ethiopic tradition, and thus omitted by Charles and VanderKam. In it, Jacob says, "Do not act thus my brother. As for me there is no evil in my heart against you," thus deploying the heart metaphor with regard to Jacob in a way that parallels Esau's statement, but in the opposite—Jacob's heart has not stored up evil toward Esau that would cause him to wish to harm him or break an oath.

59   Charles: "soul."

60   37:24.

61   Here, obviously, the function of the heart as a seat of thought, decision-making, and volition is at the fore. Note also that Esau states that that which his heart is planning is in keeping with the fact that "Mankind and beasts of the field have no righteous oath which they have surely sworn forever, but daily they *seek* (Charles: *devise*; VanderKam: *aim at*) *evil*, one against the other, and each one seeks to kill his enemy and adversary" (37:18). Again, the volitional aspect of the heart is emphasized.

62   Note the similarity to the perspective of Rosen-Zvi in "Two Rabbinic Inclinations? Rethinking a Scholarly Dogma," mentioned above in n. 7 on p. 29.

63   35:9. VanderKam: "He is devoid of virtue."

64   35:10. The juxtaposition in Rebecca's speech of the idea of Esau's completely evil *yetser* and the involvement of his whole heart in the iniquitous abandonment of his parents links the two and may be two ways of underscoring the utter depravity of Esau's moral faculties.

65   Charles, 35:13.

66   35:13. Wintermute has "injustice" for "unrighteousness," but this obscures the parallelism with "he has no righteousness in him." VanderKam preserves the parallelism by using consistently in this passage "justice" and "injustice."

67   35:15.

ENOCHIC LITERATURE

It is this sense of one's whole nature—one's genetic makeup, even—as a source of evil that is our last area to explore. As in *1 Enoch*, we see also in *Jubilees* the use of genetic or familial metaphors to explain the source of certain people's wrong-doing. Certain classes of people are portrayed as being as sinful *as a group* and essentially irredeemable. Not surprisingly, these are mainly ethnic or familial groups that are historically in conflict with the Israelites, or as we noted above, the vast multitude of Gentiles. To return to our discussion of Esau, we see that after his thoroughgoing badness is established by Isaac and Rebecca, we are told that this is a situation that will not pertain only to him but will be passed on to his "seed":

> And now my heart is vexed on account of all his deeds. And neither he nor his seed is to be saved, for they are those who will be destroyed from the earth, and they will be uprooted from under heaven, for he has forsaken the God of Abraham, and he has gone after his wives and after their defilement and after their errors, (both) he and his children.[68]

Similarly, in Abraham's warning to Jacob, when he prophesies the fate of the Canaanites, the language of "seed" is prominently invoked:

> Be careful, my son, Jacob, that you do not take a wife from any of the seed of the daughters of Canaan, because all his seed is (destined) for uprooting from the earth; because through the sin of Ham, Canaan sinned, and all of his seed will be blotted out from the earth, and all his remnant, and there is none of his who will be saved.[69]

Ham's sin is genetically passed down to his seed, such that God's people must not mingle with it lest they be polluted since the fruit of this lineage of sinfulness is that "their deeds are defiled, and all of their ways are contaminated, and despicable, and abominable." Thus, even though humanity has been renewed after the Flood and God has "made for all his works a new and righteous nature so that they might not sin in all their nature forever, and so that they might all be righteous, each in his kind, always" (5:12), the seed of humanity becomes corrupt again.[70] So, in the use of this metaphor, we have again as in *1 Enoch* the

---

68   35:14.

69   22:20–21.

70   Note that by the time of Abraham, "all the works of the children of men are sin and wickedness, and all their deeds are uncleanness and an abomination and a pollution, And there is no righteousness with them" (21:21). Abraham alone breaks away from this corrupt gene pool to be the father of God's people.

58   CHAPTER 2

invocation of ontological dualism to explain why some people are sinful. They do so because it is their hereditary nature, their very being, to do so.

Thus, *Jubilees* displays a significant diversity of perspective on the question of the source of sin and evil, both in its apparent explicit, intentional reflection on the subject as well as in the messages conveyed in the less overt, perhaps even unconsidered use of various images and metaphors related to the cause of sin. Even if these differing perspectives are in some cases the result of the melding of different traditions and perspectives of the editor(s), we have seen above that even within particular sections or even particular speeches by a character, multiple perspectives are displayed. This can be seen well at very beginning of the book in Moses' prayer to God in response to the prophecy of Israel's apostasy and in God's response:

> And Moses fell upon his face, and he prayed and said, "O Lord, my God, do not abandon your people and your inheritance to walk in the error of their heart. And do not deliver them into the hand of their enemy, the gentiles, lest they rule over them and cause them to sin against you. O Lord, let your mercy be lifted up upon your people, and create for them an upright spirit. And do not let the spirit of Beliar rule over them to accuse them before you and ensnare them from every path of righteousness so that they might be destroyed from before your face. But they are your people and your inheritance, whom you saved by your great might from the hand of the Egyptians. Create a pure heart and a holy spirit for them. And do not let them be ensnared by their sin henceforth and forevermore."
>
> And the Lord said unto Moses, "I know their contrariness and their thoughts and their stubbornness. And they will not obey until they acknowledge their sin and the sins of their fathers. But after this they will return to me in all uprightness and with all of (their) heart and soul. And I will cut off the foreskin of their heart and the foreskin of the heart of their descendants. And I shall create for them a holy spirit, and I shall purify them so that they will not turn away from following me from that day and forever. And their souls will cleave to me and to all my commandments. And they will do my commandments. And I shall be a Father to them and they will be sons to me. And they will all be called 'sons of the living God.' And every angel and spirit will know and acknowledge that they are my sons and I am their Father in uprightness and righteousness. And I shall love them."[71]

---

71   1:18–24.

ENOCHIC LITERATURE

Above, we see multiple loci for the source of sin: external sources such as evil spiritual forces, gentiles, and even the power of sin itself to entrap people;[72] internal sources such as people's hearts, "their contrariness and their thoughts and their stubbornness," and even, by implication, an "unrighteous spirit," since God's creation of a "holy spirit" in them will result in their purification. There is also a volitional aspect here, as noted elsewhere, in that it is the Israelites themselves who will repent and return to God. This plurality resists simplification to the indictment of one or even a few sources for sin and evil but insists on holding the diversity of sources together.

---

72   1:21: "Do not let them be ensnared by their sin."

CHAPTER 3

4 Ezra

Turning now to *4 Ezra*, we can note immediately some significant differences from the Enochic literature which we have just been exploring. The first is that, while *Jubilees* and *1 Enoch* exhibited some explicit interest the source of sin and evil, they also had other interests which they were exploring, interests that perhaps were more at the fore of those texts than the investigation of the source(s) of sin and evil. By contrast, *4 Ezra* is essentially a theodicy; we are told immediately that Ezra[1] is troubled by the conquest of God's people (3:1),[2] and he begins to question God about the reason for what has befallen them. *4 Ezra*'s primary and overt concern is why this evil has occurred, and further what human sinning has to do with it and why sin continues.[3]

The second notable difference is the absence of any reference to the Watchers or their offspring as sources of sin and evil, either from the introduction of sinful impurity, illicit knowledge, or through coercion, violence, or even temptation. In fact, *4 Ezra* avoids mentioning them at all: in the summary

---

1   We will use the name Ezra to denote the first-person narrator of *4 Ezra* as distinct from both of his dialogue partners, Uriel and the Lord, and also from the author of *4 Ezra*.

2   Our chapter and verse numbering will follow that of 2 Esdras and Metzger in *OTP* 1:528–555. The English translation is that of the NRSV except where noted.

3   For example, immediately in 3:20, Ezra asks God why he "did not take away their evil heart from them, so that your law might produce fruit in them." For Ezra, the question of personal sin and the corporate experience of evil are twin questions that God must address. Various interpreters come to differing conclusions about what Ezra's final position is regarding God's responsibility for these twin problems and how he arrives at his position. For our purposes, it is not necessary to come to a decision on the overall message of *4 Ezra* since *4 Ezra* would not have been an actual source for Matthew, as scholars are for the most part agreed on a late first century date for *4 Ezra* and there is no evidence of Matthew's knowledge of the text. Nevertheless, as works that share both an apocalyptic perspective and a deep belief in the importance of the Law, and as works potentially drawing from the same literary pool of images and scriptures for their reflection, they bear comparison. Thus, even though one always needs to keep in mind the dialogical nature of the text in interpreting *4 Ezra* and trying to reach a conclusion about the perspective of the author (as Bruce Longenecker has rightly noted, *2 Esdras* [Sheffield: Sheffield Academic Press, 1995], 21), this is less essential for our work since both the positions of "Ezra" and of Uriel can be assumed to represent positions present in the milieu out of which both Matthew and *4 Ezra* grew. On the dating of *4 Ezra*, see the discussions in Bruce M. Metzger's introduction to his translation (*OTP* 1:520), as well as Raymond E. Brown, *The Jerome Biblical Commentary* (Englewood Cliffs, N.J.: Prentice Hall, 1968), 2:542: "It is a Jewish work of about A.D. 100–120"; Longenecker, 13–14; Jacob M. Myers, *I and II Esdras*, AB 42 (Garden City, New York: Doubleday, 1974), 129.

© KONINKLIJKE BRILL NV, LEIDEN, 2020 | DOI:10.1163/9789004419506_005

4 EZRA

of the first twelve chapters of Genesis (3:4–13), even the brief references in the canonical text are eliminated. It simply says that, between the times of Adam and Noah, "there sprang nations and tribes from [Adam], peoples and clans without number. And every nation walked after its own will; they did ungodly things in your sight and rejected your commands, and you did not hinder them."[4]

Yet like the Enochic literature, *4 Ezra* does emphasize that humans are culpable for the sins they commit, perhaps rather more so than the texts we have previously examined. This can be seen in *4 Ezra's* unremitting insistence on the eventual judgment and punishment of those who sin.[5] Though Ezra complains to Uriel that, given the pervasiveness of sin, those who will be judged and punished will be many and those saved few,[6] *4 Ezra*, through the words of Uriel and indeed God,[7] does not concede any latitude on this point.

The fact that humans are held responsible for their sins is, indeed, part of—if not the crux of—Ezra's complaint regarding sin. Ezra concedes that humans ought to keep God's commandments, but he is pessimistic about their ability to do so. The reason for this that humans have an evil heart that prevents them from doing what they ought:

> O sovereign Lord, I said then and I say now: Blessed are those who are alive and keep your commandments! But what of those for whom I prayed? For who among the living is there that has not sinned, or who is there among mortals that has not transgressed your covenant? And now I see that the world to come will bring delight to few, but torments to many. For an evil heart has grown up in us, which has alienated us from God, and has brought us into corruption and the ways of death and has shown us the paths of perdition and removed us far from life—and that not merely for a few but for almost all who have been created.[8]

Being that humans are burdened with this evil heart, it is not surprising that they do not obey God's commands. The source of this evil heart gets at the core of Ezra's problem with the judgment that awaits sinning humans. It is the evil heart that is the source of sin, and the heart is obviously internal and integral to the human. In fact, as we have noted above, it is indeed symbolic of

---

4   3:7–8.
5   7:32–44, 7:87, 12:33–34.
6   7:45–47, 7:51, 7:59–61, 8:1–3, 8:15–16.
7   6:17–19, 7:70, 14:35.
8   7:45–48.

all the internal faculties of the human, that which is most essential in a person in the Hebrew tradition. It is unclear from the passage whether all are born with the evil heart and only a few overcome it, or if that small remnant who have not gone "into corruption and the ways of death" avoided these by virtue of having a good rather than evil heart.

Furthermore, a few verses later, Ezra claims that all, not just "many" or "almost all," are in danger of judgment, since "all who have been born are entangled in iniquities and are full of sins and burdened with transgressions" (7:68). Here, obviously, the metaphor changes to that of sin ("iniquities") entangling people, a move from a metaphor of internal causation to a metaphor of external causation. Perhaps the move is related to the move from "some" to "all"— some, many or almost all have an evil heart which causes sin but all without exception are victims of the being caught and entangled in iniquity even when it does not spring from any internal catalyst.

The blame for the introduction of this problem is, in *4 Ezra*, unlike in the Enochic literature, placed squarely on Adam, and sin's enduring presence in humans is a function of its nature, which as we will see is compared to a chronic disease or a plant that cannot be uprooted. As Ezra complains to Uriel:

> Yet you did not take away their evil heart from them, so that your law might produce fruit in them. For the first Adam, burdened with an evil heart, transgressed and was overcome, as were also all who were descended from him. Thus, the disease became permanent; the law was in the hearts of the people along with the evil root; but what was good departed, and the evil remained. So the times passed and the years were completed, and you raised up for yourself a servant, named David. You commanded him to build a city for your name, and there to offer you oblations from what is yours. This was done for many years; but the inhabitants of the city transgressed, in everything doing just as Adam and all his descendants had done, for they also had the evil heart.[9]

In this passage, sin is compared to a disease passed on from Adam—and diseases are by nature something internal to one but still foreign.[10] They are not

---

9   3:20–26.

10 This is not to suggest that *4 Ezra* anticipates the germ theory of disease, but rather to simply point out that the metaphor of illness or infirmity implies the healthy body as the norm, a norm from which one is removed. In the case of something like blindness, lameness, or deafness, the infirmity may have an obvious external cause such as a blow or other injury, but the effect becomes internal to the person's body. Similarly, with disease more generally, the change from a normal and functioning state of healthfulness to

4 EZRA

a natural part of the human. It is this evil heart that has been passed on like a disease from Adam. In this sense *4 Ezra* comes quite close to some conceptions of the traditional Christian doctrine of original sin.

Ezra recognizes that God worked against the evil of the human heart in sending the Law, but he complains that, even though God:

> ... bent down the heavens and shook the earth, and moved the world, and caused the depths to tremble ... to give the law to the descendants of Jacob, and [his] commandment to the posterity of Israel. Yet [God] did not take away their evil heart from them, so that [his] law might produce fruit in them.... The law was in the hearts of the people along with the evil root [from Adam]; but what was good departed, and the evil remained.[11]

Even the Law is not capable of overcoming the power of sin that was set in motion and passed on from Adam. Thus, Ezra laments, "O Adam, what have you done? For though it was you who sinned, the fall was not yours alone, but ours also who are your descendants" (7:118).

In discussing the original source of sin, the above passage contains both of the dominant images for the source of on-going sin in *4 Ezra*: the human heart and a "seed" of evil that is planted and has grown in it. On this point Ezra and Uriel are agreed: the source of sinful action is the human heart made evil by the seed of evil introduced by Adam and passed on to all his descendants. So, it is notable that Uriel does not disagree with Ezra's assessment of the people when Ezra questions Uriel about God's justice in punishing God's people. As noted above, Ezra says, "You did not take away their evil heart from them, so that your law might produce fruit in them.... [and] the inhabitants of the city transgressed, in everything doing just as Adam and all his descendants had done, for they also had the evil heart" (3:20–26). Uriel's response, though it does not affirm Ezra's questioning, does confirm his judgment about the condition of the human heart: "If you can solve one of [these questions] for me, then I will show you the way you desire to see, and will teach you why the heart is evil" (4:4). By giving him impossible tasks, Uriel guarantees that he will not

---

a diseased state is a change brought about by something "foreign"—the disease. Even if it was not conceptualized as germs, the disease represents the intrusion of that which is contrary to the normative state of healthfulness, and this intruder lodges in the body and incapacitates it for its intended deeds.

11   3:18–20, 22.

64   CHAPTER 3

have to explain the problem to Ezra, but he does not dispute the nature of the problem.[12]

That this is indeed the perspective of Uriel is confirmed in his later use of the same language with respect to the human heart. In 4:28–31, Uriel utilizes an organic metaphor with respect to the evil of the human heart and the agricultural metaphor of sowing and reaping for the judgment that is to come upon humans because of it:

> For the evil about which you ask me has been sown, but the harvest of it has not yet come. If therefore that which has been sown is not reaped, and if the place where the evil has been sown does not pass away, the field where the good has been sown will not come. For a grain of evil seed was sown in Adam's heart from the beginning, and how much ungodliness it has produced until now—and will produce until the time of threshing comes! Consider now for yourself how much fruit of ungodliness a grain of evil seed has produced.

The remedy for this sin-producing heart is not, however, to be attained before the end of the world. After many tribulations and the punishment of evil-doers (6:19), "it shall be that whoever remains after all that I have foretold to you shall be saved and shall see my salvation and the end of my world ... and the heart of the earth's inhabitants shall be changed and converted to a different spirit. For evil shall be blotted out, and deceit shall be quenched" (6:25–27). Whether any will be left who are sinful and indeed in need of a different sort of heart is unclear. Uriel promises Ezra that for those who are "like yourself," who have not "despised the Most High, and [been] contemptuous of his law, and abandoned his ways" (8:56), for these "paradise is opened, the tree of life is planted, the age to come is prepared, plenty is provided, a city is built, rest is appointed, goodness is established and wisdom perfected beforehand. The root of evil is sealed up from you" (8:52–53). Thus, only those who have to some extent overcome the power of the evil heart by adherence to the Law—the ability to do this being implied—will eventually be delivered from it.

The perspective that, despite the power of the evil heart to provoke sin, humans are still capable of obedience and thus culpable for any disobedience is also notably present. In one of his responses to Ezra, Uriel says:

---

12   Uriel also seems to be implicating the heart in discussing the few who will be saved, in as much as he invokes the idea of thought and thus the deliberative function of the heart, when he says, "The first order [of those saved], because they have striven with great effort to overcome the evil thought that was formed with them, so that it might not lead them astray from life into death" (7:92).

For the Lord strictly commanded those who came into the world, when they came, what they should do to live, and what they should observe to avoid punishment. Nevertheless, they were not obedient and spoke against him; they devised for themselves vain thoughts and proposed to themselves wicked frauds; they even declared that the Most High does not exist, and they ignored his ways. They scorned his law and denied his covenants; they have been unfaithful to his statutes and have not performed his works.[13]

This implication is clearly that these people knew God's Law (since they scorned it) and flagrantly disobeyed it. Uriel sees their inherited evil heart as no excuse. In fact, when Ezra comments that the mind, as an organic entity, "grows with us" (7:64), Uriel turns this to the purpose of indicting humanity:

But now, understand from your own words—for you have said that the mind grows with us. For this reason, therefore, those who live on earth shall be tormented, because though they had understanding, they committed iniquity; and though they received the commandments, they did not keep them; and though they obtained the law, they dealt unfaithfully with what they received.[14]

Yet, despite Uriel's defense of the justice of punishing those who are victims of their inherited, natural tendency toward sin and disobedience, Ezra's indictment of God remains: "Every nation walked after its own will; they did ungodly things in your sight and rejected your commands, and *you did not hinder them*" (3:8) Still, in the end, the responsibility for sin *or* obedience in *4 Ezra* rests with humanity. As Uriel says of the great number who will perish, "When they had opportunity to choose, they despised the Most High and were contemptuous of his law and abandoned his ways" (8:56), though ultimately the *source* of sin is Adam and the evil heart he passed on to all.

---

13 7:21–24.

14 7:71–72. The fact that Uriel assumes that those who are being condemned and punished have received the Law may mean that only disobedient Jews are envisioned here, but the continual invocation of Adam would implicate all humanity. Perhaps a situation where, through the Jews, all people have been made aware of God's commandments is envisioned. Alternately, perhaps some conception of God's Law as congruent with a version of "natural Law" available to all humanity is in view. In any case, those who have received the law in some form have also inherited the evil heart from Adam and thus their ability to keep God's commands has certainly been impaired through no fault of their own.

CHAPTER 4

2 Baruch

Like *4 Ezra*, *2 Baruch* is thought to be a product of the late first century c.e., and also like *4 Ezra*, *2 Baruch* is grappling with the question of God's justice in the wake of the conquest of Jerusalem and destruction of the temple. Thus, also like *4 Ezra*, the author of *2 Baruch* adopts the persona of an important figure of the era of the Babylonian conquest to pose the questions that cause portions of the text to fall into the genre of theodicy. Further, the use of apocalypses as a means of responding to the questions of theodicy raised by the misfortunes of God's people is also common to both texts.[1]

In turning to examine *2 Baruch*'s perspective regarding the source or cause of sin, however, we find some significant differences: the passages are not only less numerous but also less extensive and less diverse than the other texts we have examined, despite the length of the text.[2] The more significant difference from *4 Ezra* with which it is often compared, however, is in *2 Baruch*'s understanding of the human capacity for living according to God's law and of what

---

1   Though *4 Ezra* is generally referred to in recent scholarly works as a theodicy, the presence of future-oriented prophecy in *4 Ezra* (e.g., 4:26–32, 5:1–13, 6:18–28, 7:26–44, 8:46–62, 9:1–1, 13:21–50, 14:11–18) caused earlier scholars to label it as an apocalypse. Similarly, though *2 Baruch* has traditionally been referred to as an apocalypse, the elements of theodicy are also very apparent. The blending of the two genres in *2 Baruch* as well as in *4 Ezra* simply highlights the necessity of recognizing such genre categories as provisional and fluid rather than definitive and water-tight. Inasmuch as these designations have become common practice with these texts and do not misrepresent their overall gist and tenor, we will continue to use these labels while recognizing their non-comprehensive nature.

2   *2 Baruch*'s relative lack of interest in investigating the cause(s) of sin even led Fredrick James Murphy to concluded that "2B is not really concerned with the source of evil" (*The Structure and Meaning of Second Baruch*, SBLDS 78 [Atlanta, Ga.: Scholars Press, 1985], 37). In this statement, Murphy uses evil as a synonym for sin or moral evil, which in the case of *2 Baruch* is not technically correct: *2 Baruch* is quite interested in the cause of evil in the sense of misfortunes that befall God's people, but the term *evil* is not generally used in *2 Baruch* for sins or wickedness. The perspective of *2 Baruch* on this question is stated clearly at the outset of the book in the LORD's opening statement to Baruch: "For the former tribes were forced by their kings to commit sin, but these two of themselves have been forcing and compelling their kings to commit sin. For this reason, behold I bring evil upon this city, and upon its inhabitants" (1:3–4). In this and other similar statements, *2 Baruch* draws a nearly direct correlation between the sins of the people and the conquest and destruction of Jerusalem and the Temple, thus demonstrating a perspective similar to that of Deuteronomy as has been noted by both Murphy (120–133, 136) and Gwendolyn Sayers (*Have the Promises Failed?: a Literary Analysis of* 2 Baruch, SBLDS 72 [Chico, CA.: Scholars Press, 1984], 43 n. 4, 49–51, 77–78, 80–83).

© KONINKLIJKE BRILL NV, LEIDEN, 2020 | DOI:10.1163/9789004419506_006

2 BARUCH

impairs that ability; of particular difference is the role of Adam's sin in establishing this current condition of humanity.

Like *4 Ezra*, *2 Baruch* certainly sees humans as culpable for the sins they commit and thus liable to judgment. Whereas for *4 Ezra*, however, this was a problem given humanity's helplessness because of the inherited *cor malignum*, *2 Baruch* does not portray humanity as having any inherited internal propensity toward wrongdoing. The metaphor of the heart is significantly less utilized in *2 Baruch*, and in fact this metaphor is used predominantly in a positive sense and with the main function of the heart being thought and recollection rather than being a source of sin and wickedness in ethical decision-making.[3] The heart in *2 Baruch* is a place to store up and meditate upon God's commands and wisdom rather than a wellspring of sin.

Without the idea of an inherited wicked heart playing any role in *2 Baruch*'s understanding of the source of human sin, other ideas move to the fore. In 48:40 the Lord attributes human transgression to a mixture of disregard and pride: "The Judge shall come and will not tarry, because each of the inhabitants of the earth knew when he was transgressing. But My Law they knew not by reason of their pride." Some have actively resisted hearing and thus obeying God's law: "For over this above all shall those who come then lament, that they rejected My law, and stopped their ears that they might not hear wisdom or receive understanding" (51:4). Baruch further indicts such people and promises punishments: "And justly do they perish who have not loved Your law, and the torment of judgment shall await those who have not submitted themselves to Your power" (54:14). Without an inherently evil heart as the source of disobedience, the presence of God's law in the world leaves humans without excuse: "But now, because he transgressed wittingly, yea, just on this ground that he knows [about the law], he shall be tormented" (15:6).

For *2 Baruch*, Adam does, however, have a role in the miseries humanity experiences in this age, though it is important in analyzing it to guard against

---

3   Thus, Baruch says of himself and Jeremiah that they were among those "whose heart was found pure from sins" (9:1). The Lord commands Baruch, "Now therefore hold fast in your heart everything that I command you, and seal it in the recesses of your mind" (20:3). Baruch exhorts the people, "If you prepare your hearts, so as to sow in them the fruits of the law, it shall protect you in that time in which the Mighty One is to shake the whole creation" (32:1) and that they should "direct your heart to that which has been said to you, and understand those things which have been shown to you" (43:1) and "prepare you your hearts, that you may obey the law" (46:5). Other similar uses: 51:3, 66:1, 83:8, 84:10. On the negative side, the heart can also be troubled (55:4), can boast (67:2), and be liable to stupor (70:2), but there is nothing parallel to *4 Ezra*'s use. Here and elsewhere in this section, English translation used is that of R.H. Charles, except as noted.

68   CHAPTER 4

being influenced by *4 Ezra*'s understanding of the repercussions of Adam's sin.[4] In Ramael's response to one of Baruch's prayers, we find that Adam's transgression had serious repercussions, though it is not in the introduction of a flawed moral nature:

> And as you first saw the black waters on the top of the cloud which first came down upon the earth; this is the transgression which Adam, the first man, committed. For when he transgressed, untimely death came into being, mourning was mentioned, affliction was prepared, illness was created, labor accomplished, pride began to come into existence, the realm of death began to ask to be renewed with blood, the conception of children came about, the passion of the parents was produced, the loftiness of men was humiliated, and goodness vanished.[5]

The introduction of untimely death as the product of Adam's sin was an idea introduced in Baruch's prayer prior to Ramael's response: "Adam first sinned and brought untimely death upon all."[6] That this "untimely death" is not equivalent to a hereditary sinful nature—a kind of spiritual death—is clear when the sentence is looked at in the broader context of Baruch's speech:

> And justly do they perish who have not loved Your law, and the torment of judgment shall await those who have not submitted themselves to Your power. For though Adam first sinned and brought untimely death upon all, yet of those who were born from him each one of them has prepared for his own soul torment to come.... Adam is therefore not the cause, save only of his own soul, but each of us has been the Adam of his own soul.[7]

Thus, *2 Baruch* moves in the opposite direction of *4 Ezra*: each person is liable for his own sins; while Adam's sin did have negative repercussions,[8] an

---

4 Cf. Murphy, *Structure and Meaning of Second Baruch*, 34–37. On the differences of perspective and purpose generally in *4 Ezra* and *2 Baruch*, see Sayers, *Have the Promises Failed?*, 129–134 and 149.

5 56:5–6, ET: A.F.J. Klijn, OTP 1:641. Thus, while Murphy is right in noting *contra* Harnisch that Adam is not here credited with introducing sin into the world much less making it a hereditary handicap, he perhaps goes too far in saying that "'Untimely death' is all that Adam can be credited with" (*Structure and Meaning of Second Baruch*, 35–36).

6 54:15.

7 54:14–19. Sayler is correct in pointing out that here Baruch's "words apply to all mankind" (*Have the Promises Failed?*, 68). This *contra* Klijn, who sees this as speaking solely to "the nations" (OTP 1:619).

8 Murphy seems correct in his assessment that Adam's transgression in *2 Baruch* does not engender a major change in the nature of the world. Not only is no evil heart produced and

2 BARUCH

69

inherent propensity toward sin was not one of the things bequeathed to his descendants.[9] Each is responsible for choosing whether to imitate Moses' and his devotion to the light of the law or to imitate Adam and his darkness of sin and rejection of God's commands.[10] Thus, Adam becomes, not the originator of a sinful, evil heart in humanity, but the one who introduces untimely death and the archetype of those who reject God's command.[11]

Finally, there are a number of passages in 2 *Baruch* that utilize the image of "pollution" with regard to sin. This recalls the significant use of this motif in

passed on, but only untimely death, not death *per se*, is attributed as a result of his action; there is no mention of an expulsion from the Garden signaling the change from an idyllic created world of harmony and perfection to one of corruption, sin, and discord (though see 56:5–6, above). Murphy may be right in surmising that, for the author of 2 *Baruch*, the alternating periods of dark and bright waters being "established according to the multitude of the intelligence of him who sent it" undermines the attribution of any power to Adam to bring about a change in the *aeon*. In fact, if Murphy is correct that one of the main interests of 2 *Baruch* is making a spatial dualistic distinction between the lower, corruptible world of creation as opposed to the holy and glorious world of heaven, then the author of 2 *Baruch* may be conceiving of this created world as so flawed and negligible compared to the heavenly realm that it had no time of primeval perfection from which to fall in Adam's transgression. Cf. Murphy on the "Two-World Concept," in *Structure and Meaning of Second Baruch*, 31–70.

9   Thus, Sayler rightly assesses, I believe, the difference in the theodicies of *4 Ezra* and *2 Baruch*: for *4 Ezra*, the "basic premise is that the propensity to sin resulting from the evil heart makes it impossible for almost anyone to fulfill the Torah and thereby obtain life.... Thus, Ezra's question is actually an accusation: God places demands on his people which they cannot fulfill, and then punishes them for their failure to do so." For *2 Baruch*, however: "The individual's ability to fulfill the Torah is not an issue in Baruch's questions. Rather, all of Baruch's questions are variations on one major question: has God nullified the covenants he made with Abraham and Moses?" (*Have the Promises Failed?*, 131).

10   18:1: "And I answered and said: 'He [Moses] that lighted has taken from the light, and there are but few that have imitated him. But those many whom he has lighted have taken from the darkness of Adam and have not rejoiced in the light of the lamp.'"

11   Thus, in the final remaining references to Adam in 2 *Baruch*, though there is mention of the consequence of Adam's action for his descendants, again the consequence seems to be decay leading to death ("multitude are going to corruption"), and the overall emphasis of the passage is on the how numerous and sinful his descendants are rather than on how Adam's action inculcated a propensity toward sin that was previously not existent: "And I answered and said: 'O Adam, what have you done to all those who are born from you? And what will be said to the first Eve who hearkened to the serpent? For all this multitude are going to corruption, nor is there any numbering of those whom the fire devours. But again I will speak in Your presence. You, O LORD, my Lord, know what is in Your creature. For you did of old command the dust to produce Adam, and you know the number of those who are born from him, and how far they have sinned before you, who have existed and not confessed you as their Creator. And as regards all these their end shall convict them, and Your law which they have transgressed shall requite them on Your day'" (48:42–46).

Jubilees, where one of the concerns of the author was the pollution of God's people by the Gentiles. So, we see in *2 Baruch* that "even Israel was then polluted by sins in the days of the judges" (60:2) and that in the future "those who are polluted with iniquity will flee to" the evil and powerful fourth kingdom (39:6). King Josiah is lauded and his reign counted as a time of bright waters because "their polluted ones he burnt in the fire, and the lying prophets which deceived the people, these also he burnt in the fire" (66:4). In Baruch's prayer in ch. 21 he asks, "How long will that which is corruptible remain, and how long will the time of mortals be prospered, and until what time will those who transgress in the world be polluted with much wickedness?" (21:19). Yet, in each of these instances, the pollution is not a *cause* of sinning, but rather a result. The people become polluted by their sins, rather than sinning because they have become polluted. Thus, *2 Baruch,* though it uses the same imagery of pollution or impurity as *Jubilees,* sends a different message about the cause of sin: there is no force apart from humanity's own choice—not an evil heart nor the influence of the gentiles—that causes their sinfulness. "The choices that faced Adam face each of his descendants: and they have the same opportunity to do good or evil."[12]

---

12 Stephen Westerholm, "Paul's Anthropological 'Pessimism' in its Jewish Context," *Divine and Human Agency in Paul and his Cultural Environment,* LEC/LNTS 335 (London; New York: T & T Clark, 2006), 90.

CHAPTER 5

Sirach

Turning to the book of Sirach, immediately noticeable are its differences from the literature we have been examining.[1] In terms of its genre, certainly Sirach differs substantially from our other texts. As a collection of proverbial wisdom sayings, it shares little on a formal level with the imaginative retellings of biblical narratives, the pseudonymous posing of theodicies, and the apocalyptic visions of events past and future.[2] Even in those places where it overlaps with the previous literature in terms of subject matter related to our topic, it deploys the elements in a way unlike what we have previously seen. For example, the subject of the activity of the giants which received so much attention in *1 Enoch* and *Jubilees* but was notably skipped over in the retelling of Genesis 6 in *4 Ezra*, and went completely unmentioned in *2 Baruch*, is mentioned only in passing in Sirach. Its function in the text, furthermore, has nothing to do with a consideration of the causes of sin. The giants appear in the first verse of a warning against presuming that God will forgo punishment of evil-doers:

> He did not forgive the ancient giants who revolted in their might. He did not spare the neighbors of Lot, whom he loathed on account of their arrogance. He showed no pity on the doomed nation, on those dispossessed because of their sins; or on the six hundred thousand foot soldiers who assembled in their stubbornness. Even if there were only one stiff-necked person, it would be a wonder if he remained unpunished. For mercy and

---

1   It should be noted that, in terms of its date of composition (mid-second century BC), Sirach is quite close to the earliest portions of *1 Enoch* and closer to the later-composed portions of *1 Enoch* and *Jubilees* than it is to *4 Ezra* and *2 Baruch*.

2   As was true of the permeable boundary between apocalypse and theodicy which was noted above in reference to *2 Baruch* and *4 Ezra*, so here also. Despite the formal differences between the preceding texts and Sirach, a number of authors, based on the content as well as some formal characteristics, have argued for understanding at least portions of Sirach as theodicies. See for example: James L. Crenshaw, "Problem of Theodicy in Sirach: On Human Bondage," *JBL* 94 (Mr 1975): 47–64; Jack T. Sanders, "Wisdom, Theodicy, Death, and the Evolution of Intellectual Traditions," *JSJ* 36 (2005): 263–277, esp. 270–273; David A. Skelton, "Ben Sira's Imaginative Theodicy: Reflections on the Aaronide Priesthood Under Gentile Rule," *ResQ* 51 (2009): 1–12. Similarly, while no portion of Sirach can be classed as an apocalypse per se, the primary characteristic of apocalypticism, namely dualism, is also characteristic of Sirach, although, as will be discussed below, it does not manifest the same sorts of dualisms as we have seen in the previously examined texts.

© KONINKLIJKE BRILL NV, LEIDEN, 2020 | DOI:10.1163/9789004419506_007

72   CHAPTER 5

wrath are with the Lord; he is mighty to forgive—but he also pours out wrath.[3]

Here, unlike in the Enochic literature, the purpose of raising the topic of the giants is to present them as an example of God's faithfulness to punish the disobedient. The allusion serves as a cautionary tale rather than an aetiology for sin.

Similarly, though Adam figures prominently, as we saw, in the reflections of both *4 Ezra* and *2 Baruch* with regard to the cause of sin,[4] in Sirach, Adam, like the giants, serves a different purpose. In the first reference to Adam, he is simply pointed to as the progenitor of all humans: "Hard work was created for everyone, and a heavy yoke is laid on the children of Adam, from the day they come forth from their mother's womb until the day they return to the mother of all the living" (40:1). It is significant that the text shies away from the obvious opportunity to make a connection, as is made in Gen 3, between Adam's sin and the fact that he was forced to labor. Nor is there, in fact, any mention of Adam's sin at all, nor any mention of the idea, again as in Gen 3, that because of his sin the ground has been cursed, thus bequeathing the necessity of hard labor to his children. In fact, Adam's laboring is not mentioned, per se. Hard labor is not an inheritance from Adam brought on by sin but simply a universal human experience.[5] "The children of Adam" is merely a poetic way of saying "all people."[6] The only other reference to Adam appears in the encomium on the Ancestors (chs. 44–50). Here, Adam is simply mentioned along with three of his early descendants as "honored," though Adam is honored above them.[7]

---

3   16:7–11.

4   Though not in *1 Enoch* and *Jubilees*.

5   While it could be that the author intends to allude to the connection between Adam's sin and the universal need for labor, it is then unclear why he avoided making that connection explicit when he had such an obvious opportunity. Further, since, as we will see, Adam is nowhere else in *Sirach* indicted for passing on a dubious inheritance of sin and its consequences, to read that into this passage seems inconsistent with the rest of the text.

6   As John Levison notes, though Adam is referred to by name in the Greek text, "the Hebrew reads: ועול כבד על בני אדם and is most naturally translated 'and a heavy yoke (is) upon the "sons of man"'" (*Portraits of Adam in Early Judaism: From Sirach to* 2 Baruch, JSPSup 1 (Sheffield, U.K.: Sheffield Academic Press, 1988), 42. Levison notes that while there are allusions to Gen 1–3 (esp. in 40:2, where the earth rather than Eve is called the "mother of all living"), Sirach "dissociates death from primeval transgression" (*Portraits of Adam*, 43).

7   49:16: "Shem and Seth and Enosh were honored, but above every other created living being was Adam." The honoring of Adam also militates against the idea that the author of Sirach saw him as the initiator of sin.

SIRACH   73

Also, unlike our previous literature is Sirach's reference to Eve in connection with primordial sin. In 25:24 we find: "From a woman sin had its beginning, and because of her we all die." Here we have something rather close to an attribution of responsibility for sin in the world. This is a change from our previous literature which focused either on the Watchers and their offspring or on Adam in any attributions of guilt for the introduction of sin in the pre-Abrahamic era. It is important to note here, however, that what is not said is as important as what is said: it is said that Eve's action had the fatal ramifications ensuring that all after her would die, but it does not say that her first sin had the consequence of guaranteeing that all after her would sin; her sin as the "beginning" had the consequence of providing the option to sin for all those after her, but perhaps not the obligation. As Samuel Cohon notes, Sirach "definitely links [sin] with Eve.... However, this idea is completely isolated, and contrasts with the general trend of the book ... The full consequences of this statement are not drawn by him nor formulated into a doctrine of original sin, i.e., of the transmission of sinfulness from the parents of the race."[8] The context of this verse may further mitigate its significance for an investigation into the source of sin. The verse just prior reads, "Dejected mind, gloomy face, and wounded heart come from an evil wife. Drooping hands and weak knees come from the wife who does not make her husband happy," and the two verses following read, "Allow no outlet to water, and no boldness of speech to an evil wife. If she does not go as you direct, separate her from yourself."[9] Given that the context of this statement about Eve is a discussion of the behavior of a bad wife and the consequences of her behavior (verse 23) and the way to deal with such a wife (vv. 25–26), it could be that the function of the verse is simply to show Eve as the paradigmatic example and nadir of a bad wife's behavior and its consequences.[10] Still, for someone in Matthew's milieu who might have been looking for answers to the question of the source of sin, the text can be read in that light and does offer another option from what we have seen previously.

Sirach's possible consonance with another aspect of our previous texts' conception of the source of sin—that is, their shared but various traits of apocalypticism—is harder to trace than its similarities and differences in its treatments of the giants and Adam and Eve. As noted above, the primary

---

8   "Original Sin," *HUCA* 21 [1948]: 284.

9   25:23, 25–26 NRSV.

10   For another reading that tries to understand this verse in its context of the "bad wife" discussion, see John Levison, "Is Eve to Blame? A Contextual Analysis of Sirach 24:25," *CBQ* 47 (1985): 617–23.

74 CHAPTER 5

feature of apocalypticism is dualism.[11] In this issue, Sirach is notably congruent with our previous texts, since Sirach explicitly proposes dualism as the fundamental structure of the world when it says, "Good is the opposite of evil, and life the opposite of death; so, the sinner is the opposite of the godly. Look at all the works of the Most High; they come in pairs, one the opposite of the other" (33:14–15). While this understanding could play out in a number of emphases or types of dualism, the one primarily apparent in Sirach is ethical dualism—the conception that the world is made up of two types of people: the "righteous" and the "sinner," or the wise and the foolish, or the godly and the wicked.[12] One of the features of this dualism, however, is that, on an individual level, it is not a rigid, unchangeable dichotomy. Because the designation of one as righteous or sinful is based on one's actions and not on an ontological difference, one can move from the category of sinner to that of righteous by repentance and amendment of life. Similarly, one can fall away from righteousness and be ultimately counted as a sinner despite many wise and righteous deeds earlier in life.[13]

While the ethical dualism we see in Sirach usually leaves room for people to move from one category to the other, in the verses immediately preceding those above, there may be however, a different, more deterministic perspective. Here the author discusses the source of the differences in the lots of humanity:

> All people are of clay, for from earth humankind was formed. Yet in the fullness of his understanding the Lord makes people unalike; in different paths he has them walk. Some he blesses and makes great, and some he sanctifies and draws to himself. Others he curses and brings low and expels them from their station. Like clay in the hands of the potter, to be molded according to his pleasure, so are all people in the hands of their Maker, to give to them as he decides.[14]

---

11   On the relation of Sirach and wisdom literature more generally to apocalyptic literature and apocalypticism, see Richard J. Coggins, *Sirach*, Guides to Apocrypha and Pseudepigrapha (Sheffield, U.K.: Sheffield Academic Press, 1998) 73–75; Gabriele Boccaccini, *Middle Judaism: Jewish Thought, 300 B.C.E. to 200 C.E.* (Minneapolis: Fortress Press, 1991), 77–160; Benjamin G. Wright, "*1 Enoch* and Ben Sira: Wisdom and Apocalypticism in Relationship," *The Early Enochic Literature*, JSJSup 121 (Leiden; Boston: Brill, 2007), 159–176.

12   The contrasting of the godly versus the wicked can be seen in many passages, for example, 1:25, 2:12–18, 12:1–6, 16:13, 23:11–12, 27:9–10, 28:22–23, 29:14–17, 31:6–8, 32:15–18, 34:21–24 + 35:8–13, 40:14–17.

13   This ethical dualism is, of course, similar to some of the sections of Matthew influenced by wisdom literature, particularly the parable of the wise and foolish builders (7:24–29) and the wise and foolish maidens (25:1–13).

14   33:10–13. Translation based on that of Patrick W. Skehan and Alexander A. Di Lella, *The Wisdom of Ben Sira*, AB 39 (New York: Doubleday, 1987), 394, with slight modification

SIRACH 75

Taken on its own, this passage could have a number of possible meanings. Some have seen it as God determining not simply the seemingly-fortuitous events of a person's life but the very quality of that life, such that the God's activity is construed as more or less deterministic and thus predestinarian since if God determines that one will be a sinner, there are definite and unavoidable consequences in the economy of righteousness in Sirach. Since, as we will see, this is quite at odds with other passages in Sirach (particularly 15:11–20), we will try to make sense of the 33:10–15 passage as a unit, and ultimately a unit in relation to 15:11–20.

It should first of all be noted that verse 10 indicates that the context of the discussion is all humanity, not specifically Israel or all those who fear God. Though it may be tempting to see the verses that follow in terms of moral determination or even something like salvation or damnation, the text does not move in either of these directions.[15] Verse 11 could simply mean that the Lord in his boundless wisdom has set up two possible courses for humans—the course of righteousness and wisdom or the course of sin and folly—and in so doing has set in motion the distinguishing of what sort of person one is. In this construal, the Lord does not determine the individual path of any person but has simply set up the dichotomous categories.[16] The verse itself and that which follows, however, point more to God's active involvement in the lives of individuals rather than simply the establishment of various courses or tracks in life one might pursue. God appoints a particular path for each person, "that is he assigns to them different *destinies*."[17] These destinies are not, however, morally weighted categories. God makes some to be honored and successful and others to be humbled. The fact that one can be humbled and poor and yet be wise and righteous—often more so than those whose wealth and honor traditionally indicated the favor of the Lord—is, in fact, a theme of Sirach[18] and provides a link to other wisdom literature, the most notable character in this regard being, of course, Job whose misfortunes were not caused by sin but

---

(following the RSV translation of ἀποδοῦναι αὐτοῖς κατὰ τὴν κρίσιν αὐτοῦ in v. 13; Skehan and Di Lella's version, "to be requited according as he judges them," introduces overtones of eschatological judgment that do not fit the context).

15   Thus, it is especially important to resist the influence of Paul's use of the potter-clay analogy in Rom 9:18–31, where the context is clearly both moral and eschatological (honor/dishonor, righteousness, mercy/wrath, glory/destruction, salvation) with respect to the election and salvation of Gentiles and Israel.

16   The limit of two possible courses for humans rather than three or more seems required by the material in verses 14 and 15.

17   Skehan and Di Lella, *Wisdom of Ben Sira*, 400; italics theirs. As Di Lella notes, referencing Smend (*Die Weisheit des Jesus Sirach erklärt*, [Berlin: Reimer, 1906], 298), "'path' in the OT often means 'destiny'" (Skehan and Di Lella, 400).

18   E.g., 3:17–20, 4:17, 10:14–31, 21:5, 35:17–25.

76 CHAPTER 5

rather quite the opposite. Even the idea that he "sanctifies" some does not have the moral weight we might be inclined to give it. On a larger scale, this section actually begins with verse 7 and in vv. 7–9 we find God acting with regard to the times of the year in a way that is parallel to what we see with regard to humans: the days are "distinguished" from one another (v. 8); seasons, like human paths, are designated; and some days are exalted and sanctified. The sanctification here is cultic: days become holy by being designated as feasts to the Lord. Thus, the parallel sanctification of certain persons in verse 12 also is likely cultic and thus refers to God's calling of priests. Sanctification here then is not moral sanctification but the setting apart and raising up of priests for Temple service.[19] Thus, in the section dealing with God's formation and control of the destinies of humans, no moral distinctions are implied, and no source of sin is posited; the topic of sinfulness is not even addressed. It is only when we arrive at vv. 14 and 15 that the ethical dualism becomes manifest in the contrasting of good with evil and the sinner with the just.

It should be noted that, as we saw in the subsection on "Dualism" earlier in this chapter, while the dichotomies in 33:14–15 might not be counted as properly dualistic by some scholars of religion,[20] they are generally viewed as such in our field. This is particularly the case here and in apocalyptic literature where the contrasting elements are not seen as simply necessary polarities in the structure of the world (and thus each element is to be accepted as the indispensable counterpart to the other), but rather one is viewed as good and in accord with God's will and the other is counted as wrong and opposed to God's will. The fact that these dualistic pairs seem to be the very fabric of the universe does not make the presence of the evil elements acceptable, but rather makes their presence inescapable—at least in the present age. This perspective can be engendered simply by observation of the way of the world. The fact, however, that in our present passage the author portrays God as the *creator* of these dualities while also asserting that the negative elements are not a desirable or even acceptable way of being in the world forms the crux of the investigations

---

19   See Skehan and Di Lella, 400. This connection is strengthened by the frequent use of στάσις (and related forms) in the LXX apparently translating מַעֲמָד/עָמַד/עָמְדָ for those involved in temple service (e.g., 2 Ch 23:13, 30:16, 35:10, 35:15; Neh 8:7, 9:3, 13:11) and its use in v. 12d where God is depicted as able to expel people from their place/station (στάσις). In this, the author of Sirach may be issuing a covert warning to the priests of his day that, while God can sanctify them for their office, he can just as easily remove them, especially since Isa 22:19 uses στάσις /מַעֲמָד in the Lord's warning "I will thrust you from your office and pull you down from your station" (NAB). This *contra* Di Lella who sees here a reference to the Gentiles, particularly the Canaanites "whom the Lord expelled 'from their place'" (*Wisdom of Ben Sira*, 400).

20   Bianchi, *Encyclopedia of Religion*, 4:506.

SIRACH 77

related to theodicy and Sirach's view of God's sovereignty. Thus, by the time we reach the end of this passage, if the passage makes any point about the source of sin, the author's unrelenting commitment to the utter sovereignty of God places him in the position of counting God as the source of human sinfulness, since he is the source of everything.

The conundrum of this perspective is brought into sharp relief as we finish exploring the previous passage and turn now to the Sirach passage that tends to receive the most attention when discussing the source of sin: 15:11–20. This passage reads:

> Do not say, "It was the Lord's doing that I fell away"; for he does not do what he hates. Do not say, "It was he who led me astray"; for he has no need of the sinful. The Lord hates all abominations; such things are not loved by those who fear him. It was he who created humankind in the beginning, and he left them in the power of their own free choice. If you choose, you can keep the commandments, and to act faithfully is a matter of your own choice. He has placed before you fire and water; stretch out your hand for whichever you choose. Before each person are life and death, and whichever one chooses will be given. For great is the wisdom of the Lord; he is mighty in power and sees everything; his eyes are on those who fear him, and he knows every human action. He has not commanded anyone to be wicked, and he has not given anyone permission to sin.

Here we find that, although as we saw in 33:14–15, dualism—including the dualism between righteous and sinner—is the God-willed structure of creation, it is not part of his will (expressed here as command) that any should participate in the negative aspect of the dualism and *be* sinners. God neither causes nor approves of people going astray. Though God has set in place the dualities ("he has placed before you fire and water ... Before each person are life and death") it is in the power of each individual to decide which side she will choose. Since "if you choose, you can keep the commandments, and to act faithfully is a matter of your own choice," humans are without excuse. The source of sin (or obedience) is thus within the human himself. If one feels it important to demonstrate a logically consistent perspective in Sirach on why people sin,[21] this very straightforward statement will have to be given its due in relation to the somewhat less clear statements in 33:10–15.

---

21   A project that is not necessary for our purposes.

78   CHAPTER 5

Yet, this passage does have its ambiguities. As is almost universally noted with regard to this passage, the statement that God "left them in the power of their own διαβούλιον/יֵצֶר" raises a number of questions. Obviously the LXX Greek has already made an interpretive choice about the meaning of יֵצֶר, and it is not a baseless choice, though διαβούλιον is significantly clearer in meaning than יֵצֶר. The most basic meaning of the Hebrew is "that which is formed or framed" from the verb יָצַר as in Gen 2:7: "The Lord God formed the 'adam from the dust of the earth." In at least half of uses in the OT, however, יֵצֶר is joined with heart (לֵב) or thoughts (מַחֲשָׁבָה).[22] Thus, by combining the form/frame aspect with the deliberative aspect of לֵב and מַחֲשָׁבָה one could perhaps justifiably use the English idiom "frame of mind" as a translation of יֵצֶר. The awkwardness of this in our Sirach passage,[23] however, makes "inclination" perhaps a better choice,[24] though especially granting that the translators of the LXX were much closer to the lived usage of יֵצֶר, we might want to think of it as "deliberation" or "discernment" or "counsel" (KJV).[25] Sirach's only other use of

---

22   1 Ch 28:9, 1 Ch 29:18.

23   This is not the case in other passages where יֵצֶר is used. For example, the passages cited in the previous footnote as well as Ps 103:14 where it is often translated "imaginations."

24   Though no small amount of ink has been spilt on "the two inclinations," often with Sirach coming significantly into play, it is important to note here that, if there is such an idea as "the inclinations" here, there seems to be but one inclination. Sirach, for all his dualism, does not seem to conceive of humans themselves as internalizing that dualism in the form of a battle waged in each person's mind and heart between the *yetser hara* and *yetser hatov*. Johann Cook concurs that in this passage only one inclination is present, but he argues that it is the *yester hara* ("The Origin of the Tradition of the YSR HTWB and YSR HR," *JSJ* 38 [2007]: 86–87). This seems unfounded since, if it were the case, it would be unfathomable how, if this was Sirach's perspective, he would immediately assert that "if you choose, you can keep the commandments, and to act faithfully is a matter of your own choice." Rather, it seems that Sirach does not present the יֵצֶר as a fully formed "inclination" (good or bad) as the Rabbis would later develop the doctrine, but, as I argue below, as a "frame of mind" or with some merited influence from the LXX, "discernment." As Rosen-Zvi says in his article "Two Rabbinic Inclinations? Rethinking a Scholarly Dogma": "Scholars have long pointed to the fact that the older meaning of the term *yetzer*, which is attested to in the Bible, and probably in Ben Sira as well, is natural: man's tendency, proclivity or choice. A similar meaning (or, better yet, semantic field) appears in R. Akiva's homilies."

25   The use of "free choice" to translate יֵצֶר (so the NRSV and AB) seems to ignore the "framing" aspect which is inherent in the word and to give the impression of a level of human autonomy from the "forming" work of God. Such an autonomy would undoubtedly be foreign to the author of Sirach since just the opposite view—that is, humanity's total dependence on God—is clear elsewhere in the text (e.g., in 33:7–15, discussed above). This is especially the case since the use of יֵצֶר forms a link back to our passage in 33:10–15 via Isa 29:16. In this passage of Isaiah, the prophet uses the metaphor of the potter and clay, although with a somewhat different emphasis from what we saw in Sir 33:13: "Shall

SIRACH 79

יֵצֶר is in 27:6: "The fruit of a tree shows the care it has had; so too does a person's speech show his יֵצֶר." Here again, something like "frame of mind"[26] seems in order since, if we turn again to the LXX for a check, we see that there is a definite intellectual cast to its understanding of the term in this context as well, using, as it does, ἐνθύμημα for יֵצֶר, "which has the nuances of 'thought,' 'reflection' or 'idea' in different contexts."[27]

Further, as many commentators have noted, though this passage is adamant that God "has not commanded anyone to be wicked, and he has not given anyone permission to sin," the fact that he has "created humankind in the beginning and left them in the power of their own discernment" means that God has provided the means and opportunity for sin.[28] Perhaps in this sense, some ultimate responsibility for sin lies with God, but in this passage of Sirach, the *source* of sin is definitely attributed to humanity's own flawed or malicious choices. As Jonathan Klawans has noted, the author of Sirach may, as many scholars believe, be arguing in response to people or groups that hold to a more deterministic view of sin:

> By denying human beings the freedom of choice—and the moral responsibility that comes along with it—Ben Sira believes his opponents implicate God in the commission of evil. Only by separating God from evil (as we find in both Ben Sira and Josephus's Sadducees)—and by asserting that evil comes about as a result of human choice—is God's punishment of the wicked both deserved and just.[29]

the potter be regarded as the clay; that the thing made should say of its maker, 'He did not make me'; or the thing formed (יֵצֶר) say of him who formed it (יֹצְרוֹ), He has no understanding'?" Is the author of Sirach making an intratextual allusion via an intertextual allusion? Perhaps. Di Lella's argument (*Wisdom of Ben Sira*, 400) that the context following יֵצֶר justifies the translation of "free choice" has some merit, but given the ongoing connection in Sirach between keeping the commandments/Torah (v. 15) and wisdom which is undoubtedly a gift from God and not an attribute of humans apart from God's activity, perhaps "discernment" with its sapiential connotations, would be a better choice.

26   NRSV: "the bent of his mind."
27   Cook, "Origin of the Tradition," 83. Despite this observation, Cook discounts 27:6 as useful for illuminating Sirach's use of יֵצֶר in 15:14, claiming that "the latter seems less significant, since the context is geared towards establishing the criteria for determining the value of a person" (*ibid.*)
28   This is obviously the same dilemma as God's prohibition against eating of the Tree of the Knowledge of God and Evil when he himself placed it in the midst of Eden.
29   Jonathan Klawans, "Josephus on Fate, Free Will, and Ancient Jewish Types of Compatibilism," *Numen* 56 (2009): 52–53.

80   CHAPTER 5

Thus, God's ultimate goodness is preserved. For this passage of Sirach then, the message is clear: human choice is the source of sin.

Beyond these two passages, however, there are yet others that speak to the source of sin, albeit sometimes less explicitly. In 5:4–5, the reader is warned that presumptuousness with regard to God's mercy can cause sin: "Do not say, 'I sinned, yet what has happened to me?' for the Lord is slow to anger. Do not be so confident of forgiveness that you add sin to sin." Here, obviously, the problem is not simply pride within the sinner or even over-confidence in God's forgiveness, but an incorrect perception of God becomes the source of sin. As we saw above with respect to 16:7–11, Sirach is at pains to point out that God can be depended upon to punish disobedience, no matter who may be guilty (including the giants), and one must remember that "even if there were only one stiff-necked person, it would be a wonder if he remained unpunished. For mercy and wrath are with the Lord; he is mighty to forgive—but he also pours out wrath."[30] Thus, it is a misconception about the character of God (i.e., that he is so merciful as to overlook sins) that is portrayed here as a potential source of sin.

It could be argued that this idea is not beyond the previous perspective that sin is a result of human choice. Certainly, one can choose to ignore a truth that is inconvenient for the fulfillment of one's desires. One can also, however, be genuinely ignorant or misinformed, though obviously Sirach is endeavoring, through his exhortation, to eliminate this possibility for his readers by removing their ignorance. There are other things about a person, however, that are not as easily removed as misinformation and that are also portrayed as causing sin: these are various parts of the human self.

In an extended section in which the author of Sirach addresses God and prays for protection from sin, the author cites three body parts that he is concerned will cause him to sin: his heart, his belly, and his mouth and lips:[31]

> Who will set a guard over my mouth, and upon my lips a prudent seal, so that I may not fall because of them, and my tongue may not destroy me? O Lord, Father and Master of my life, do not abandon me to their counsels, and do not let me fall because of them!
>
> Who will set whips upon my thoughts, and upon my heart the discipline of wisdom, so as not to spare me in my errors, and not overlook my sins? Otherwise my ignorance may be multiplied, and my sins may

---

30   22:27–23:6.

31   Though "haughty eyes" are mentioned in 23:4, there is no indication that they lead one into sin.

SIRACH   81

abound, and I may fall before my adversaries, and my enemy may rejoice over me.

O Lord, Father and God of my life, do not give me haughty eyes, and remove lust from me. Do not let the appetite of the belly or sex seize me, and do not hand me over to a shameless soul.

Listen, my children, to instruction concerning the mouth; the one who guards it[32] will never be caught. By his lips a sinner is seized, and the reviler and the arrogant are ensnared and caused to sin[33] by them.[34]

The portrayal of personified body parts as agents of sin within a person is unlike our previous literature, except in the case of the "heart." Here, it should be noted, the emphasis of the verse above is on the deliberative faculties of the heart: the parallel between the plea that God would give whips (instruments of discipline) for the thoughts and give discipline for the "heart" makes it clear that the author is utilizing καρδία/לֵב as metaphor for one's ability to consider, decide, and will a course of action. This is in contrast to its use in *Jubilees* and *4 Ezra*, discussed above,[35] where, for the most part, although the deliberative faculties were certainly not excluded from the portrayal of the sin-causing potential of the heart, the emphasis was more holistic—the heart serving as a metaphor for a person's essential inner self in its totality, though including mental and volitional faculties.

The second body part implicated in sinning is the belly (Greek: κοιλία). There are two options for what Sirach is saying about the particular way the belly causes sin. The first is through gluttony: "the appetite of the belly" being

---

32   Taking στόματος rather than παιδείαν to be the implied object of the participle φυλάσσων, since this is the same sense as the opening verse (22:27) and the following verse as well, the reiterated point in each being the potential for the mouth/tongue/lips (i.e., speech) to cause sin and thus the need to control them in order to avoid transgression.

33   σκανδαλισθήσονται. The dual meaning is important here, thus I include the literal meaning of "ensnared"/"tripped up" (NRSV) as well as the metaphorical sense "caused to sin." The sense of being "tripped up" is important because it forms a conceptual connection to the multiple uses of "fall" (πίπτω) in the passage, although the use of "ensnared" for σκανδαλισθήσονται draws attention to the parallelism with the first half of the sentence where sinner is "caught" or "grabbed" and thus ensnared by his lips. The use of forms of σκανδαλίζω with respect to body parts will be a significant aspect of our investigation of the causes of sin in Matthew, so it is important to recognize the similar use of such language here.

34   22:27–23:8, my translation of the LXX.

35   Although it is consonant with the much of the use of the metaphor in the canonical wisdom literature. Cf. Prov 6:14, 6:18, 15:14, 15:28, 16:21, 23:7; Eccl 1:13, 1:16–17, 2:3, 7:25, 8:9, 8:16, 9:1, etc., as well as, for example, Ps 131:1, 140:2. The connection is so significant that לֵב is often translated as "mind" or "sense" in the RSV and NRSV of Proverbs and Ecclesiastes.

understood to refer to physical hunger for food. This is consistent with Sirach's admonitions elsewhere to avoid overindulgence.[36] Since, however, κοιλία can mean womb or inward abdominal parts more generally and ὄρεξις can mean not simply physical appetite but desire and longing as well, the two elements of the compound subject—κοιλίας ὄρεξις and συνουσιασμός—may be reiterating the same idea rather than offering two possible agents of that might overtake one. This would fit also with the following clause where Sirach prays to be protected from the influence of a "shameless soul." The use of ἀναιδεῖ in Proverbs in connection with sexual sin[37] strengthens the possibility that each part of this sentence in Sirach is referring to the same thing, and thus that κοιλίας ὄρεξις ought to be taken in a sexual sense. Thus, just as in Matthew where one's eye and hand are connected with leading one into sexual sins (5:27–30), so here the appetites of the "belly" can cause one to be seized or overtaken, particularly if one's soul lacks a sufficient sense of shame. It is not explicit here that such an "overtaking" would be tantamount to sin, though Sirach's use of the same verb in 23:8 with respect to the sinner clarifies any ambiguity.[38]

The depiction of the mouth and its parts as sources of sin[39] forms the frame of the section and thus is of particular importance. In the first section, the mouth is personified in terms that suggest a criminal—it ought to have a guard set over it (22:27), it can destroy you (22:27), and its counsels can cause one to fall (23:1). In the second section (23:7–8), despite the repetition of the guarding motif, the dominant image for the way the mouth induces sin is inanimate: the mouth is like a trap or a snare that catches one and trips one up.[40]

In the use of these metaphors, and indeed those explored with respect to other body parts, there exists an interesting dynamic: the source of sin is within the human—it is a part of the body—but it is only a portion of the person. The whole person is not implicated,[41] but the source of sin, while internal, is localized and, in the case of the mouth in 22:27–23:1, personified as a lawless

---

36 E.g., 29:21–23, 30:12–22, 37:27–31.

37 In the description of the activities of the adulteress in Prov. 7:3–27, it is noted that she has an ἀναιδεῖ face (v. 13).

38 The use of the verb in 7:1 is along similar lines: "Do no ill (κακά) and you shall by no means be seized by ill (καταλάβῃ κακόν)."

39 Here also depicted metaphorically as a "fall."

40 For a discussion of the image of the σκάνδαλον and its original sense of snare, see TDNT 7:339–340.

41 Again, as opposed to the use of heart elsewhere in our literature and, indeed in the various places in the OT (see TDNT, "καρδία," 3:605–614), where the heart is a metaphor for the whole person or one's essential self.

SIRACH 83

person.[42] Thus, this section, while more metaphorical than that in 15:11–20, fits well with its message: the greater part of the person must exercise control over the portions that would lead one into sin and thus one may choose to be obedient. In both passages, the source of sin is not beyond the control of the person, but as an internal issue "to act faithfully is a matter of your own choice."

Our final set of passages presents a different perspective, however. In these, sin is compared to attacking animals and thus is pictured as wholly external. In 21:2 we read: "As from the presence a snake, flee from sin; for if you should approach, it will bite you. Its teeth are lion's teeth, killing the soul of a person." Here sin is pictured as an external entity that lies in wait for a person to walk past. The warning is that, once it is recognized, one ought to flee "as from a snake." If one does not, the deadly consequences are also comparable to those experienced with a fierce animal, in this case a lion.

An almost identical sentiment is expressed in 27:10: "A lion lies in wait for prey; just so does sin for the unrighteous."[43] Again, sin is pictured as a deadly animal that will attack the unwary.[44] The message of these passages complexifies, probably unintentionally, the picture painted by the more explicit reflections in ch. 15. In picturing sin as an entity that is external to the human and by which a person can be attacked unawares, the element of choice and volition with respect to any individual's participation in sin so vehemently asserted in ch. 15 is undermined. Although the purpose of these passages is to put the reader on her guard against sin, the possibility that one could, completely unintentionally, be ambushed by sin in one's walk through life is also a possibility raised by these analogies, the use of ἐνεδρεύει here being analogous to the use of σκανδαλίζω that we saw above in our discussion of 22:27–23:8.[45] Thus, even in a text like Sirach where there apparently has been some intentionally systematic reflection on the source of sin, diversity of perspective exists within the text.

---

42   This is notably similar to the sentiments of Jas 3:4–8, in which the tongue is portrayed as an unrighteous body part, evil and filled with poison, that guides the actions of the whole body and thus must be "bridled" (controlled).

43   My translation.

44   The comparison with God's words to Cain (Gen 4:7) is tempting, and despite the difference in vocabulary ("ἥμαρτες ἡσύχασον πρὸς σὲ ἡ ἀποστροφὴ αὐτοῦ" versus "λέων θήραν ἐνεδρεύει") perhaps valid.

45   ἐνεδρεύω: lie in wait for, lay snares for; passive: to be caught in an ambush, to be ensnared (LSJ 562).

CHAPTER 6

Qumran Texts

As we turn to the literature of Qumran,[1] it is necessary to note that, as with *2 Baruch* and *4 Ezra*, there seems to be little likelihood that there was any direct literary connection between these texts and the Gospel of Matthew. Yet, given that Josephus asserts that "many [Essenes] dwell in every city," their contribution to the general fund of ideas current and available in the first century needs to be taken into account. As Jean Duhaime notes in his introduction to the PTSDSSP edition of 1QM, while "the similarities between the War Scroll and the New Testament do not indicate direct influence in one way or another," an exploration of Qumran texts does "contribute, however, to a better contextualization and understanding of early Jewish and the earliest 'Christian' documents."[2]

As with the apocryphal and pseudepigraphic texts, our study will attempt to be representative rather than exhaustive its survey of Qumran texts. The texts selected for examination below are the major texts composed by the Qumranites or their Essene predecessors and thus likely to be the most indicative of their particular perspective and to indicate areas in which their ideas were markedly influential.

1   War Scroll (1QM)

We begin with the War Scroll for a number of reasons. First, it presents perhaps the most consistent (and accordingly least complex) picture of the source of sin and evil found in any of our texts. Second, though most of the scroll (columns 2–12) has little to contribute to our study, being detailed descriptions of the plans and procedures for the eschatological war against Belial and the Sons of Darkness (the Kittim, *et al*), the dualistic language in the passages that frame these practical matters is arresting in its intensity and significant for understanding the depth of the dualism found in at least some segments of,

---

1   The inclusion of the Damascus Document (CD), though in its most complete form not technically a text from Qumran, is justified by its apparent presence in the Qumran library, based on fragments of manuscripts found there that match the text of CD. See the "Introduction" to the Damascus Document in PTSDSSP 2:4–9, esp. 6–8.

2   2:90.

© KONINKLIJKE BRILL NV, LEIDEN, 2020 | DOI:10.1163/9789004419506_008

and perhaps the whole of, the Essene movement and so important for appreciating how that may have contributed to Matthew's milieu. Finally, the War Scroll utilizes in a very clear and specific way some terms that appear in other Qumran literature and thus helps us appreciate the significance of the use of those terms in the other texts.

In columns 1 and 13–15 there is consistent reference to two groups of people: those who are allied with God and those who are allied with his spiritual opponent, Belial.[3] These are often referred to as "Sons of" (בני) either element of a dualistic pair, usually light[4] or darkness,[5] although other conventionally dualistic elements are also employed as descriptors of God's people—such as sons of righteousness,[6] sons of truth,[7] and sons of his covenant[8]—without the use of their opposites to describe Belial's followers. The use of this familial language conveys a sense that those in each group are allied with these powers not by some choice, but by their very nature: they are spiritual "genetic heirs" of these powers and as such share their very nature.[9]

The language of sonship, however, is not the only metaphor employed in the War Scroll in describing the followers of God and Belial. The term "lot of" (גורל) is used seemingly interchangeably with "sons of"[10] and even in combination

---

3 Though Belial is cast as God's opposite, the inequality of this opposition is demonstrated by the failure of Belial and his followers and the ultimate, though hard-won, victory of God and God's people in the War.

4 1.1, 1.3, 1.9, 1.13, 1.14.

5 1.1, 1.7, 1.10, 1.16, 13.16, 16.11.

6 1.8.

7 17.8; perhaps also 1.16.

8 17.8.

9 Obviously, the metaphors here cannot be taken over literally, but should be understood in the context of OT usage of "sons of" wherein the phrase indicates participation in a group identity perhaps more than an individual in heritance of characteristics. Still, in that case as well, there is the sense that that participation carries with it identifying characteristics—often dictated by God's determination—whether it be the sons of Israel as participants in the covenant with the subsequent characteristic of Torah observance or whether it is the sons of Ham (Canaanites) who are cursed by God and thus are predicted to display the characteristic of servitude, etc. Thus, the metaphor of "sons of" carries the nearly indistinguishable dyad of identity and characteristic behavior. Somewhat complicating the picture in 1QS is that the "parent" is a dualistic symbolic entity: Light, Deceit, etc. Yet the connection of those abstractions with the dualism of God and Belial clarifies the message, such that it is clear that the sons of light or sons of darkness have not actually been generated by these symbolic "characters," but are offspring of the greater entities (God and Belial) with whom these symbolic entities are seen to be inherently identified.

10 The interchangeability of the terms is particularly evident in 1.9–11 since in line 9 God's people are referred to as "Sons of Light" and in line 10 Belial's are called "Sons of Darkness,"

86 CHAPTER 6

with it.[11] The use of this image, however, suggests a different but complementary aspect of the nature of these groups: that their allegiance to their respective spiritual forces was the result of predetermination. In the OT, the basic, literal meaning of גורל is the stone (originally) that was thrown to prophetically indicate the will of God with regard to some question,[12] and particularly in Numbers and Joshua, to allocate land to the various tribes.[13] Obviously, the apportioning of the land was understood to have been determined by God and thus the result of the casting of the lots to have been controlled by him and used as an instrument of his will in this instance, and in general practice as well. This idea is articulated explicitly in Proverbs 16:33: "The lot is cast into the lap, but its every decision is from the Lord."[14]

From this very tangible sense of the Lord "allotting" a portion of land to a person or group sprung a more abstract idea of the "portion" that God allots to one, an idea that encompasses not simply physical space but all the "givens" of one's life and various things that happen to one.[15] From this it is not a far step to understanding a person's spiritual disposition to be one of these givens and thus part of one's "lot" in life.

The use of גורל in 1QM draws upon this deterministic sense and also brings in the sense of a "lot" as the portion or property given to one. Thus, the "lot of darkness/Belial"[16] are those persons given to him by the divine determination of the Lord, and those who are of the "lot of light/God"[17] are those whom God has chosen to be God's own portion.[18]

---

    yet in line 11 it is said that the two groups, "the Sons of Light and the lot darkness, shall fight each other." Note also the use of גורל with light and darkness in 13.5–6.

11   E.g., 1.1.

12   For example, which goat was to be the scapegoat (Lev. 16:8–10) and on which day to destroy the Jews (Est 3:7 and 9:24) and which person was the cause of the storm threatening the ship of Tarshish (Jon 1:7). Proverbs 18:18 articulates the general understanding: "The lot puts an end to disputes and decides between powerful contenders."

13   Thus, in English a portion of land that you own is a "lot."

14   ESV.

15   E.g., Isa 17:14: "At evening time, behold, terror! Before morning, they are no more! This is the portion of those who despoil us, and the lot of those who plunder us"; Jer 13:25: "This is your lot, the portion I have measured out to you, says the LORD, because you have forgotten me and trusted in lies."

16   1.5, 1.11. Though in 13.1–12, it may be tempting to take the גורל רוחי as non-human spiritual entities that are also allied with Belial, the use of רוח in other Qumran texts, notably 1QH, to refer to human beings, especially with reference to their spiritual condition, indicates that the writer is still speaking of humans here, although the use of מלאכי חבל as an apparent appositive for רוחו in 13.12 complicates the matter.

17   13.9 and 13.5. See also 1.5 and 13.12: "lot of truth."

18   It seems however, that גורל still retains some of its generic, "secular" usage and has not become strictly a *terminus technicus* with reference to persons' spiritual condition, as evidenced by its use in 1.13–14 to refer to the seven periods of time in the War, though

QUMRAN TEXTS

Thus, in 1QM, people's violent opposition to God, the epitome of sin, and their allegiance with the powers of evil in this opposition, has its source in their very nature which is articulated in the language of sonship, a nature that apparently has been allotted to them by God. These people sin in opposing God and warring with God's people because they have a genetic-spiritual connection with—a kinship to—the entity that is God's opposite. In this sense, their fate as sinners and adherents of evil is inescapable.

2   The Hodayot (1QH)

In the collection of Hymns of Thanksgiving, we see a much greater diversity of images and ideas regarding the causes of sin in humans. The hymns' divergent perspectives and varying images are sometimes complementary but also sometimes at odds with one another, the recurring motifs and themes even being combined with each other within a particular passage in ways that sometimes reinforce the meaning of a particular motif and sometimes seemingly undermine the implications of individual images.[19]

Exploring the Hymns, we find three recurring ideas related to the hymnist's[20] perspective on the cause of sin: the human as animated but impure clay, a

certainly the sense is that these periods are "allotted," ordained, and predetermined by God.

19   For example, in 11.21–25 we find the combination of a number of key terms that will be explored below with regard to the source of sin, and while in this passage the focus is not so much on the cause of human sinfulness, these terms play important roles elsewhere in the Hodayot in reflection on the cause of sin, and thus, from those more explicit reflections, these terms carry with them an accrual of meaning: "You created (יצרתה) from the dust for the eternal council. The perverse spirit (רוח נעוה) you have cleansed from great transgression that he might take his stand with the host of the holy ones, and enter together (ביחד = "in the community") with the congregation of the sons of heaven [בני שמים]. And for man, You have allotted (גורל) an eternal destiny with the spirits of knowledge, to praise your name together [ביחד = "in the community"]... But I, a creature of clay (יצר החמר) what am I? Kneaded with water, for whom am I to be reckoned, and what is my strength? For I have taken my stand within the domain of wickedness, and I am with the wretched by lot (בגורל)." ET here and throughout the *Hodayot* section is that of *The Dead Sea Scrolls Reader: Part 5: Poetical and Liturgical Texts*, Donald W. Parry and Emmanuel Tov, eds., (Boston; Leiden: Koninklijke Brill, 2005), 2–76, except as noted.

20   For convenience, I refer to the author(s) of the Hodayot as one person, though the actual authorship of hymns—whether by the Righteous Teacher, someone writing in his *persona*, or by a number of writers over a period of time—is a question that may be impossible to answer. Fortunately, this issue does not significantly affect our study since these texts, as articulations of understandings of the self—individually and as representative of people generally—remain representative of perspectives present and apparently "canonized" by the group through their preservation and reproduction of the Hymns. As Carol

88   CHAPTER 6

dualism articulated as the division of all humans between two families or "lots"[21]
or spirits, and the divine determination of a person's nature or disposition
by God.

The writer in describing himself often refers to himself as a "vessel of clay/
dust" (עפר / חמר יצר), particularly with respect to his sinful impulses or his life
before he experienced some apparent conversion-like experience. In 9.21–23,
he writes:

> You have opened my ears to wonderful mysteries even though I am a ves-
> sel of clay (חמר יצר) and kneaded with water, a foundation of shame and
> a spring of filth, a melting pot of iniquity and a structure of sin (מבנה
> החטאה), spirit (רוח) of error, perverted, without understanding and terri-
> fied by righteous judgments.

Here we see the writer describing his sinfulness in terms that indicate it is
something inherent to him: he is a "structure of sin."[22] The reference to formed
(יצר) clay (elsewhere "dust;" see below) calls to mind the physical formation
(יצר) of Adam by God in Gen 2:7 as well as the use of the potter/clay analogy
in Isa 64:8 noted above in the section on Sirach with respect to the use of יצר.
Given the obvious associations of this language with the physical creation of
humanity, the hymn writer seems to be pointing to humanity's physical nature
as at least contributive to if not completely to blame for human sinfulness.[23]
Further, he depicts himself as both containing sin ("a melting pot of iniquity")
and also engendering it out of his most inner self ("a spring of filth").[24] Yet this

---

Newsom says, "Even if they are understood as representing the perspective of a leader-
ship class or of a single, historical leader, they would still be in many respects a model of
ideal sectarian subjectivity" ("Apocalyptic Subjects: Social Construction of the Self in the
Qumran Hodayot," *JSP* 12 [2001]: 9). The entire section on "Authorship and *Sitz im Leben*"
(pp. 8–16) is applicable here, as is the rest of Newsom's argument to the methodology
of mine.

21   As in 1QM.

22   "Structure of sin" = מבנה החטאה, as noted above; "structure" being "that which is built,"
from בנה, "to build."

23   This obviously would be analogous to the possible perspective of *2 Baruch* already mentioned and the attribution of sin-causing capabilities to various body parts in Sirach, as
discussed above. It is interesting to note, here and in the previous example, the author's
somewhat unique addition of the element of "water" to the clay or dust when discussing
the sin and impurity inherent in human bodies. Perhaps he is thinking of the impurity-
carrying propensity of moisture that was of such concern to the Essenes and perhaps
Pharisees (based on rabbinic texts) as the source of the problem.

24   The Hebrew here for spring—מקור—is used regularly in the OT with חי (Ps 36:9, Prov
10:11, Prov 13:14, 14:27, 16:22, Jer 2:13, Jer 17:13) to indicate one's most inward motivation
and sustenance. Thus, the law, understanding, and the fear of the Lord are all pointed to

iniquity isn't confined to his physical self: he is also a "spirit (רוח) of error, perverted, without understanding."[25]

This characterization, however, is not restricted to himself, as if he sees himself as particularly iniquitous compared to others and is hyperbolically depicting his own state which is now apparent to him but is not the case for others. No, he sees the aspects of his own sinfulness as anything but idiosyncratic; they are one instance of the general condition of humanity, as we see in 5.20–22: "What is one born of woman among all [Your] awesome [works]? He is but an edifice of dust, kneaded with water, [ ] his foundation is obscene shame, [ ] and a perverted spirit (רוח נעוה) ruled him." In language quite similar to that used to describe himself, the hymnist poses this rhetorical question regarding *not* himself but anyone "born of woman."[26] A similar universal perspective is evident in 12.29–30: "Where is the vessel (יצר) of clay that is able to carry out wondrous deeds? For he is sinful from the womb and in the guilt of unfaithfulness until old age." Thus, the hymnist portrays all persons as originally and thoroughly sinful, perverse, and guilty. Sin characterizes the very being of humanity, and individual sins springs from this.

This assertion of inherent sin and guilt for every "vessel of clay" seems at odds with one of the Hodayot's other main themes: the dualistic division of people between two families or lots or spirits.

As in the War Scroll, so we see also the Hymns of Thanksgiving a variety of expressions of the fundamental dualism of the Essenes. This dualism is sometimes expressed, as in 1QM, in familial terms. This is especially the case in 14.17ff where the hymnist predicts the coming judgment of God and war against those who have disbelieved and persecuted him:

> As far as Sheol [ ] the spring of light shall become an everlasting fountain
> without end. In its brilliant flames all the child[ren of injustice][27] shall

---

as a spring or fountain of life, whereas the writer is, because of his sinfulness, a fountain of filth.

25 Thus, 1QH is not positing a "physical" or "anthropological dualism" as discussed above, since the hymnist does not see one's body as evil and sinful in contrast to one's spirit that is good and moral.

26 The hymnist does apparently, however, use the phrase "vessel of dust" (יצר עפר) to refer specifically to himself over against his opponents in Frg. 3.5–9: "I keep the vessel of dust (יצר עפר) from being shattered ... they hide trap after trap, the shares of wickedness [ ] with injustice (in sinfulness, unrighteousness: בעול), and every deceitful vessel (יצר רמיה) is destroyed," although, the fragmentary condition of the text makes further interpretation difficult.

27 Or "sons of iniquity" (Wilfred Watson, trans., *The Dead Sea Scrolls Translated: the Qumran Texts in English*, edited by Florentino García Martínez [Leiden; New York: E.J. Brill; Grand Rapids: Eerdmans, 1996], 341).

90   CHAPTER 6

> burn [and it shall] become a fire which burns up all the men of guilt com-
> pletely…. Then the sword of God shall hasten to the time of judgment and
> all the children of his truth shall awaken to put an end to [the children of]
> wickedness, and all the children of guilt shall be no more … there is no
> escape for the creatures[28] of guilt.[29]

The dynamics that were present in the familial and genetic language of the War
Scroll are at work here as well: some people are characterized as descendants
of wickedness and guilt and thus as sharers in that "family resemblance,"[30] but
some are "children of his truth." This is in significant contrast to the characterization we saw above of *all* humans as sharers in thoroughgoing sinfulness
from the womb.

   Also similar to 1QM is 1QH's use of גורל. Though the use is not as extensive,
we see some similar dynamics. In XIX.10–14 we find the combination of filial
language with the use of גורל:

---

28   "Creatures" here translates יצר. The sentence in which it is found—"There will be no es-
     cape for the creatures (ליצר) of guilt"—seems to parallel XIV.30: "All the בני of guilt shall
     be no more," Yet, the flexible use of יצר allows here for some word-play. Since יצר can
     simply mean "that which is formed" it can mean a "creature" like Adam formed by God
     (so the translation of Parry and Tov) or, playing on the "frame of mind/inclination" mean-
     ing, the phrase might be rendered "for those of guilty inclination" (so Watson). In either
     case, the combination of יצר with the dualistic filial language implies that a יצר is analo-
     gous to or at least related to one's heredity—a given that is inescapable. Unlike 1QS, how-
     ever, 1QH does not appear to conceive of there being two *yetsers*, one good and one bad.
     The Hymnist sees the יצר of humans as generally sinful, as we see in 19.19–20: "But as for
     me, a fountain for bitter sorrow has been opened [ ] distress is not hidden from my eyes
     when I come to know the inclinations (יצרי) of man and [consider] the response (or "re-
     turn") of human-kind [and recognize] sin and the grief of guilt." Yet, it is not universally
     so. The hymnist apparently has a יצר that is not sinful since he writes: "You know the
     intention (יצר) of every work [or "of every creature"] and every reply you discern…. You
     know the inclination (יצר) of your servant that [I have] not relied on [ ] to exalt myself"
     (XV.13, 16–17). It is questionable, however, whether the use of יצר here really indicates
     any sort of inherent, determinative, animating principle (such as we will see, below, רוח
     does). Rather, it seems, we are back to a meaning more on the order of "frame of mind"
     based on the context of God's omniscience seen in the parallelism of "every reply you
     discern" with "You know the intention (יצר) of every work [or "of every creature"]," such
     that the message is the same as that of 1 Ch 28:9: "For the Lord searches all hearts, and
     understands every יצר and thought." Thus, while 1QH uses יצר with some frequency, it is
     usually, as we saw above, in the sense of a vessel or one's "formed" physical self, or as a
     mental intention which can be good or bad, but it is not used in a dualistic way as we see
     in some other texts such that it might be considered a source of sin.
29   XIV.17–19, 29–30, 32. The same dualism is evident in 15.29–30, 17.35, 18.27, 19.9, 19.11.
30   It seems that col. XV is a continuation of the same text as col. XIV and thus the statement
     in XV.3 that "Belial is manifest when the true nature of their being is revealed" aptly sum-
     marizes the ontological dualism of both these sections and 1QM.

For Your glory's sake You have cleansed man from transgression, so that he can purify himself for You from all filthy abominations and the guilt of unfaithfulness so as to be joined wi[th] the children (בני) of your truth, in the lot (ובגורל) with your saints. That bodies, covered with worms of the dead, might rise up from the dust to an et[ernal] council; from a perverse spirit (ומרוח נעוה) to Your understanding ... to be renewed with all that be and to rejoice together with those who know.

Just as in 1QM, the hymnist apparently sees people's status as "sons" and their membership in one or another "lot" as analogous concepts, since the second is used as an appositive of the first. Unlike 1QM, however, here we have the assertion of a change in people's status. Whereas in 1QM there was no indication that there was any possibility of change if you were of one "lot" or the other, here the hymnist claims that through God's cleansing, a human is made fit to change his "lot." This work of God even contravenes the apparent sin-producing impurity of human bodiliness articulated, as we saw above, in the image of the vessel of clay or dust and evoked here in the use of "dust" in "bodies, covered with worms of the dead, might rise up from the dust to an et[ernal] council." That there is more than one possible גורל is evident in xv.34: "[I give thanks to Y]ou, O Lord, for You have not cast my lot (גורלי) in the fraudulent assembly, nor have You set my portion in the council of the pretenders." Thus, 1QH affirms the dualism of 1QM's use of גורל, yet asserts the possibility that these are not unchangeable, static categories.

The text of xix.10–14 also includes another important term that we have touched upon above in our exploration of the concept of the vessel of clay: that is, the רוח and its importance for the hymnist's understanding of the source of sin.[31]

---

31   It should also be noted that the final phrase in xix.10–14 above that is translated by Parry and Tov as "and to rejoice together with those who know" could also be translated "and with those who know in a community (ביחד) of jubilation" (so Watson). As will be seen particularly in our exploration of 1QS, in the Qumran texts, the community is seen as the appropriate "habitat" for those of God's lot and entering the יחד is linked to rejection of and cleansing from sin. Thus, the rendering of that phrase as "and with those who know in a community (ביחד) of jubilation" appropriately draws attention to this aspect of Qumran identity, though it does not apply directly to our exploration of the causes of sin. It is also worth noting that the same constellation of terms—מרוח נעוה, גורל, יחד, and עפר, as well as the ideas of knowledge and "the council"—appears also in the text of 11.21–25, as discussed in note 19, above: "You created (יצרתה) from the dust for the eternal council. The perverse spirit (רוח נעוה) you have cleansed from great transgression that he might take his stand with the host of the holy ones, and enter together (ביחד = "in the community") with the congregation of the sons of heaven. And for man, You have allotted (גורל)

As we saw above in our exploration of the "vessel" image and in the passage above from col. XIX, the hymnist posits the he has (or had) a wicked and perverse רוח; yet, while he may have had a perverse spirit that caused him to sin, this was not a situation that was either inevitable or irreparable. Elsewhere, he also indicates that that was not the only possible רוח; one can have a good spirit as well, for we see in VI.11–12 that "by their spirits (רוחות) You [God] distinguish between the good and the evil."

Distinguishing is not the only thing, however, God does with regard to רוחות. 1QH also claims that God "determines" the spirits. In XIX.8–9 the hymnist says, "[For apart from You no]thing is done, and without Your will nothing is known. You have formed every spirit (רוח יצרתה כול) and [Yo]u[determined its] de[eds] and judgment for all their works." If one has a good or an evil spirit, it is, apparently, the work of God.

The idea of divine moral pre-determination by God is even more evident in an extended passage from col. VII:

> I know by Your understanding that it is not by human strength [nor can] a man [fathom] his way, nor is a person able to determine his step. But I know that in You is the inclination of every spirit (יצר כול רוח) [and all] his [works] You have determined before ever You created him. How should any be able to change Your words? You alone have [creat]ed the righteous one, and from the womb you established him to your covenant at the appointed time of grace and to walk in all things.... But the wicked You created for [the time of] Your [w]rath, and from the womb You set them apart for the day of slaughter. For they walk in a way which is not profitable, and they reject your covenant and their soul abhors Your [truth], they have no delight in all that You have commanded, but they choose what You hate.... What indeed is a mere human that it might have insight into [ ] how is dust able to determine its steps? You Yourself have formed (יצרתה) the spirit (רוח), and its activity You have determined [ ] and from You is the way of all life.[32]

Thus, whether one is righteous or wicked has been determined by God. This firm insistence on the complete sovereignty of God and on God's formation of

---

an eternal destiny with the spirits of knowledge, to praise your name together [ביחד = "in the community"]... But I, a creature of clay (יצר החמר), what am I? Kneaded with water, for whom am I to be reckoned, and what is my strength? For I have taken my stand within the domain of wickedness, and I am with the wretched by lot (בגורל)."

32 VII.12–22.

everything in creation leaves the hymnist, of course, in the same theological predicament that we have seen above with Sirach and others: he is put in the position of having to assert that a person's wicked moral character is the result of God's predetermined creative will, and thus that God is the source of sin and evil. Further, the passage is in contrast with the previously examined passages in which the hymnist portrays himself as having once had a perverted spirit but now to have been cleansed.

Even if one can reconcile the "conversion" passages with the divine determination passages by asserting that the hymnist would understand even his conversion as part of the divine determination of God, there are yet other passages that cannot be so easily discounted in their disagreement with the message of col. VII. For example, in the passage from col. XIX that we examined above, even though the hymnist asserts that it is God who has "cleansed man from transgression" this is done "so that *he can purify himself* for You from all filthy abominations and the guilt of unfaithfulness so as to be joined with the children of your truth."[33] There is thus a level of cooperation implied in the action of humans and God or at least some subsequent action on the part of an individual is expected after the initial cleansing action of God if the person is "to be joined with the children of your truth in the lot with your saints."

Further, when writing of his enemies, the hymnist indicates that they themselves are guilty of causing their own sin through their choices. He says in XII.17, "For they did not choose the wa[y of] Your [heart] nor attend to your word," and in XIX.14–16 that "with a willful heart they look about and seek You in idols. They have set the stumbling block of their iniquity before themselves, and they come to seek you through the words of lying prophets corrupted by error." The image of putting a stumbling block before themselves is particularly telling. The people are depicted as knowingly, intentionally setting themselves up to sin. Thus, in these passages, some people are portrayed as the cause of their own sinning.

Finally, there are also hints that evil spiritual powers play a role in people's sinful behavior. In col. XIV, which we saw was highly dualistic and utilized the language of both "sons of" and "lot," the hymnist claims that, for his enemies, "Belial is the counselor of their heart [ ] schemes of wickedness, they wallow in guilt."[34] Thus, Belial, if not actually completely motivating their wicked schemes, at least has a significant "voice" in their hearts and is thus aiding and perhaps instructing them in wickedness. As noted above, "Belial is manifest

---

33   XIX.10–11.

34   XIV.21–22.

94   CHAPTER 6

when the יצר of their being is revealed."[35] This points to Belial's hidden but dominating presence and activity in their thoughts and perhaps even in their very being.

Thus, in 1QH, we see a diversity of potential causes of sin: the physicality of one's body, the "lot" or family of which one has been destined to be a part, the divine predetermination of God or the work of his adversary, or even one's own choices.

3   Damascus Document (CD)

The perspectives on the source of sin in CD, though not demonstrating the diversity of 1QH, manifest some of the same tensions.

In the early sections of the Admonition, there is a notable use of images and metaphors of the body when attributing the cause of sin. Thus, we see in II.14–18:

> And now, O sons, hearken to me and I will uncover your eyes, so you may see and understand the works of God and choose that which he wants and despise that which he hates: to walk perfectly in all his ways and not to stray in the thoughts of a guilty inclination [במחשבות יצר אשמה] and licentious eyes. For many have failed because of them ... (thus, for example,) walking after the wantonness of their heart(s) [בשרירות לבם], the Watchers fell. They were held by it (the wantonness of their heart), for they did not keep God's ordinance.

There are several aspects of this passage that deserve attention. First there is the command to hearken and choose. The image of choosing is connected with walking in God's way (an image we have discussed previously) and not being led astray by 1.) a guilty יצר, and 2.) licentious eyes. As with its use in 1QH, יצר is here again paired with "thoughts" and thus refers more to one's "frame of mind" than some catalyzing moral force in the human. This is paired with "licentious eyes." The potential of a particular body part to lead one to sin has been discussed above, and the propensity of eyes in particular to lead to sexual sin is biblical commonplace.[36] This image of the "licentious eye" indeed

---

35   XV.3.

36   See the section on eyes in part 2. It is also important to recognize that eyes apparently can also play a positive role in moral choices, since we see in line 11 that "uncovering" the eyes is part of the process by which a person can come to choose what God wants and despise

QUMRAN TEXTS

forms a conceptual link to the image at the end of the passage, that of "wantonness of heart." The use of the metaphor of the heart we have also considered already above, but here, in its conjunction with wantonness with regard to the Watchers, the reader is again put in mind of the sexual trespasses of the Watchers which is held up as paradigmatic of the types of going astray that result from the influence of these body parts.[37] Given the importance of *Jubilees* for the Qumran community and perhaps for other Essenes, the flouting of God's "ordinances" with reference to the Watchers may in particular evoke the sense of the trespassing of divinely ordained boundaries, especially through sexual activity.

"Wantonness of heart" does seem, based on other passages, however, to encompass a broader range of sins than just the sexual. Discussing the Israelites who left Egypt, the author of CD writes: "The first one who entered the covenant became guilty through it; and they were given up to the sword, having departed from God's covenant and chosen their own will, straying after the wantonness of their heart each doing his (own) will."[38] Here again we see a connection between wantonness of heart and choosing one's own will against the will of God, and thus straying into sin. The images of straying (turning away) and the wantonness of heart are again combined with reference to God's ordinances in a warning of judgment in VIII.18–19: "And thus is this judgment against anyone who despises God's ordinances and abandons them and turns away in the wantonness of their heart."

It should be noted that these warnings of judgment seem to apply both to those inside and those outside; being taken into the covenant[39] does not exempt one from the possibility of turning away from God's commands into sin. We see this possibility expressed in two passages. In XIX.13–17, we read:

> And thus is the judgment for all who enter his covenant and who will not hold firmly to these statutes: They will be visited unto destruction by the hand of Belial[40].... For although they entered into a covenant of

---

what he hates. Thus, the eyes, metaphorically, are perhaps neutral, and it is only when an eye is "licentious" that it is a source of sin.

37   Obviously, however, the Watcher's sin is not being portrayed as causing sin in humans in any on-going sense. They are being referred to, as the Giants were in Sirach 16:7, as a negative example, this time of the effects of "wantonness of heart."

38   III.10–12.

39   Notice that the ideas of covenant (ברית) and congregation (עדה) seem to play the same role in CD that יחד does in other Qumran texts. יחד is only used once in CD, in XX.32.

40   Note that Belial here has no part here in causing sin, only in punishing it.

repentance, they did not depart from the ways of the traitors but wallowed in the ways of unchastity and wicked wealth.

And in XX.1–10, we read:

> And this is the judgment for all those who entered the congregation of the men of perfect holiness but recoiled from doing the regulation of the upright: He is the man 'who is melted in the midst of a furnace.' When his works become apparent, he shall be expelled from the congregation as one whose lot (גורלו) did not fall among those taught by God … And thus (is) this judgment concerning anyone who rejects, the first and the last, who put abominations upon their heart and walk in the wantonness of their heart: they have no portion in the house of the Torah.

The emphasis in both these passages, but especially the second, on the intentional activity of humans in choosing and perpetrating sin is conspicuous, particularly in the imagery of the heart: not only is the heart wanton—a condition which could be attributable to a number of causes—but the backsliding congregants are portrayed as having themselves "put abominations upon their heart" just as when in the previous passage they "wallowed in the ways of unchastity and wicked wealth." This very active and intentional rebellion and participation in sin portrays the choice and desire of the sinner as the true cause behind the sinning.[41]

While this perspective in CD is fairly consistent, there are hints at other possible conceptions of the cause of sin as well. To return to our opening passage, II.14–18, before the call to hearken, understand, choose, and walk, we are told, regarding prior generations, "During all those (years), (God) raised up for himself those called by name so as to leave a remnant for the land and fill the face of the world with their seed.… But those whom he hated he caused to stray."[42] Here, the obvious cause of straying is God himself. Further, in XX.3–4, it was noted within the quotation that the writer invoked the idea of the גורל and that the backslider's "lot did not fall among those taught by God." The use of גורל alone would not be enough necessarily to indicate a conception of some type

---

41 According to Joseph Baumgarten and Daniel Schwartz ("Damascus Document: Introduction," PTSDSSP 2:7), "The whole point of the Admonition [col. I–VII and XIX–XX] is that evil men can and should repent so as to gain access to salvation and that even members of the sect can backslide or betray." This is seen as a significant contrast to 1QS and 1QH which "assume that individuals are assigned by divine will to one 'lot' or the other, and they themselves have no role to play in the process."

42 XX.11–13.

QUMRAN TEXTS

97

of predetermination, but the fact that it is "when his works become apparent" that "he shall be expelled from the congregation as one whose lot did not fall among those taught by God," does point in that direction. It is not that he was in the lot of the congregation and then forfeited his place, but it was when his works came to light that it was recognized that his lot never was among them.[43] Also, there is some indication that it was held that evil spiritual forces could be the cause of someone's sinning in the line "Each man who is ruled by the spirits of Belial and speaks apostasy ... shall be judged."[44]

Thus, as with the other texts we have examined, CD manifests multiple, often divergent, perspectives on the cause of sin.

4   The Rule of the Community (1QS)

The Community Rule has provoked much scholarly reflection and debate regarding our topic of the cause of sin. Significant study has been done on "The Treatise on the Two Spirits," and while we will examine that passage, we will not focus solely on it, but also explore other passages in 1QS as well.

The conventional designation of 3.13–4.26 as the "Treatise on the Two Spirits" gives a clear and, for the most part, valid summary of the theme of this passage, particularly in the perspective it offers on our topic. To briefly rehearse some of the most pertinent and oft cited lines: in 3.17–19 we are told that God "created the human for the dominion of the world, designing for him two spirits in which to walk until the appointed time of his visitation, namely the spirits of truth and deceit."

The potential ambiguity of this passage—whether the dualism is ontological or psychological—is clarified in 4.15–16. Before this, however, the author delineates in an extended section the "principles" that are characteristic of the spirit for the Sons of Truth and of the Spirit of Deceit (3.20–4.14). Then the author says that "In these generations/races/families* [are] all the sons of man, and in their divisions of inheritance* all their hosts of their generations have a share; in their ways they walk, and the entire reward* of their works (falls) within their divisions according to a man's share, much or little, in all the times of eternity."[45] Both of these passages—4.15–16 and the section preceding

---

43   Further the use of גורל in XIII.12—"Let them inscribe him in his place according to his inheritance in the lot of light"—supports the possibility of a dualistic predetermination, despite the lack a balancing reference to a "lot of darkness."

44   12.2–3.

45   ET of PTSDSSP, with slight modification at points with an asterisk.

98 CHAPTER 6

it—demonstrate a use familial language (sons, generations) combined with terms pertaining to ontological dualism (two spirits, two divisions). Thus, the consequent implication for our question is that people sin because their nature is one that participates in the Spirit of Deceit. For those who are of the Spirit of Deceit, they sin because it is their nature to do so. This is perhaps the dominant or even consensus reading of the Treatise and its dualism.

There are other images and perspectives to be found in the Treatise, however. In 3.20–23, we read that:

> In the hand of the Prince of Lights (is) the dominion of all the Sons of Righteousness; in the ways of light they walk. But in the hand of the Angel of Darkness (is) the dominion of all the Sons of Deceit; in the ways of darkness they walk. By the Angel of Darkness comes the aberration of all the Sons of Righteousness; and all their sins their iniquities, their guilt, and their iniquitous works (are caused) by his dominion, according to God's mysteries until his end.... And all the spirits of his lot cause to stumble the Sons of Light.[46]

This is not necessarily incompatible with the previous perspective. In fact, it may be a necessary clarification, for if those who are Sons of Deceit sin because it is their nature to do so, the sins of the Sons of Truth remain unexplained. This passage seems an attempt at clarification: even those who are by nature righteous can be caused to sin by the Angel of Darkness; even though they are not part of his "dominion" (ממשלה), his dominion can cause them to stray or err (תעה). This dominion is conceived of as a sphere of rulership that is both spiritual (with respect to the Sons of Darkness) but also temporal, as is clear from the use of ממשלה (generally with Belial) in 1.18, 1.23–24, 2.19 as well as the coupling of ממשלה with temporal language in 3.23[47] and 4.18–20.[48]

---

46   The use of גורל here to signify a company of people under a certain dominion or defined by a certain trait (see previous discussions above), is actually not the overwhelmingly dominant use of the word in 1QS, despite the text's considerable dualism. Though we do see it used this way also in 2.2 and 5 (contrasting the lot of God and the lot of Belial), 3.24, 4.24, 11.7, and perhaps 2.17 and 4:26 (the fragmentary character of the latter making interpretation tricky), just as often it is used to denote a person's place of standing within the community or council (so 1.10, 2.23, 5.3) or the apparent casting of lots in the decision-making of the community (6.16, 6.18, 6.22, 9.7).

47   "The appointed times of their suffering [are caused] by the dominion of his hostility."

48   "But God ... has set an end for the existence of deceit. At the appointed time for visitation, he will destroy it forever. Then truth will appear forever in the world, which has polluted itself by the ways of ungodliness during the ממשלה of deceit until the appointed time for judgment."

QUMRAN TEXTS   99

The perspective that sin is caused by the rulership of an evil spiritual entity constitutes a different image and thus a different understanding than the familial/ontological understanding. It also, as we see in the previous passages, utilizes different dualisms, i.e., metaphysical and temporal dualism. In this image, evil exercises authority over those of its dominion, but because its dominion is temporal as well as spiritual, it also exercises influence over those outside its direct rule who are forced to live during the time of its temporal rule.

Elsewhere in 1QS, however, there is also an indication that people's own choice is the cause of sin. Particularly with regard to their rejection of sin as a condition for entrance and continuation in the community, 1QS portrays people as able, by the choices they make, either to continue sinning or not.

In 1.16–17, one of the initial regulations of the community is that "All those who are entering shall cross over into the covenant before God by the Rule of the Community … They must not turn back from following after him because of any terror, dread, affliction, or agony during the reign of Belial." Here the choice—whether to turn from God or to continue in the covenant of the יחד which makes one a Son of Light—rests with the person himself.

We see a similar but more complex explanation of the process in 5.1–2 and 4–5:

> This is the rule for the men of the Community who devote themselves to turn away from all evil and hold fast to all which he has commanded as his will: they shall separate themselves from the congregation of the men of deceit, in order to become a Community … No man shall walk in the stubbornness of his heart, to err following his heart, his eyes, and the plan of his inclination.[49] He shall rather circumcise in the Community the foreskin of the inclination[50] (and) a stiff neck.[51]

Here it is the entrants themselves who are called upon to "devote themselves to turn away from all evil," "to hold fast to all which he has commanded," and

---

49   לוא ילכ איש בשרירות לבו לתעותאחר לבבו ועינוהי ומחשבתיצרו.

50   עורלת יצר.

51   Line 5 has some significant textual variation in MSS B and D: both omit "following his heart, his eyes, and the plan of his inclination" and "circumcise in the Community the foreskin of the inclination (and) a stiff neck." As noted earlier, however, our purpose here is not to trace the original form of the document nor adjudicate what might be additions or deletions; since we are simply interested in what were the options for perspectives on the cause of sin available in Matthew's milieu, the presence of these phrases in any of the manuscripts represents a viable passage for examination.

100 CHAPTER 6

to "separate themselves from the congregation of the men of deceit." These are necessary "in order to become a community" as the Sons of Light. Here we also have the recurrence of the images of body parts as potential sources of sin: the eyes and the heart are capable of leading the whole person into error. Still, even the heart—an image that elsewhere indicates the essential and potentially predetermined and determinative moral character of a person—appears to be under the control of the new entrant to community: he must not choose to follow its stubbornness which would cause him to err. He can also resist his יצר and circumcise it, presumably thereby bringing it in line with the covenant. Each is to "circumcise the foreskin of his inclination" so that he will no longer sin, and it is in his power to do so, to change the nature of his יצר.

The metaphor of the heart appears again in 2.11–12: "And the priests and Levites shall continue and say: 'Because of the idols of his heart which he worships, cursed be he who enters into this covenant and puts the stumbling block of his iniquity before him so that he backslides, stumbling over it.'"[52]

Here again, though it could be argued that the "idols of his heart" are something which he worships because he cannot remove them and thus cannot do anything but worship them, the overall thrust of the statement is the indictment of the entrant for not ceasing his idolatry and for willfully causing himself to stumble by placing the מכשול of iniquity in his own path.[53]

The final section of 1QS (10.6ff.) features a first-person narrator who, in 11.7 first asserts that "those whom God has chosen, he has set as an eternal possession. He has allowed them to inherit the lot of the holy ones. With the sons of heaven, he has joined together their assembly for the Council of the Community." He asserts about himself, however:

---

52 C.f. 1QH XIX.14–16: "With a willful heart they look about and seek You in idols. They have set the stumbling block of their iniquity before themselves."

53 Despite the assertion by the editors of PTSDSSP v.1 that the entrant's statement immediately following in line 14 ("I walk in the stubbornness of my heart") "denotes the period before the person became a member of the community" (p. 11 n. 33), the context makes it clear that the person has already become a member ("those who cross over into the covenant" [ln. 10], "he who enters into the covenant" [ln. 12], "when he hears the words of this covenant" [ln. 13]). The context does not indicate that the statement refers to a previous time when "he walked blindly and was stubbornly committed to the ways of the Sons of Darkness (although in essence being a Son of Light)" (PTSDSSP 1:11, n. 33). In fact, because of this person's willful actions of idolatry and iniquity, the author says "May God set him apart for evil ... May he put his lot among those who are cursed forever" (2.16–17). It seems as if his "lot" (גורל) was previously undetermined or, if previously determined, then subject to change based upon his actions.

QUMRAN TEXTS 101

> ... and I (belong) to wicked Adam, to the assembly of deceitful flesh. My iniquities, my transgressions, my sins, as well as the perverseness of my heart (belong) to the assembly of maggots and of those who walk in darkness. For my way belongs to Adam. The human cannot establish his righteousness.... When I stumble over fleshly iniquity, my judgment is by God's righteousness which endures forever.... In his righteousness he cleanses me of the impurity of the human and the sin of the sons of Adam.[54]

Here the author cites a number of loci as the sources of sin. As we have seen in other passages, the "perverseness of the heart" is again pointed to, and as in 1QH this is again in the mouth of a member of the community, so again this points to something deep-seated, almost ontological as the cause of sin, something that is present in the human even if one is a Son of Light. We again have also the suggestion that sin is cause by some shared familial inheritance ("I belong to wicked Adam" and "he cleanses me of the impurity of the human and the sin of the sons of Adam") perhaps based simply on being corporeal ("I belong ... to the assembly of deceitful flesh" and "When I stumble over fleshly iniquity").

So, in 1QS we see a fair diversity of depictions of the cause of sin. Besides the oft-noted participation of a person in the lot of either the Sons of Darkness (deceit, etc.) or the Sons of Light (truth, etc.) which employs genetic and familial imagery, we also see indications that sin springs from human choice, corporality, descent from Adam, one's "heart," and one's inclination(s). In all the depiction is multifaceted but consistent with the portrayals in the other sectarian documents.

5   Summary of Qumran Literature

Thus, while some of the writings found at Qumran are explicitly interested in the possible generative locus of sin and evil in humans, their reflections

---

54   11.7–15. Note also 11.20–22: "What, indeed, is the son of Adam among your wondrous works? Born of a woman, how can he dwell before you, he whose kneading (is) from dust and whose corpse food for maggots? He is but a discharge, (mere) pinched-off clay whose urge is for the dust. What can clay that is shaped (by) hand dispute; and what counsel does it comprehend?" Though here corporeality is not directly indicated as a source of sin, the fact that "he whose kneading is from dust and whose corpse food for maggots" cannot "dwell before you" perhaps indicates something more than the inability of the finite to stand before the infinite. Although, perhaps not.

are by no means univocal and there are a number of images and statements used that are in tension or outright opposition to the explicit reflection.[55] Be that as it may, the variety and tensions present are consistent with the range and tensions found both within and among other examples of Second Temple literature.

---

55 Sanders in *Paul and Palestinian Judaism* addresses the dual aspects of election to and participation in the sect and thus the members' identity as "sons of truth" but the continuing reality of sin and the power of the Angel of Darkness: "Transgression is not altogether avoidable.... there is no solution to the unavoidable transgressions ... [yet] these profound views of human sinfulness do not touch soteriology. They do not state a plight to which a soteriological solution within this life is offered ... Man needs to be cured of his nothingness, and those in the covenant and will be cured; but confessions of nothingness are not confessions of 'lostness', and nothingness will not lead to the damnation of those in the sect. It is rather the transfer from the outside of the sect to within the sect (a transfer that does not correct nothingness and which does not altogether eradicate the power of the Angel of Darkness) which constitutes the operative soteriology of the sect.... There is a kind of two-stage soteriology. One stage involves joining the elect, the other the final purification of the elect ... The transfer from outside the sect to within it, then, involves repentance of avoidable transgression and 'volunteering' ... There is, however, no outside salvific force which breaks the power which the Angel of Darkness exercises over the elect" (p. 283). In this sense, Sanders' understanding of the interaction of the various articulations of sin may be simultaneously more complex and less problematic than the simple opposition of sinless sons of truth with wicked and sinning sons of darkness, for in his interpretation the sectarians saw no opposition between being sons of truth and continuing to be mired in sin. Yet the frequent portrayal—sometimes explicitly and sometimes subtly—of the wicked (variously described and labeled) as those who reject God and God's way and ally themselves with Belial, indicates that such people are seen as not simply having sinned (as all do sometimes, even the elect) but as having rejected God's covenantal election and call. The issue is not just that they sin, but that they actively reject God and God's way (as understood by the Qumranites). Still, the source or cause of sin—whether to the level of rejection of God or common transgressions that plague all—is variously ascribed, regardless of its role in Qumran soteriology.

CHAPTER 7

Conclusion on Texts of Matthew's Milieu

Thus, as we can see, the first century milieu offered the author of the Gospel of Matthew a wide variety of perspectives and metaphors for understanding and portraying the source or sources of sin in humans. Some texts such as the Enochic literature and portions of Sirach evidence explicit concern with this issue, while in others such as *2 Baruch*, *4 Ezra*, and the Qumran sectarian documents, the reflections formed part of their concerns about other issues such as theodicy and the shape and nature of community life. These explicit reflections cite a number of causes for sin and evil in humans: external causes such as the activity of the Watchers and Giants or Belial or the sin of Adam passed down to all his descendants or the leading or coercion of other humans; internal causes such as an evil heart or inclination; or causes that spring from human choice and will. Yet alongside these potential causes that are explicitly asserted, within each text there are metaphorical statements which present competing pictures of the source or cause of sin—body parts, illness, stumbling blocks, inadvertent straying, or images of a familial or genetic inheritance. Thus, the range of options available to Matthew for portraying the cause of sin was quite large and some of these options were in significant tension with one another. Further, the fact that most of these portrayals are on some level metaphorical adds an inherent level of tension because of the metaphorical dynamics. While Matthew does not manifest quite the entire range of options we have explored in the Second Temple literature, he does, as we will see, utilize a full range of images from external to internal in portraying the causes of sin and evil in humans, and in this his portrayal reflects much of the core diversity of his milieu and the tensions involved in the use of multiple metaphors of causation.

© KONINKLIJKE BRILL NV, LEIDEN, 2020 | DOI:10.1163/9789004419506_009

PART 2

The Portrayal of the Causes of Sin and Evil in the Gospel of Matthew

∵

CHAPTER 8

Review of Previous Scholarship

Despite the fact that our topic would seem to be a crucial question to ask of any Gospel or indeed any religious text, there has been no work that specifically addresses the Gospel of Matthew's perspective of on the cause or causes of sin in humans. The significant literature sometimes touches on the topic in analyzing the themes of righteousness and salvation in Matthew, but there are no monographs or articles that devote sustained attention to the topic. Thus, although these studies, particularly those focused on soteriology, do sometimes discuss sin and evil, the discussion centers on how one might achieve the "greater righteousness" needed to enter the kingdom. Inasmuch as these studies may shed light in Matthew's view of sin by way of its opposite, they provide some limited and indirect help in our work. The two most important works in this area are the monographs by Benno Przybylski and Robert Mohrlang.

1 *Righteousness in Matthew and His World of Thought* by Benno Przybylski

The subject of Przybylski's book is the scholarly disagreement regarding the meaning of *dikaiosynē*[1] in Matthew, a disagreement that has revolved, in recent history, around whether *dikaiosynē* is the demand of God or an eschatological gift of God, i.e., whether for Matthew *dikaiosynē* represents "achieved" or "imputed" righteousness. According to Przybylski, the problem—and lack of agreement among scholars—however, is caused by imposing Pauline categories on the Matthean material. The Pauline definition of righteousness and consequent understanding of its soteriological significance are foreign to Matthew's way of thinking, and thus the use of this understanding serves mainly to muddy the Matthean waters.[2] A more appropriate approach is to

---

1   In this section, the alternation between original-language terms and transliterated terms reflects Przybylski's usage not the approach of this study.

2   Pauline scholars might also point out that the Pauline definitions and understandings that are most problematic when applied to Matthew (righteousness, the Law, grace, etc.) have been under significant reassessment in the last 30 years with regard to Paul's writings vis-à-vis Judaism, and thus the presenting problem (at least as Przybylski sees it) is probably not as acute as it was, at least within the scholarly community, or at least stands in need of reassessment.

© KONINKLIJKE BRILL NV, LEIDEN, 2020 | DOI:10.1163/9789004419506_010

108   CHAPTER 8

study the meaning and significance of צדק and related words in the DSS and the earliest Rabbinic writings since these are closer to Matthew's frame of reference.[3]

In Chapter 2, Przybylski examines the use of צדק-based words in a dozen Qumran documents (including the Damascus Document, 1QS, 1QM, and 1QH) and finds that there is not a uniform use of צדק in the DSS. There is little sustained use of the terms except in CD, but "in CD and 1QS apart from the Hymn (10:9–11:22), it is clear that *tsedeqah* refers to God's saving, gracious activity and that *tsedeq* designates the norm for man's conduct" (31–38). In the rest of the documents, however, Przybylski finds that "there is some overlap in meaning between *tsedeq* and *tsedeqah*" such that sometimes *tsedeq* is used for God's saving activity and *tsedeqah* is used to refer to human conduct. Przybylski feels, however, that "the instances of overlap ... are not so extensive to obliterate the trend to differentiate between the terms between *tsedeq* and *tsedeqah*," and "in contrast to the Old Testament where it was difficult to ascertain whether in fact *tsedeq*/ *tsedeqah* referred to a norm or a relationship, in the Dead Sea Scrolls, *tsedeq* is considered a norm."

Przybylski sees that trend continued in the Tannaitic literature. His survey finds that when *tsedeq* is used, it designates "the norm by which every aspect of man's behavior ... is to be measured" (external). It is not the gift but the demand of God which, when one lives according to it one possesses it (internal).[4] It is not an initiatory gift of God which results in corresponding actions. Przybylski finds, however, that *tsedeqah* is primarily used with regard to almsgiving[5] and thus as a synonym for mercy or "deeds of lovingkindness" (*gemilut ḥasidim*).[6] Finally, with regard to the use of *tsaddiq*, Przybylski finds that:

> The adjective *tsaddiq* plays a decisive role in designating those who lead a properly religious life. Being righteous is not viewed as the gift of God. Rather the righteous are those who practice the commandments. This is not to say that God does not give any help to the righteous.... This help however, is not construed as making being righteous the gift of God. Being

---

3 Przybylski sees the OT as only of limited help: in terms of date, the DSS and earliest Rabbinic writings are much closer to Matthew. Our current understanding of the meaning of צדק as it is used in the OT may not have been the meaning of the term as it was used by people of Matthew's time. To gain insight into the climate of Matthew's time, Przybylski feels it is more instructive to look at how the DSS and Rabbinic materials interpreted these OT passages (p. 4).

4 Przybylski, 65.

5 Przybylski, 66–74, esp. 74.

6 Przybylski, 66.

REVIEW OF PREVIOUS SCHOLARSHIP   109

righteous (*tsaddiq*) is the result of man's actions. Salvation on the other hand is the gift of God insofar as God's forgiveness on the basis of man's repentance cannot be viewed as having been earned by man. It must be stressed that being *tsaddiq* and salvation are not equivalent concepts.[7]

In summary, צדק-terms are used to designate that which is properly religious. As such, it is concerned not with soteriology but with conduct. It is the demand of God and living according to this demand indicates that one wants to continue to live in relationship with God (rather than rebel), culminating in relationship in the world to come.

Following this usage, *dikaiosynē* in the Gospel of Matthew is not a gift of God; it is the observance of the Law. It is not, however, salvific nor is it specifically Christian. Those who led properly religious lives according to Jewish standards were called "righteous," but those who followed the teaching of Jesus were "disciples" who followed "the will of God." This raises the question of whether *dikaiosynē* is then expected of followers of Jesus? The Sermon on the Mount seems to say yes (5:20), but looking at Matthew as whole, Przybylski is forced to answer no. The emphasis is on doing God's will. This is not the same as *dikaiosynē*. Przybylski finds that *dikaiosynē* is used in polemical contexts or those where Jesus is speaking to both disciples and others. Jesus in 5:20 is contrasting his teaching and practice with that of Judaism. The will of God is more inclusive and incorporates both God's demand upon man and also the gift of God for man.[8] Thus, the concepts of "disciple" and "will of God" are more central to Matthew's overall message than "righteousness."

What then is the significance of *dikaiosynē* in Matthean theology? Przybylski find that while "the concept of righteousness does not pervade Matthean theology,"[9] the concept of righteousness functions as a bridge to Jesus' teaching for first century Palestinian Jews, "from the known to the unknown." The use of *dikaiosynē* is provisional and does not fully express the view it points to. When the new understanding is reached, the provisional concept can be discarded. Thus, the Matthean use of *dikaiosynē* is different than the Pauline in

---

7 Przybylski, 52. One of the weaknesses of Przybylski's work here is that he nowhere defines what he means by "salvation" or the "saving work" of God. Given that the work is, on the one hand concerned to show the connection or lack thereof between righteousness and "salvation," and on the other to show how our inherited assumptions about the meaning of "righteousness" need to be reexamined, the fact that he does not also reexamine the assumed understanding of salvation leaves his conclusions about righteousness without a clear connection to the whole of Matthew's (and the Qumran and Tannaitic) theology.

8 Przybylski, 115.

9 Przybylski, 115.

that, for Matthew it is not a Christian theological concept but a Jewish ethical/behavioral concept that is employed provisionally to make Matthew's message accessible to his audience.

Przybylski's work is particularly helpful in regard to present study in that it clearly lays out the context of Matthew's use of δικαιοσύνη and related terms and finds that Matthew's use is consistent with that of his milieu: "righteousness" consists in living rightly as defined by Torah. In this sense, it stands as the opposite of "sin." Further, Przybylski's conclusion that more than Torah observance is necessary to enter the Kingdom, particularly doing God's will (which includes recognizing Jesus as the Messiah), is also clear and accords with the conclusion of the present study. Przybylski's view, however, that for Matthew δικαιοσύνη is not a significant concept but is used merely as bridge "from the known to the unknown" seems less well-founded; on the contrary, as will be shown below, righteousness is a consistent characteristic of those who enter the kingdom of heaven, just as unrighteousness, ἀνομία, and causing σκάνδαλα will result in expulsion from the Kingdom and condemnation at the Judgement.

2   *Matthew and Paul: A Comparison of Ethical Perspectives* by Roger Mohrlang[10]

Mohrlang's stated purpose is to compare the "basic structures" of Matthew's and Paul's ethics, rather than to detail their teachings on specific issues. To do so, Mohrlang looks at five aspects: the law, reward and punishment, relationship to Christ, and the role of grace, love, and "inner forces."[11]

In ch. 1, "Law," Mohrlang finds that in Matthew there are passages that affirm the continuing validity of the Law (5:17–19, 12:1–14, 15:1–20, 19:3–9, 22:34–40) and even the radicalization of it, but the polemic against the Pharisees shows that the priority of the Love Command permits the breaking of specific

---

10   Roger Mohrlang, *Matthew and Paul: a Comparison of Ethical Perspectives*, SNTSMS 48 (Cambridge; London: Cambridge University Press, 1984).

11   For each topic, Mohrlang outlines what he sees as Matthew's perspective on the issue, then Paul's, then compares them. It is not clear that the book, however, really succeeds in making clear the "basic structure" of Paul's and Matthew's ethics since the format of the book militates against this by, first of all, predetermining the topics rather than letting each book or corpus set the semantic field and the relationships between the terms and issues, and second, by not first developing an overall picture of each writer's ethics and comparing those, but rather jumping back and forth from one to the other without developing how the issues are related to one another for each writer.

commands and that the real emphasis is on heartfelt radical obedience. Both Paul and Matthew agree that true righteousness is more than formal observance of the Law and that truly doing the will of God is an internal as well as external matter.

While Paul sees Christian community as not ordered by law at all, Matthew sees his Jewish-Christian community as still under Mosaic Law. Though both Paul and Matthew have broken with certain elements of traditional understanding and practice of the Law, Matthew's view of the Law is overall positive and setting aside commands and teaching others to do so makes one least in the Kingdom. Matthew expects the Christian to fulfill the commands in radicalized form (the law was given to be obeyed) and there is no explicit indication that the power of the spirit is needed. Thus, *dikaiosynē* is conceived in traditional Jewish terms in Matthew, i.e., as obedience to the Law.

In the second chapter on "Reward and Punishment," Mohrlang argues that, as a result of their common Jewish heritage, both Matthew and Paul presuppose personal accountability and divine recompense for one's behavior. Grace in Jesus does not eliminate the demand for moral living—to set such aside invites God's judgment, but ethical conduct brings eschatological reward. For Matthew, there are two kind of judgment: one relating to ultimate destiny and one relating to rewards, and the threat of punishment is a significant motivator.

The "Relationship to Christ and the Role of Grace" is the subject of ch. 3. Mohrlang seems to conceive of grace as the working of God or the Spirit in fulfilling righteousness or doing ethical things. Thus, Peter's confession that "with men it is impossible but with God all things are possible" is an example of "grace," as is the central position of the Lord's Prayer in the Sermon on the Mount and the affirmation that God gives his children what they need and ask for. Hence, Mohrlang sees in Matthew an underlying "structure of grace," but Matthew does not explicitly bring this to bear in his ethics; rather, it remains in the background and "the overall emphasis is certainly elsewhere," i.e., on the responsibility of the humans to do what they are supposed to, and "the sense of demand predominates and characterizes Matthew's ethics."[12]

Chapter 4 explores the role of "Love" in the ethics of Paul and Matthew. In Mohrlang's opinion, Matthew sees love as a commandment to be followed— the most important in fact. Love of neighbor is not, however, the main concern of Matthew in the Sermon on the Mount or elsewhere. The main concern is *dikaiosynē*—the point of reference is God and his command to love. One loves one's neighbor not out of concern for the neighbor but out of obedience and submission to the will of God.

---

12   Mohrlang, 81.

Of all the scholarly literature on Matthew, the material that comes closest to dealing with our topic is Mohrlang's ch. 5, "Inner Forces." Mohrlang says that for Matthew, "what lies at the heart of ethical behavior in this Gospel is 'an essential inner goodness,'" i.e., *dikaiosynē*.[13] This is not merely outwardly correct behavior but inner attitude (which is lacking in the hypocritical Pharisees), including love and mercy as well submission and obedience. Thus, *dikaiosynē* is consistently used not in a forensic sense but in an ethical. It is something one *does* but it is also something one *is* inside that issues in obedient behavior. In Matthew it is one's heart, one's inner being, that determines behavior. Essential inner goodness—*dikaiosynē*—is essential for truly doing God's will. Though Matthew asserts the presence of Christ in the community, he does not develop its implications for ethics or otherwise to any great degree, as Paul does on a very significant, even comprehensive, scale.

According to Mohrlang, "the underlying assumption appears to be a traditional Jewish one: if God commands something to be done, it must be within the power of humans to do it."[14] Matthew does not raise the question of how one finds the power to live a moral life but seems to simply presuppose its possibility. Yet, Jesus is ever present to help those who hunger and thirst for *dikaiosynē*.

This possibility is only presupposed for some, however. Mohrlang finds Matthew's understanding of humanity dichotomous: there are those who are "good" (righteous) and those who are evil, the terms applying equally to attitude ("heart") and behavior. A fundamental aspect of the eschaton and coming of the Kingdom is the Judgment, wherein it is made clear who is good and who is evil.

Several aspects of Mohrlang's work agree with both Przybylski and this study: namely, the essential definition of δικαιοσύνη as Torah observance and thus the assumption of its continued importance, but also the expectation for more beyond that—doing God's will through love of neighbor and showing mercy. Beyond this, the most helpful aspect is his emphasis on Matthew's dualistic understanding of human beings. Mohrlang's treatment of this is brief, however, and Matthew's dualism is deeper and more complex and multifaceted than a simple dualism of "good" and "evil" might indicate, as this study will show.

---

13   Mohrlang, 113.

14   Mohrlang, 114.

CHAPTER 9

Exegesis of the Portrayal of the Causes of Sin and Evil in Matthew

Turning now to the Gospel of Matthew itself, we begin by exploring Matthew's use of the two most common words for sin, ἁμαρτία and σκάνδαλον (and related terms), as well as the use of πλανάω. Following that, we will investigate Matthew's use of various metaphors for sin, including those passages that connect these behaviors to the concept of evil (πονηρός/πονηρία). These metaphors can be grouped into three broad categories: those that relate to body parts as a cause of sin, those that indicate something inherent or genetically ingrained in the human as the cause of sin, and those that attribute the cause of sin to the activity of the devil.[1] Thus, the progression of our examination will be from those causes which are most obviously external (the σκάνδαλον) to those which are most holistically internal (genetic metaphors) and conclude by looking at how the language of satanic activity connects both the sense of external causation (as in the use of σκάνδαλ-) and the language of pervasive internal causation of the genetic and familial metaphors such that the two end of the spectrum meet. In the conclusion of this section, we will discuss how Matthew's underlying apocalypticism, expressed most clearly in his understanding of the enmity between God and the devil, helps tie together the disparate metaphors for the cause of sin by locating their source in the work of the devil.

1 The Use of ἁμαρτ- in Matthew

We begin our investigation of the causes of sin in Matthew by looking at Matthew's use of words with the ἁμαρτ- root. While a word study will be seen ultimately to be inadequate for giving a complete picture of sin in Matthew, it

---

1 Though it would seem an important first task to define what Matthew means by "sin," we find Matthew little interested in spelling out what constitutes sin, so the task cannot be approached straightforwardly. This is particularly the case since, in his uses of ἁμαρτία and in his use of other words for sinning, it appears he assumes that he and his readers share a common understanding of "sin" which he does not need to explicate. Even so, through the course of the study, a basic definition will emerge.

© KONINKLIJKE BRILL NV, LEIDEN, 2020 | DOI:10.1163/9789004419506_011

114   CHAPTER 9

seems a necessary starting point.[2] This will lead us to a broader examination of the use of ἀμαρτ- in the LXX and the potential fruitfulness of its etymological background for assessing its use as a metaphor and thus its significance for our investigation. With this as background, we will then return to looking at Matthew and the use of ἀμαρτάνω.

Matthew most frequently talks about ἁμαρτία in the context of forgiveness. In three of the four passages that use ἁμαρτία, sin is explicitly connected to forgiveness (9:2–6,[3] 12:31–32,[4] and 26:28[5]),[6] and in another (3:5–6) forgiveness is implied[7] since sins are confessed and apparently repented of. Except for 9:10–13 (which will be discussed below in our examination of bodily metaphors for the source of sin), these passages are surprisingly unfruitful for our investigation of the *causes* of sin, although some are certainly interested in forgiveness

---

2   As Luomanen points out regarding his project on Matthean soteriology: "It goes without saying that we cannot form the overall view of Matthew's soteriology on the basis of word study, by analyzing how the word σῴζω is used in Matthew's gospel, since we cannot assume that everything pertinent to salvation is expressed using this particular term. On the other hand, it is reasonable to presume that a connection exists between Matthew's understanding of salvation and his use of the verb most expressly referring to it." (Petri Luomanen, *Entering the Kingdom of Heaven*, WUNT[2] 101 (Tübingen: Mohr Siebeck, 1998), 37–38.) The same applies, *mutatis mutandis*, to a study of Matthew's depiction of sin and its causes.

3   Jesus to the paralytic: "Your sins are forgiven."

4   All sins will be forgiven but the blasphemy against the Holy Spirit.

5   Jesus' blood is shed for the forgiveness of many.

6   Of the five passages, the first two and the fifth are paralleled in Mark and Luke and the third in Luke; thus, the connection of ἁμαρτία with forgiveness could be attributed simply to Matthew's sources of Mark and Q. The only passage that connects sin and forgiveness in which the language is uniquely Matthean is 26:28. Both Mark and Luke have the covenant language ("new" in Luke), but only Matthew claims that the blood is "poured out for many for the forgiveness of sins."

7   3:5–6 People confess and are baptized by John. Davies and Allison (*A Critical and Exegetical Commentary*, 1:301) seem to miss the implied forgiveness in John's call to repentance and the people's response of confession: "For his part, Matthew says no more than that those who came to John confessed their sins. He does not use the word forgiveness ... forgiveness was apparently too central a feature of Jesus' work to be associated with another (cf. 1:21, 26:28). In Matthew's eyes John only brought people to repentance in order to make them ready for the Messiah. It was then the Messiah's task to bring the world forgiveness." This presumes that Matthew believes God would not forgive sins confessed to a prophet prior to the work of Jesus, a perspective I find unlikely (see, for example, David's confession before Nathan [2 Sam 12:13]), or given the final sentence of the quote, that Matthew believed there was no forgiveness at all before the work of Jesus, a sentiment that again seems unlikely, especially given Jesus' statements in 6:12–15, where forgiveness from God is apparently conditioned on one's forgiveness of others not on anything done by Jesus. For further on forgiveness through prayer and confession in Early Judaism, see James H. Charlesworth, "Forgiveness (Early Judaism)," ABD 2:833–835.

EXEGESIS OF THE PORTRAYAL OF THE CAUSES OF SIN AND EVIL 115

as the remedy for sin, or perhaps part of the remedy. There is no clear indication of the cause of the sin—whether it is caused by the choice of the sinner, by some defect of character or nature in the person, by the workings of some external force, or by simple accident or misjudgment.

The one remaining use of ἁμαρτία is in 1:21. Here we read that an angel tells Joseph that Mary "will bear a son, and you are to call his name Jesus, for he will save his people from their sins." The verse, and indeed the entire passage reporting Joseph's interaction with the angel, is unique to Matthew, and this being the case, the designation of Jesus as one who will "save his people from their sins" would seem a prime locus for insight into Matthew's understanding of sin, especially as it relates to the person and work of Jesus.

Some, certainly, have seen this passage as yet another reference to forgiveness (and thus to be grouped with the others above).[8] The fact, however, that Matthew does *not* connect ἁμαρτία with "forgiveness" in this passage when he certainly could have, and apparently elsewhere was in the habit of doing, perhaps militates against this. Further, the exact meaning of "save from sins"— which would potentially give us a clue as to the cause of sin—remains unclear since Matthew's narrator spends no time explicating what is meant by "he will save his people from their sins" but moves directly onto pointing to Jesus as the fulfillment of Isa 7:14 and the designation of him as Emmanuel. As Davies and Allison write:

> Our verse is not very illuminating with regard to exactly how Jesus saves. The atoning death must be in view; but given the connexion in Matthew's world between sickness and sin, Jesus' healing ministry could also be thought of as having saved people from their sins. Furthermore, Jesus' revelatory imperatives and abiding presence are salvific in so far as they encourage and enable believers to obtain the 'better righteousness' (5:20). Perhaps Matthew thought Jesus saved his people from their sins in a variety of ways.[9]

As noted in the introduction, the naming of the baby "Jesus" at the beginning of the Gospel because "he will save his people from their sins" has a similar parallel near the end of the story in Jesus' declaration that the wine of the Last

---

8   Davies and Allison (*A Critical and Exegetical Commentary*, 1:210) claim that here "The atoning death must be in view," but just what shape that atonement would take and how it would be brought about by Jesus' death—whether in some form of a classic sacrificial or penal substitutionary model or something else altogether—is not developed by the commentators.

9   Davies and Allison, *A Critical and Exegetical Commentary*, 1:210.

116 CHAPTER 9

Supper is his blood of the covenant "poured out for many for the forgiveness of sins" (26:28). If these two passages in fact form a second *inclusio* in tandem with the Emmanuel/"Lo I am with you" pair, then the theme of Jesus as savior from sin through forgiveness must be counted as on par with the Emmanuel theme. Whether this forgiveness comprehends all that Matthew conceives of as forming "salvation" is not clear. It may be that the forgiveness of ἁμαρτία effected through the pouring out of Jesus' blood is specifically for "the many," i.e., Gentiles, since Jews had always had access to forgiveness, and thus their salvation from their sins will be effected by some other aspect of Jesus' salvific work.

Thus, although 1:21 seems to present perhaps the greatest opportunity to understand clearly what Matthew might see as the cause of sin—at least indirectly by indicating Jesus as the agent of being saved from sin—it does not present any clear evidence. Still, it does perhaps help us to make progress in our investigation inasmuch as it pushes us to the assessment that "perhaps Matthew thought Jesus saved his people from their sins in a variety of ways," and thus that there may be multiple ways in which sin is a problem or a problem with multiple causes.

One direction we might take in searching for the cause of sin from Matthew's use of ἁμαρτία and related terms is to recognize that, etymologically, the word is a metaphor. In the classical Greek use of its verbal form, it means to miss the target or mark at which one is shooting or to err or wander from the path, and in its nominal form it means a failure, fault, or error.[10]

While classical usage of this word-group may have had some influence on Matthew's thinking, the use of ἁμαρτία in the Septuagint is undoubtedly also an important consideration, perhaps far more so.[11] In looking at the use of words with the ἁμαρτ- root, we find that they are used to translate a number of Hebrew words, the most common by far being those of the חטא word group.[12] Some have found this unsurprising since the underlying meaning of חטא is "to

---

10 ἁμαρτάνω and ἁμάρτημα, LSJ 77.

11 The difficulty of assessing the LXX's use by and/or influence on Matthew versus the MT or its predecessor(s) is a notoriously thorny question. Even if, however, Matthew was in the end more reliant on a Hebrew OT than a Greek, he likely wrote in Greek and thus the way ἁμαρτία is used in the Gospel undoubtedly owes a good deal to how it was used in the broader Greek-speaking Christian community, which itself was influenced both by classical and Septuagintal usage. For classic discussions of the problem of Matthew's use of a Greek versus a Hebrew OT, see Bacon, *Studies in Matthew*, 470–477, and Sherman E. Johnson, "Biblical Quotations in Matthew," *HTR* 36, no. 2 (Ap 1943): 135–153.

12 The various nominal and verbal forms of ἁμαρτ- are used to translate words with the חטא root approximately 450 times. Other Hebrew roots that are often translated with a form of ἁμαρτ- include רשׁע (81 times), עוֹן (78 times), פשׁע (26), and אשׁם (7). For more detailed statistics on the correspondence of particular forms, see *TDNT* 1:268.

EXEGESIS OF THE PORTRAYAL OF THE CAUSES OF SIN AND EVIL   117

miss [the mark]" and thus is etymologically analogous to ἁμαρτ- and also meta-phorical when used in an ethical or religious sense. Quell in his TDNT article on the OT background of ἁμαρτάνω is confident that, for those who employed חטא, the metaphor was indeed a living one: "The root is basically metaphori-cal and all who used or heard it must have been aware of this."[13] Quell bases this claim on the fact that חטא is used not exclusively in a religious or ethical sense, but "in a limited way the OT uses the same word חטא in a secular sense as a verb of movement to indicate 'missing the right point'.... Although there are only a few instances of this secular usage, they give us good grounds for concluding that חטא never quite lost in Hebrew its sense of erroneous action."[14] Obviously, this accords well with the underlying meaning of ἁμαρτ- and could make sensible the common substitution of words in the ἁμαρτ- family for those in the חטא group.[15]

It is further noteworthy that ἁμαρτία is the Greek term often used by LXX translators of the Pentateuch and Psalms in dealing with verses regarding for-giveness and offerings for atonement.[16] In Leviticus, ἁμαρτία is the word used for the propitiatory sin-offering itself. This being the case, it is not surprising that, as noted above, Matthew tends to use ἁμαρτία in the context of forgive-ness rather than, for example, σκάνδαλον/σκανδαλίζω.

Further, if Quell is correct that the use of חטא indicates that it was still a liv-ing metaphor, we might assume that this was also the case for Matthew's use of ἁμαρτία, since the translation is consistent in the LXX and the roots have a similar meaning. This is especially the case if, as noted above, Matthew was familiar with both the LXX and the Hebrew OT and was, in his quotations, sometimes developing his own translations from the Hebrew.[17] Further, the etymological meaning of "missing the mark" would also explain its consistent

---

13   *TDNT* 1:271.

14   *TDNT* 1:271–272.

15   This obviously excludes uses of חטא in the piel since in that form it means "to purify." Ἀνομία, though also widely used in the LXX, is used to translate a number of words (esp. עָוֹן, but also פשע, and רשע) but seldom those of the חטא group. Similarly, ἀδικία/ἀδίκημα translates a number of Hebrew words (particularly חָמָס) but only occasionally חטא.

16   Exod 29:14, 29:36, 30:10, 32:30–32, 34:7, 34:9; Lev 4:3, 4:8, 4:14, 4:20–35, 5:5–13, 6:17, 6:25, 6:30, 7:7, 7:18, 7:37, 8:2, 8:14, 9:2–3, 9:7–10, 9:15, 9:22, 10:16–17, 10:19, 12:6, 12:8, 14:13, 14:19, 14:22, 14:31, 15:15, 15:30, 16:3–16, 16:21, 16:25, 16:27, 16: 30, 16:34, 19:22, 23:19; Num 5:6–7, 5:15, 5:31, 6:11, 6:14, 6:16, 7:16, 7:22, 7:28, 7:34, 7:40, 7:46, 7:52, 7:58, 7:64, 7:70, 7:76, 7:82, 7:87, 8:8, 8:12, 14:18, 14:19, 15:24–25, 18:9, 28:25, 28:22, 28:30, 29:5, 29:11, 29:16, 29:19, 29:22, 29:25, 29:28, 29:31, 29:34, 29:38; Ps 25:7, 25:11, 25:18, 32:1–2, 32:5, 38:18, 40:6, 51:2, 51:9, 78:38, 79:9, 85:2, 103:10. See also Sir 2:11, 3:3, 3:14, 3:15, 4:26, 5:5–6, 17:25, 28:5, 34:23, 47:11; and Isa 1:18, 27:9, 33:24, 38:17, 40:2, 44:22, 53:4–6, 53:10–12, 55:7, 59:2, 64:9.

17   Johnson, "Biblical Quotations," 152–153.

118   CHAPTER 9

use in the context of forgiveness. If sin (אטח/ἁμαρτ-) is "missing the mark" or "erring" then there is certainly a sense in which the person might more easily be forgiven since the error was unintentional.

But is Quell correct? As noted above, Quell admits that there are only a few examples of the secular use of אטח that support his assertion of its continued vitality as metaphor when applied to the ethical and religious realm.[18] Quell's conclusion that "the most common Heb[rew] term for sin did not have the predominantly religious emphasis proper to the English 'sin'"[19] is undermined by overwhelming number of instances where אטח is used with an obviously religious, ethical meaning with no indication of the metaphorical background. Rather, אטח seems to have just the same ethical and religious use, force, and emphasis as the English "sin." The metaphorical background seems to have receded to the point that אטח is a dead metaphor, no longer evoking the imagery of erring.[20] In fact, the sense of unintentional erring is much more clearly communicated in some other aspects of OT vocabulary and usage.

Both the MT and the LXX appear to have technical terms for unintentional sins: in Hebrew שְׁגָגָה is used and in Greek ἄγνοια.[21] Further, especially in the LXX Pentateuch, we find the use of ἀκουσίως—"unintentionally"—as a modifier of ἁμαρτία, and particularly in Leviticus in the context of offerings for atonement and forgiveness.[22] In the LXX passages from Leviticus and in Num 15:24 and 15:27–29, we have ἀκουσίως combined either with ἄγνοια or with ἁμαρτία,

---

18   "There are only a few instances." These are Prov 19:2 and 8:36, Job 5:24, Judg 20:16, Ps 25:8, and possibly Isa 65:20 (*TDNT* 1:271–272). Quell's citation of a number of juridical examples, while not unimportant, does not expressly support the assertion that "missing the mark" was still in the background of all uses of the word. Further, his claim based on these examples that "there is certainly no thought of a purely cultic or religious transgression [in the use of אטח], since the authorities concerned are secular" (1:272) is likely true, but probably says more about the overlap of religious and "secular" legal categories for offenses in ancient Israel than about the liveliness of the underlying metaphor of the word.

19   *TDNT* 1:272.

20   In this respect, it is perhaps more analogous to the English term "trespasses," the use of which in the Lord's Prayer has freighted it with connotations more related to religion than property rights.

21   שְׁגָגָה is used 18 times: Lev 4:2, 4:22, 4:27, 5:15, 5:18, and 22:14; Num 15:24–29 and 35:15; Jos 20:3 and 20:9, and Eccl 5:5 and 10:5. In the LXX (including Apocryphal texts), ἄγνοια is used 18 times to mean a "sin committed in ignorance": Gen 26:10; Lev 5:18; 1 Sam 14:24; 2 Chr 28:13; 1 Esdras 8:72 (NRSV 8:75) and 9:20; Ps 24:7 (NRSV 25:7); Eccl 5:5; Wis 17:12 (NRSV 17:13); Sir 23:3 and 28:7; Ezek 40:39, 42:13, 44:29, 46:20; Dan 4:33–34 and 6:5. It is apparent that ἄγνοιον was also used to simply mean "ignorance" in general (cf. Lev 22:14 and 4 Macc 1:5 and 2:24).

22   Lev 4:2, 4:13, 4:22, 4:27, 5:15; Num 15:24–29 (related words in this passage: in 25 and 26, ἀκούσιον; in 25, ἀκουσίως; in 28, ἀκουσιασθείσης), 35:11, 35:15; Deut 19:4; Jos 20:3 and 20:9. The verses in Num 35:11 and 35:15; Deut 19:4; and Jos 20:3 and 20:9 all deal with the provision of refuge for one who unintentionally slays another. The use of the related ἀκούσιον

EXEGESIS OF THE PORTRAYAL OF THE CAUSES OF SIN AND EVIL 119

and in the Hebrew, there is the combination of חטא with שְׁגָגָה, such that שְׁגָגָה brings the sense of "unintentionally." Since the writers of the Hebrew OT found it necessary to utilize a different word for unintentional erring (שְׁגָגָה) and also used that word to modify חטא (the most common word for sin) such that it might become clear that certain kinds of חטא were unintentional, there seems to be little support for Quell's assertion that חטא retained its metaphorical live-liness as "missing the mark." If it had, the practice of combining it with שְׁגָגָה would have been unnecessary since חטא would have sufficiently conveyed this on its own. The same appears to be true for the LXX and ἁμαρτία (as the word most often chosen to render חטא) since the translators also deemed it neces-sary either to augment ἁμαρτία with ἀκουσίως when unintentionality is empha-sized or to replace it altogether with ἄγνοια.

In addition, the MT's use of תָּעָה indicates that it was another and perhaps more obviously lively metaphor for unintentional sin. The metaphorical vital-ity of תָּעָה ("to stray") is apparent in its use: of the 45 verses in the MT using תָּעָה, eight use it in a literal sense[23] while 37 use it metaphorically[24]—a propor-tion of almost 2:9 in contrast to the disproportionate use of חטא in a non-literal sense. More importantly, in four of the metaphorical uses, the *straying* itself is literal in the passage, but the straying is done by a metaphorical character (sheep) to stand for the moral (thus, metaphorical) straying of the real group (God's people) represented in the metaphor.[25] The combination of literal and metaphorical in these passages, combined with the greater proportion of liter-al uses of תָּעָה (compared to חטא), indicates that תָּעָה was a common and living metaphor for erring in the MT. If, then, חטא had in large part lost its meta-phorical vitality and had simply become a word denoting sin in general, the use of a word that remained obviously metaphorical like תָּעָה is a reasonable choice to communicate the idea of unintentional erring (even, as Quell defines

---

    ("error") in Eccl 10:5 also indicates a negative but unintended result given the context of vv. 8 and 9.

23   Gen 20:13, Gen 21:14, Gen 37:15, Ex 23:4, Job 38:41, Ps 107:4, Ps 107:40, and Isa 28:7.

24   These include 2 Kgs 21:9, 2 Chr 33:9, Job 12:24 and 25, Job 15:31, Ps 58:3, Ps 95:10, Ps 119:110, Prov 7:25, Prov 10:17, Prov 12:26, Prov 14:22, Prov 21:16, Isa 3:12, Isa 9:15, Isa 19:13 and 14, Isa 21:4, Isa 29:24, Isa 30:28, Isa 35:8, Isa 47:15, Isa 63:17, Jer 23:13, Jer 23:32, Jer 42:20, Ezek 14:11, Ezek 44:10, Ezek 44:15, Ezek 48:11, Hos 4:12, Amos 2:4, and Mic 3:5.

25   Ps119:176: "I have gone astray like a lost sheep; seek out your servant, for I do not for-get your commandments"; Isa 16:8: "For the fields of Heshbon languish, and the vines of Sibmah, whose clusters once made drunk the lords of the nations, reached to Jazer and strayed to the desert; their shoots once spread abroad and crossed over the sea"; Isa 53:6: "All we like sheep have gone astray; we have all turned to our own way, and the LORD has laid on him the iniquity of us all"; Jeremiah 50:6: "My people have been lost sheep; their shepherds have led them astray, turning them away on the mountains; from mountain to hill they have gone, they have forgotten their fold."

120   CHAPTER 9

it, in its nature as "deviation from a required norm,"[26] that norm being the will of God[27]). That being the case, it is likely that ἁμαρτία as the most common LXX translation of חֵטְא [28] also was no longer evocative since ἁμαρτία is not the word commonly used in LXX translations of passages where the MT uses תָּעָה in the qal; there the LXX almost invariably uses πλανάω to translate תָּעָה.[29]

There thus appears to be no significant evidence that the metaphorical background of ἁμαρτ- or חטא as "missing the mark" exerted much influence on the use of either root in the Hebrew or Greek OT. Most likely, both had simply become the common, dormant-metaphorical words for sin in their respective languages and were not used with an eye toward inadvertent sin and the external or possibly fortuitous causes of sin.

Turning again to Matthew, the use of ἁμαρτάνω follows a similar pattern to what we saw with the use of ἁμαρτία. As we will see below, the possibility that the metaphorical root of ἁμαρτάνω played a role in Matthew's word choice is contravened (just as the use of חטא and ἁμαρτ- in the Hebrew and Greek versions of the OT was) by the fact that ἁμαρτάνω is not used in any contexts where inadvertence ("missing the mark") is an obvious aspect of the sinning. On the contrary, Matthew's use of the verbal form particularly indicates the

---

26   Quell, *TDNT* 1:278.

27   Quell, *TDNT* 1: 276–277.

28   Of 33 uses of the nominal form חֵטְא rather than the verbal (חָטָא) in the MT, the LXX uses ἁμαρτία in 29 of them. Of the four remaining verses, one uses ἁμάρτημα (Deut 22:26), one uses a form of ἁμαρτάνω (Hos 12:9), one eliminates the word (Isa 31:7; from "idols which your hands have sinfully made" to "idols which your hands have made"), and one uses ἀσχημοσύνη (Lev 20:20). Similarly, of the 296 uses of חַטָּאת, only four times was something other than ἁμαρτία, ἁμάρτημα, or a form of ἁμαρτανω is used to translate it (ἀνομία three times [Lam 4:6, Ezek 18:21, Ezek 33:10]; ἀσεβήματά once [Lam 4:22]). At some points where the MT pairs חַטָּאת with עָוֹן, the LXX tends to transpose the usual translations of the two terms. Thus, for example Isa 5:18: "Woe to those who draw iniquity [עָוֹן] with cords of falsehood, who draw sin [חַטָּאת] as with cart ropes" becomes "οὐαὶ οἱ ἐπισπώμενοι τὰς ἁμαρτίας ὡς σχοινίῳ μακρῷ καὶ ὡς ζυγοῦ ἱμάντι δαμάλεως τὰς ἀνομίας." (However, cf. the MT and the LXX of Isa 6:7.) We find this primarily in contexts where the two terms are paired for emphasis, such as in Ex 34:9: here "and pardon our iniquity (עָוֹן) and our sin (חַטָּאת)" becomes "καὶ ἀφελεῖς σὺ τὰς ἁμαρτίας ἡμῶν καὶ τὰς ἀνομίας ἡμῶν." Though this does point to a certain level of interchangeability between the two terms, the fact that when they are used apart from each other, חטא-based words are almost always translated with ἁμαρτ-based words and עון-based with ἀνομ-based, seems indicate a stylistic quirk of translating the terms when paired, since this happens primarily in these contexts. Because of this, I do not count these as exceptions to the pattern of translating חַטָּאת with ἁμαρτία or ἁμάρτημα.

29   Of the 40 MT verses using תעה in the qal, I find only one that does not use πλανάω to translate it: Prov 7:25, where the LXX uses ἐκκλίνω.

EXEGESIS OF THE PORTRAYAL OF THE CAUSES OF SIN AND EVIL 121

opposite—that the sense of intentionality and knowing disobedience are at least a possible, if not the dominant, aspect of ἁμαρτάνω.

The possibility that unintentionality is not an implication of ἁμαρτάνω is strengthened by the fact that Matthew elsewhere uses πλανάω. This word obviously has a much stronger sense of unintentionality (as noted above and as will be seen below in examining the use of πλανάω in Matthew), and thus Matthew does not use ἁμαρτ- in a general way to indicate all kinds of sinning but makes a verbal distinction between "sins" in general or those obviously intentional (ἁμαρτ-) and those that are apparently unintentional ("straying" or "stumbling" [using σκανδαλ-; see below]).[30]

The intentionality of ἁμαρτάνω is particularly clear in 18:21. In 18:15–17, Jesus had given instructions on how a believer ought to respond when another disciple sins against him or her; the instructions are particularly focused on proceeding in such a way that there can be forgiveness and reconciliation. In response, Peter wonders in 18:21 about the limits of this protocol: how often ought he to forgive a fellow believer who sins (ἁμαρτήσει) against him, even up to seven times? The fact that the sin is repeated multiple times after the person has apparently been confronted about it indicates that the sinning is willful and deliberate. Also of note is that the connection of sin and forgiveness is here again manifest, and in this context, it is obvious that the forgiveness is not premised in any way by the inadvertence of the sinful act, but in fact, just the opposite.[31]

---

30   Apparently, the use of πλανάω is Matthew's preferred way of indicating unintentionality since, neither ἄγνοια nor words of the ἀκουσι- group are used by Matthew to modify ἁμαρτ- or otherwise imply that the sin was a "mistake" or "error." (We will further explore πλανάω below in conjunction with our discussion of σκανδαλ-.) It should also be noted that ἀδικ-, which is used often in the OT and seems to be particularly connected to violent injustice, is used only twice in Matthew: in 5:45 Jesus says that God makes the rain to fall on the δικαίους and ἀδίκους, and in and 20:13 the vineyard owner tells those paid last "οὐκ ἀδικῶ σε"—"I am not being unfair to you." Neither use seems to reflect the common usage of the LXX; in 5:45 the term is the obvious necessary complement to δικαίους needed to complete the chiasm with the sun rising on the πονηρός and the ἀγαθός, and in 20:13 the emphasis is on redefining God's "justice" as based not on the "work" done by the individual but on God's generosity. This limited use of ἀδικ- is rather surprising given Matthew's extensive use of δικαι- words, but neither use gives us any real indication of the cause of ἀδικία.

31   Further, if we take as an underlying premise that ἁμαρτία refers primarily to deliberate sins, this would shed some light on Matthew's use of ἁμαρτωλοί. Three passages use the term to classify certain people as "sinners"—ἁμαρτωλοί: the first two (9:10–13 and 11:19) refer to Jesus' offensive fellowship with sinners, and a third passage (26:45) notes that the Son of Man is handed over into the hands of sinners. If the sense of ἁμαρτία as deliberate sin holds, then those people counted as "sinners" knew that the actions that earned them

The use of ἁμαρτάνω in 27:4 also supports the idea that Matthew uses this word to refer to deliberate wrong-doing rather than with an underlying conception of missing the mark. This final use is by Judas: when, upon seeing the condemnation of Jesus, he regrets[32] his betrayal and returns the silver pieces, he says, "I have sinned (ἥμαρτον) betraying innocent blood."[33] Judas' careful initiation and planning of the betrayal (26:14–16 and 26:46–49) makes it obvious that his sinning was not unintentional.

1.1 Summary

Matthew's use of both ἁμαρτία and ἁμαρτάνω follows conventional usage of the terms in the LXX and the analogous Hebrew terms in the Hebrew Bible. Although both ἁμαρτ- and חטא share similar metaphorical etymologies, the metaphors seem no longer to be living since the ramifications of the metaphorical sense do not appear to play any part in their contextual usage in Matthew, the LXX, or in the Hebrew Bible. In fact, the opposite of the metaphorical sense—that is intentional, knowing sin rather than unintentional "missing the mark"—is the underlying connotation in Matthew, and in Hebrew and the LXX, the original metaphorical sense is only revived by the use of an auxiliary word to make clear the inadvertent nature of the act or by the choice of a different word altogether. Thus, our investigation of ἁμαρτ- with regard to the cause of sinning remains relatively unfruitful. The term is used in situations where people sin deliberately—and thus the source of the sin is essentially their own will. Whether there is some underlying, perhaps metaphysical, cause for this wrong use of their will is not clear, however. Perhaps they had the power (moral or spiritual) to do otherwise and perhaps not. As we will see below, there are indications that some people do not have free choice

---

the name were contrary to what is right. The uses in 11:19 and 26:45 do not give us much indication of a cause of the sinning of the ἁμαρτωλοί, but 9:10–13 draws a metaphorical connection between sin and illness (Οὐ χρείαν ἔχουσιν οἱ ἰσχύοντες ἰατροῦ ἀλλ ἀ οἱ κακῶς ἔχοντες), a connection that will be explored below in the section on bodily metaphors for sin.

32   Literally, "repenting [μεταμεληθείς] he returned the thirty silver coins." Though here ἔστρεψεν certainly means "returned" since it has the coins as its object, the use of this verb which can also mean "to turn around or repent" may serve as a punning emphasis on Judas' remorse for his act.

33   This too seems to be a passage where ἁμαρτ- is connected with forgiveness. Not only does Judas confess his sin (as did those who were baptized by John), but here the confession is made to the chief priests. Though the priests do not in turn fulfill their duty by performing any sacrifice for atonement, Judas' repentance and confession implies forgiveness for the sin, as it did with John's followers.

EXEGESIS OF THE PORTRAYAL OF THE CAUSES OF SIN AND EVIL 123

in whether they will act in line with God's law and will, but passages that use ἁμαρτ- portray at least some people as having chosen not to do so.[34]

There are, however, places in Matthew that do portray a person's wrong-doing as unintentional. It is to these terms and passages that we now turn.

2   Πλανάω, σκανδαλίζω, and σκάνδαλον

As we continue to investigate Matthew's portrayal of the cause(s) of sin, we find some fruitful ground in examining the use of the terms πλανάω and σκανδαλίζω/σκάνδαλον, terms that are both significant in their use in Matthew and related to one another in their meaning and thus in their portrayal of the cause of sinning. Both, as we will see, are used in ways that portray sin as, on the one hand, an unintended mishap for some. On the other hand, one who engineers the stumbling or straying of another also sins, and in this case the sinning is intentional and malicious. We will look first at passages in Matthew where words of the σκάνδαλ- group are used alone, and following that, we will look at the use of πλανάω in Matthew which, apart from one brief use, always occurs in conjunction with σκανδαλίζω/σκάνδαλον. The last passage to be examined, 18:6–22, employs πλανάω, σκανδαλ-, and also ἁμαρτάνω (as discussed briefly above). As we will see, through the various uses of these three groups of terms, Matthew sometimes depicts the cause of sin as some external force (particularly when using σκανδαλ- or πλανάω), but other times the cause is ambiguous or complicated by the context or use of ἁμαρτάνω.

There are eight passages in Matthew that use σκανδαλ- without πλανάω or ἁμαρτ- in the context. Of these, five indicate Jesus as a potential or actual σκάνδαλον. These present something of a special case and will be examined

---

34   That obedience and disobedience are equally possible alternatives for Jesus' hearers seems to be the underlying assumption in Matthew 7:24–27, "The Wise and Foolish Builders." This is perhaps the passage that most clearly indicates the possibility of real moral agency for humans with regard to sin. The question remains, however, whether "wise" and "foolish" are in a sense pre-existing moral conditions in humans and thus their obedience or disobedience to Jesus' word is the manifestation of that quality or whether they make something like a free decision that then results in their being labeled wise or foolish. The passage seems to call for contextualization with the previous two pericopes: the immediately previous context is Jesus teaching that not all who call him Lord will enter the kingdom but only those who do God's will (7:21–23), but prior to that we are informed that, while there may be many who appear to be doing God's will, they will, like good and bad trees, be known by their fruit (7:15–20). This passage then sets the tone for the two that follow, and its use of a genetic metaphor will be further discussed below, but it does indicate that outward actions are manifestations of one's inner nature.

124   CHAPTER 9

together below. Of the three remaining, two are found in the explanations of the parables of ch. 13 and one in Jesus' interaction with Peter in ch. 16. Before we begin, however, to look at what we can glean regarding the cause of sin from the use of this word in these passages, we need a clear sense of the traditional definition and connotations of the term.

The terms σκανδαλίζω and σκάνδαλον are particularly rich in their imagery. As Ulrich Luz says commenting on their use in 18:6:

> There are hardly suitable translations for the verse's keywords, the verb σκανδαλίζειν and the substantive σκάνδαλον. The root meaning of σκάνδαλον is 'snare.' It seldom appears with a figurative meaning in Hellenistic sources, but the LXX offers numerous examples of such usage. We have no instances of the causative verb σκανδαλίζω ("cause to fall") that are not dependent on the LXX.... Frequently the Old Testament text still contains the image of the root meaning 'snare,' but sometimes the image is no longer recognizable.... However, the root contains much more than is suggested by the weak expression 'offense/to offend'; it speaks of something that is destructive to human life or the life of the people of God.[35]

The image of the "snare" evokes the relation of hunter and prey. The (moral) trap will snare the foot of the prey and trip it up.[36] The snare's action of entrapping the prey's foot and thus tripping leads logically to the conception of the σκάνδαλον as a "stumbling block," and subsequent English translations along such lines.[37] There seems to be some distinction in the use of σκάνδαλον versus σκανδαλίζω: "Whereas σκάνδαλον is only an 'occasion of falling' which might lead to a fall or not, σκανδαλίζω is the causing of an ensnarement and fall and σκανδαλίζομαι the experience of ensnarement or fall."[38] The tripping action also becomes applied more broadly, beyond moral stumbling, to the situation of being mentally "tripped up" or "offended"—scandalized—by an idea or situation.[39]

---

35   Ulrich Luz, *Matthew 8–20*, Hermeneia (Minneapolis: Fortress, 2001), 432.
36   G. Stählin, "σκάνδαλον, σκανδαλίζω," TDNT 7:339–340.
37   Stählin, TDNT 7:341.
38   Stählin, TDNT 7:345.
39   As will become clear, while Luz is on whole correct in his last statement about the force of σκάνδαλον/σκανδαλίζω being significantly greater than simply "offense/to offend," the fact that Jesus and his words and actions can "trip up" (σκανδαλίζειν) those who do not understand requires nuancing of σκανδαλ- beyond "something that is destructive to human life or the life of the people of God," though it could be argued that those who are scandalized

EXEGESIS OF THE PORTRAYAL OF THE CAUSES OF SIN AND EVIL 125

Thus, in looking at Matthew's use of σκανδαλ-, we see that in Jesus' explanation of the Parable of the Sower and Soils, the seed that is sown on the rocky ground is not productive because those who have no root in themselves are tripped up and ensnared/trapped (σκανδαλίζεται), and the *cause* of the ensnarement is trials and persecutions on account of the word.[40] Their sinning is caused by these outside forces. While it can be argued that their lack of rootedness plays a role in their sinning, perhaps by providing the necessary condition, it is the trials and persecutions that provide the effective, causative force.

The second use in ch. 13 comes in Jesus' explanation of the Parable of the Wheat and the Tares.[41] Here, Jesus is explaining what will happen at the end of the age: the angels will come and gather up the σκάνδαλα together with those who do lawlessness and throw them into the furnace of fire, just as weeds are gathered and burned in a fire. If one takes this verse on its own, it is possible to interpret the σκάνδαλα in a variety of ways. While the τοὺς ποιοῦντας τὴν ἀνομίαν almost certainly must be humans, it might be possible to understand the σκάνδαλα to be something else. One might assert that there are situations or forces that might cause a person to be tripped up and ensnared into sin such as the "trials and persecutions on account of the word" in the Parable of the Sower and Soils.[42] Even simple fortuitous events might cause one to do something wrong inadvertently without the direct action of another person being the effective cause. People also might be included, but the πάντα might allow for other causes as well.

---

by Jesus' words or actions do indeed see them to be "destructive to the life of the people of God."

40   Matthew 13:21: οὐκ ἔχει δὲ ῥίζαν ἐν ἑαυτῷ ἀλλ ἀ πρόσκαιρός ἐστιν, γενομένης δὲ θλίψεως ἢ διωγμοῦ διὰ τὸν λόγον εὐθὺς σκανδαλίζεται. There is a certain amount of metaphor mixing in the Parable of the Sower. This happens elsewhere in Matthew as well. See the end of the section on genetic "Tree and Fruit Metaphors" for other instances where different but complementary metaphors are blended.

41   It is difficult to overemphasize the importance of ch. 13 for our study. The five-discourse structure of the Gospel puts ch. 13 at the chiastic center of Matthew's telling of the story of Jesus. The discourse itself focuses on righteousness and eschatological judgment (key themes in Matthew and related to our study), and some of Matthew's clearest portrayals of the causes of sin and evil are in the parables of Seeds and Soils, the Wheat and the Tares, and the Net, and "judgment" as the distinguishing of reality from appearance (see Excursus, below). For a classic discussion of the importance of plot structuring and the extension of narrative time in extended discourses, see R. Alan Culpepper, *Anatomy of the Fourth Gospel: a Study in Literary Design*, Foundations and Facets: New Testament (Minneapolis: Fortress Press, 1983).

42   The NRSV translation leans in this direction, choosing to translate πάντα τὰ σκάνδαλα as "all causes of sin."

In the larger schema of the parable explanation, however, both πάντα τὰ σκάνδαλα and τοὺς ποιοῦντας τὴν ἀνομίαν are humans. Earlier in Jesus' explanation, he has already informed the disciples that "the field is the world, and the good seed is the children of the kingdom. The weeds are the children of the evil one." So, "all σκάνδαλα and those who do lawlessness" are not two different things—perhaps the second being humans and the first being something else—but either they are two kinds of children of the evil one/devil[43] or two ways of describing the same people.[44] In either case, it is clear that the σκάνδαλα that are to be removed and burned like weeds at the end of the age are people who now are mixed in among the children of the kingdom.[45] The coming of the end of the age will include the removal of all people who might induce or coerce others to sin and thus be an outside cause.

The third use of σκανδαλ- that we will examine occurs in Jesus' interaction with Peter following Peter's confession in ch. 16. After Jesus predicts his upcoming rejection and death in Jerusalem and Peter rebukes him, Jesus in turn replies, "Get behind me, Satan! You are a σκάνδαλον to me, because you do not think things that are of God but of humans."[46] Here, there are a number of connections to be noted with the interpretation of the Parable of the Wheat and the Tares. The first connection is between the σκάνδαλον and human beings. In looking at the Wheat and the Tares, it became clear that the σκάνδαλα to be removed were people, though not people generally, but those designated as children of the evil one/devil. In our current case, Jesus points to one particular person as the σκάνδαλον of that situation: Peter.

The other similarity between the Peter situation and the explanation of the Parable of the Wheat and the Tares is the connection between the person

---

43   That the weeds are the sons not just of "evil" (a possible reading of οἱ υἱοὶ τοῦ πονηροῦ) but that τοῦ πονηροῦ is synonymous with the devil (ὁ διαβλος) is clear from the following verse (39).

44   It is quite possible that this is a distinction that would not really be sensible to the author of Matthew. If one causes people to sin, one is not following the law, and if one is doer of lawlessness, one will undoubtedly prove a snare to others.

45   The presence of the tares among the wheat is one of the classic examples used to support the idea that Matthew was concerned to reflect upon the situation of the church as a *corpus mixtum*. The explanation, however, given at the beginning of the interpretation indicating that the field into which the wheat and tares are sown is the *cosmos* indicates a much broader scope to the parable than simply the *ekklēsia*. Thus, rather than being a parable reflecting a concern about unrighteous persons in the church, this parable reflects the ongoing theme of the difficulty of distinguishing between the righteous and unrighteous generally prior to the judgement (since many are not as they seem) but also the reassurance that eventually all will be shown for what they truly are, and God will reward accordingly.

46   Matthew 16:23.

EXEGESIS OF THE PORTRAYAL OF THE CAUSES OF SIN AND EVIL 127

functioning as a σκάνδαλον and the devil or Satan. It is clear that same person/ entity is being referred to by both of these names (ὁ διάβλος in Wheat and the Tares, 13:39, and Σατανᾶ in Jesus' rebuke, 16:23) from looking at the narrative of Jesus' temptation in the wilderness. There we see the tempter (4:3) referred to as ὁ διάβλος in 4:1, 5, 8, and 11 and referred to as Σατανᾶ in 4:10. The similarity of language in the two passages—ὕπαγε, Σατανᾶ in 4:10 and ὕπαγε ὀπίσω μου, Σατανᾶ in 16:23—reinforces the identification of Peter with the devil/ Satan/the Evil One. Thus, in both the Wheat and the Tares and in the rebuke of Peter, the person or people who are snares are portrayed as incarnating the instantiation of evil (ὁ πονηρός), called either ὁ διάβλος or Σατανᾶ. While in the Wheat and the Tares this is portrayed as a permanent condition comparable to one's parentage ("children of the evil one") and thus part of one's genetic make-up or fundamental nature,[47] in the case of Peter, his seeming embodiment of the devil is evidently temporary. As we can see from the previous passage, Peter's actions (or at least his words) can just as easily be swayed by the Father (16:17) as by the devil.[48] It is worth noting that both 16:17 and 16:23 make mention of the role of human opinion. In the first, Peter is blessed because his revelation is from God and not from "flesh and blood" (17: σὰρξ καὶ αἷμα οὐκ ἀπεκάλυψέν σοι) while in the second, Peter is rebuked and called Satan and a σκάνδαλον for thinking like a human (23: οὐ φρονεῖς τὰ τοῦ θεοῦ ἀλλὰ τὰ τῶν ἀνθρώπων). The connection back to the Temptation is obvious here as well: the temptation for Jesus in both cases is to utilize his status as the Christ and Son of God as a way to achieve glory and avoid suffering or to understand the nature of those designations as precluding suffering—a path that is apparently consistent with "thinking like a human" but not with God's perspective. Although the temptation narrative does not specifically utilize any σκανδαλ- terminology,

---

47   The dynamics of this portrayal and others that display a similar perspective will be discussed further in the section on familial and genetic imagery, below.

48   This instance does, in fact, fit to some extent into one of the possible of our originally conceived paradigms: sin or its opposite as motivated by the agency of spiritual forces outside the human. There is certainly the sense (as will be explored at the end of this chapter) that Satan is an active force working against God's will being done in the world, that is, in causing sin. This passage seems to fit the category of Satanic rulership which will be discussed below. Oftentimes in Matthew, however, those who are under Satan's control are characterized as his offspring, thus using a genetic metaphor. Without reiterating here what will be discussed at length later, it is simply worth noting that Matthew portrays some people (those who are "offspring of Satan") as being inherently evil but others (like Peter here) to be only temporarily influenced or overcome by him, so Matthew demonstrates a certain blending of ontological and ethical dualism. Yet Satan's power even over those who are not inherently evil is such that even Jesus in the Temptation narrative is portrayed by Matthew as having to resist coming under the dominion of Satan.

the dynamics of ensnarement are apparent in the temptations presented by the devil. Thus, in the voice that encourages one to seek glory (4:8–9) and to avoid suffering (16:21–22), the temptation of the devil himself becomes indistinguishable from what Matthew sees as thinking in as a typically human way (thinking τὰ τῶν ἀνθρώπων), at least if we take Peter as paradigmatic example. Proposing such ways of thinking to others makes one a snare such that one can be labeled a σκάνδαλον and makes one an opponent of God such that one can be called "Satan."

2.1   Jesus as a σκάνδαλον

So far, the examples that we have looked at have supported Luz's assertion that, when looking at the use of σκανδαλ-, we see that the force is "much more than is suggested by the weak expression 'offense/to offend'." According to Luz, those who "scandalize" are engaging in an activity that is destructive to individual and communal life and thus opposed to the will of God. There is, however, a group of texts utilizing σκανδαλίζω that complicates this picture. In each of these texts, Jesus is portrayed as potentially able to "scandalize" people (ensnare them, cause them to stumble morally) or actually does cause this.

The first instance where this possibility is introduced is in 11:5–6. Here, John the Baptist's disciples come to Jesus to ask if he is "the one who is to come." Jesus instructs them to report the works that Jesus has been doing: the blind see again and the lame walk about, lepers are cleansed and the deaf hear, the dead are raised and the poor are proclaimed good news, and Jesus says that those who are not σκανδαλισθῇ by him are blessed. Apparently, the works that Jesus does or perhaps what they indicate about who he is, is something that could ensnare or trip people up. It is easy to see that perhaps his works and person might cause some people to "stumble" mentally in the sense that they are confused or have trouble reconciling the apparent meaning of words and deeds with their expectations of "the one who is to come." Does the simple fact that it is Jesus who is causing the stumbling, however, compel us to think of σκανδαλίζειν differently than we might if the actor were someone else? Does anything in the context compel us to change definitions because of the actor? Or is the alternative—that Jesus could potentially be a cause of sin—a possibility to consider?

In the next example, people's offense/stumbling on account of Jesus moves from a possibility to an actuality. In 13:53–58, we read about Jesus' return to his hometown and his teaching in the synagogue there. Afterward, people are astonished—they are unable to reconcile his wise teaching and his "mighty works" with what they expect from the son of Mary and the sibling of their neighbors. In 13:57 it says, "καὶ ἐσκανδαλίζοντο ἐν αὐτῷ." Jesus has "stumbled them" or tripped up or ensnared them. For his part, Jesus is unapologetic and seemingly unsurprised, since "a prophet is not without honor except in his home town and in his house." This statement of Jesus' suggests that the sin or stumbling which he is causing is not really a confounding of the minds of his hearers. The σκάνδαλον that trips up Jesus' hearers is their rejection of him. Jesus becomes an occasion for or cause of sin in that, like so many other prophets, his message is not received by those who need it, and thus they put themselves in opposition to God, the sender of the prophet. They are not simply "offended" by him but caused to sin by Jesus' deeds and message and, indeed, his person. Jesus' actions and presence make plain the people's unwillingness to recognize and accept these as having their source in the will of God.

A similar dynamic is present in 15:10–14. Here Jesus teaches that one is not defiled by what goes into one's mouth but by what comes out. After delivering this pronouncement, Jesus is informed by his disciples that the Pharisees ἐσκανδαλίσθησαν by this saying (15:12). Again, Jesus is unapologetic, and in his response, we find evidence that what has happened to the Pharisees goes beyond simply being offended. Jesus responds parabolically: "Every plant that is not planted by my father in heaven will be uprooted. The blind are leaders of the blind, and if the blind lead the blind, both will fall into a pit."[49] Jesus likens his "scandalized" opponents to plants that are not planted by his father, thus hearkening back to the parable of the Wheat and the Tares and implying that they are planted by the devil, and although he calls them guides or leaders, they are leaders who are blind and who themselves cause those who follow them to be tripped up and fall with them into a pit.[50] Thus, ironically (and in contrast to the uses we will explore in the next section), although Jesus is the cause of their sinning, they alone are counted as culpable for their tripping.

While not as explicit, Matthew is presenting a perspective analogous to the assessment of Luke's Simeon: "This child is destined for the falling and the rising of many in Israel, and to be a sign that will be opposed" (Lk 2:34). Matthew presents this perspective only slightly less clearly in Jesus' comments after the Parable of the Wicked Tenants:

---

49   15:13–14: ὁ δὲ ἀποκριθεὶς εἶπεν· Πᾶσα φυτεία ἣν οὐκ ἐφύτευσεν ὁ πατήρ μου ὁ οὐράνιος ἐκριζωθήσεται. ἄφετε αὐτούς· τυφλοί εἰσιν ὁδηγοί τυφλῶν· τυφλὸς δὲ τυφλὸν ἐὰν ὁδηγῇ, ἀμφότεροι εἰς βόθυνον πεσοῦνται.

50   In Isaiah and Jeremiah in the LXX, falling into a βόθυνος is used in to signify punishment for infidelity to God, and the punishment is part of a larger apocalyptic scenario. See Isa 47:11 and the parallel passages of Isa 24:17-and Jer 31:43–44. There is also here obvious connection back to 13:13–15 and the blindness that prevents those "without ears to hear" from comprehending the meaning of the parables and overall thematic links to Jesus' indictment of the scribes and Pharisees in ch. 23.

Jesus said to them, "Did you never read in the Scriptures, 'The stone which the builders rejected, this became the chief cornerstone. This came about from the Lord, and it is marvelous in our eyes'? Therefore, I say to you, the kingdom of God will be taken away from you and be given to a nation producing the fruit of it. And he who falls on this stone will be broken to pieces; but on whomever it falls, it will scatter him like dust." And when the chief priests and the Pharisees heard His parables, they understood that He was speaking about them.[51]

Jesus here, while not technically using the language of σκανδαλίζω/σκάνδαλον, presents himself as a σκάνδαλον, a thing that causes people to stumble and trip. The rejection of Jesus and his message, however, by the Pharisees (the "builders") and their stumbling and falling over this "stone," while remaining contrary to the will of God and thus a sin, is apparently divinely ordained. Jesus, despite being the cause of their sin, remains innocent of guilt since the way in which they "fall" is by rejecting him as God's chosen emissary and, following the scenario of the parable, his son.[52]

---

51   21:42–45.

52   The same issue pertains to the passage on the sin of blasphemy against the Holy Spirit, mentioned previously regarding the connection between ἁμαρτία and forgiveness. The core issue is whether Jesus acts under the impetus of God's spirit or that of Satan. Jesus' words and actions lead his opponents to the assessment that he is not motivated by God's spirit (though Matthew's narrator has specifically informed the reader that he is, via the quotation of Isa 42:1 in 12:18) and thus it could be argued that here also Jesus acts as a σκάνδαλον tripping up his opponents and causing them to sin, although this terminology is not used. The immediately following context, however, points in a different direction. In 12:32 Jesus says, "Whoever speaks a word against the Son of Man will be forgiven, but whoever speaks against the Holy Spirit will not be forgiven, either in this age or in the age to come." The next statement seems at first to represent a change of topic: "Either make the tree good and its fruit good, or make the tree bad and its fruit bad, for the tree is known by its fruit." Though proverbial and perhaps not original to the context since a very similar statement is found in Jesus' warning about false prophets (7:15–20) and also in John the Baptist's preaching (3:10), yet in this context it becomes a comment on the source of the speaking "against the Holy Spirit," as the next verses make clear:
    "You brood of vipers! How can you speak good, when you are evil? For out of the abundance of the heart the mouth speaks. The good person out of his good treasure brings forth good, and the evil person out of his evil treasure brings forth evil. I tell you, on the day of judgment people will give account for every careless word they speak, for by your words you will be justified, and by your words you will be condemned."
    Thus, in this section, it is not Jesus that is indicated as the cause of the evil speaking that brings sin and thus condemnation (a σκάνδαλον) but rather the fundamentally evil nature of the speakers. Jesus and his words and actions are merely an occasion, albeit the preeminent one, by which these people's inherent opposition to God becomes manifest,

EXEGESIS OF THE PORTRAYAL OF THE CAUSES OF SIN AND EVIL   131

Jesus, however, proves to be a σκάνδαλον not only for his opponents but for his followers as well. As we saw above in discussing Jesus' rebuke of Peter, Peter becomes a σκάνδαλον to Jesus and a manifestation of God's opponent, Satan, because of his attempts to deter Jesus from suffering and death, an action based on his misconception of what it means to be "the Christ, the Son of the living God." As the time draws near for that suffering to be undertaken, Jesus predicts that his actions—or his allowance of the actions of his opponents—will cause his disciples to be σκανδαλισθήσεσθε by him.[53] Ironically, it is Peter, the one who has previously been a σκάνδαλον to Jesus, who is shown to protest most vehemently that he will never be "scandalized" (σκανδαλισθήσομαι) by Jesus. That the σκανδαλίζειν which Jesus predicts for his disciples involves real sinning, not merely intellectual stumbling over the incomprehensibility of a suffering Messiah, is made clear by Jesus' next statement: "Truly I tell you, this very night, before the rooster crows, you will deny me three times" (26:34). The disciples' abandonment of Jesus and Peter's denial constitute a lack of faithfulness to Jesus and thus sin. Jesus' commitment to the way of suffering and death proves a snare and a cause of sin for the disciples for, just like the Pharisees, they are unwilling to accept God's working in Jesus, either because it does not conform to their ideals of Messiahship or because of fear born out of a lack of faith. Jesus' faithfulness to his own identity and work becomes the occasion for the stumbling of many in Israel, including the real acts of sinful unfaithfulness in the disciples' abandonment and denial.

Jesus, however, is not portrayed as consistently willing to σκανδαλίζειν those around him. In 17:27, Jesus instructs Peter to pay the half-shekel tax for himself and Jesus "in order that we not σκανδαλίσωμεν them." Here is another instance where the question of Jesus' identity—and his opponents' seeming ignorance or misunderstanding of it—plays a major role in the issue, at least as Jesus frames the issue. Jesus' opponents do not understand who Jesus really is (in this case, a son and free) and thus his true nature and the living out of it has the potential to σκανδαλίζειν his opponents. What is especially unclear here is how Jesus' non-payment of the temple tax would cause others to sin. It might be argued that he would be setting an example which, if it were followed by those who are not sons, would result in them not fulfilling a rightful obligation toward the Temple. Given the fact, however, that the "them" (αὐτούς) apparently

---

and thus this passage is more closely related to the two examples above from ch. 13: the "seed" that is stumbled by trials because of the rocky soil and the σκάνδαλα that will be removed at the end of the age because of their inherent, genetic connection to the Evil One. We will return to this passage in our discussion of genetic metaphors.

53   26:31–33.

132   CHAPTER 9

refers to those who collect the temple tax, it seems unlikely that they would
be tempted to not pay their tax simply because Jesus did not pay his. The most
sensible way to understand the passage is, I would argue, to look at it in the
light of the passages that follow it. We will thus return to this question when
we explore the beginning of ch. 18, below.

So, setting aside for the moment this last example, when Jesus is portrayed
as the one who does or could σκανδαλίζειν someone, it is because those people
are setting themselves in opposition to God's will as it is being carried out in
Jesus. Rather like in our discussion of the use of σκανδαλίζειν in the interpretation of the Parable of the Sower and the Soils, the attitude of Jesus' opponents
is analogous to the rocky soil—while it is not the effective cause of the sinning,
it provides the necessary conditions for it. Jesus, like the trials and persecutions, is the effective cause of the stumbling. One could argue, however, that,
had Jesus or the trials encountered a different intellectual or spiritual "environment" in the hearers, the result would not have been stumbling at all but bearing fruit, thirty-, sixty-, or one hundred-fold. Jesus, while the cause of their sin,
remains an occasion—albeit the paramount instance—for the manifestation
of the sinful tendency already present in his opponents. He activates a poten-
tiality already present in the ones who sin.

2.2   *Πλανάω, σκανδαλίζω, and ἁμαρτάνω in Conjunction*

As we saw above in our exploration of ἁμαρτ-, the LXX often makes use of
πλανάω rather than ἁμαρτάνω to indicate unintentional sinning. Matthew also
uses the metaphor of straying, and in fairly specific contexts.[54] In the two passages in which Matthew uses the verb most intensively, Jesus is talking both
to and about his followers. In the apocalyptic discourse of ch. 24, Jesus begins
his speech by warning his disciples, "Watch out! lest anyone πλανήσῃ you. For
many will come in my name, saying, 'I am the Messiah!' and they will lead
many astray (πολλοὺς πλανήσουσιν)." The essence of the warning is reiterated
in 24:11 and 24:24: "And many false prophets will arise and lead many astray
(πλανήσουσιν πολλούς)"[55] and "False messiahs and false prophets will appear

---

54   Matthew's only use of the nominal form, πλανή—deception—is in 27:64 where the Jews
        express concern that if the news of Jesus' resurrection is not discredited, "the last πλανή
        will be worse than the first."

55   While the immediate context of the other verses makes it clear that those in danger of
        being led astray are Jesus' followers, here it might be possible to argue that a more general
        deception and straying of the populace is envisioned in verse 11. The use of πολλούς in 11,
        however, mirrors the use in the verses before and after where it seems obviously to be a
        marker for disciples, and thus makes it clear that here also the "many" who are led astray
        are those who were previously on the right path—Jesus' followers.

EXEGESIS OF THE PORTRAYAL OF THE CAUSES OF SIN AND EVIL   133

and produce great signs and omens, in order to lead astray (ὥστε πλανῆσαι), if possible, even the elect." In each of these warnings, it is Jesus' followers who are being led astray or in danger of it. They are not deliberately leaving the path but are the victims of the activity of others. Thus, the use of πλανάω in this passage, indicates that the sinning is caused, at least in some cases, by an outside force—the activity of others.

The use of σκανδαλίζω in this passage is of a similar tenor but is put in conjunction with some complicating material. In 24:10 we read, "καὶ τότε σκανδαλισθήσονται πολλοὶ καὶ ἀλλήλους παραδώσουσιν καὶ μισήσουσιν ἀλλήλους." Here, in the first clause, the use of σκανδαλίζω in the future passive portrays the moral stumbling of Jesus' followers as caused by some force outside themselves. This obviously fits with the previously noted uses of πλανάω in the passage and continues to portray the disciples' sinning as unintentional and thus the "sinners" as victims, a depiction that fits well with the theme of apocalyptic *thlipsis*. In the next two clauses, however, the verbs are active, indicating that the sins of betrayal and hatred are being actively engaged in: "... and they will betray one another and will hate one another." We could perhaps take the two *kais* as inferential rather than copulative.[56] In that case, the σκανδαλισθήσονται would govern the sense of the other two verbs such that the verse would be best translated "And then many will be tripped up/stumbled/ensnared, [so that] they will even betray one another and hate one another."[57] This would fit well with the content of 24:12 in which the increase of ἀνομία causes the love of many disciples to wane. If this ἀνομία is the cause the hatred of v. 10 (as the opposite of ἀγάπη in v. 12), then the sinning would be caused by an outside force—namely the rise of ἀνομία. Thus, though the grammar of verse 10 allows for the possibility that Jesus' persecuted followers may sometimes be active agents of sin, the overall tenor of this passage is dominated by metaphors that indicate causes of sinning that lie outside the sinner and thus it is likely the case here as well.[58]

---

56   The terminology of "inferential" comes from Adolf Kaegi, *A Short Grammar of Classical Greek* (London: Herder, 1936), §208.19, but see also "Parataxis" in H.W. Smyth, *Greek Grammar*, revised by Gordon M. Messing (Cambridge, Mass.: Harvard University Press, 1956), §2168–2170, esp. §2169.

57   The same construction is evident in English in a sentence such as "He called and told me about the incident." Here it is obvious that the second action is conditionally dependent on the first.

58   The one use of πλανάω that is not in reference to Jesus' followers comes in the controversy with the Sadducees regarding the woman who had seven husbands. Jesus tells the Sadducees, "You stray, because you know neither the scriptures nor the power of God" (22:29). Here again, the actor is not so much the Sadducees themselves—they do not stray intentionally—but it is ignorance that causes them to stray, although in this case the

134   CHAPTER 9

The second passage in which we see a conjunction of the use of πλανάω and σκανδαλίζω is 18:6–22. The immediate context of the passage is an instruction on greatness in the kingdom as demonstrated in the humility of a child (18:1–5), but the passage quickly transitions into an exhortation on sin.

In the initial section of the exhortation, terms of the σκανδαλ- group are used. The sense of σκάνδαλον as a snare (and σκανδαλίζω as "to ensnare") is particularly fruitful for our investigation of the causes of sin here. The similarity to πλανάω is obvious—in both situations the sinner is the metaphorical victim of forces outside him- or herself that cause her or him to sin, albeit unintentionally.

In the later portions of the passage, however, the use of σκανδαλ- has a dual dynamic analogous to the dynamic of πλανάω. Here the terminology speaks about both the one who is caused to stumble and the one who causes the stumbling. We have, in a sense, dual sinning by the perpetrator of the ensnarement and by the victim. In the beginning of this passage, although it mentions the sinning/stumbling of Jesus' followers, Jesus' teaching emphasizes the seriousness of being the one who is that outside cause—one who ensnares one of "these little ones who believe in me":

> If one should trip up/ensnare (σκανδαλίσῃ) one of these little ones who believes in me, it would be better if he were to have a great millstone hung around his neck and then be thrown into the heart of the sea. Woe to the world because of snares (σκανδάλων)! Snares (σκάνδαλα) are bound to come, but woe to the person through whom the snare comes!

While there is no denying the sin of one of Jesus followers here,[59] the culpability of the one who caused the sin is emphasized. While a norm has been transgressed by the one who has stumbled or been tripped up, albeit inadvertently,

---

      straying is less a moral failure than a straying from the path of correct doctrine, though these are not unrelated.

59   There is little debate among scholars about Matthew's use of μικροί; used here and also in 10:42 and 11:11, it stands clearly for Jesus' followers. Beyond the obvious contextual evidence here (τῶν μικρῶν τούτων τῶν πιστευόντων εἰς ἐμέ), Matthew's emphasis on humility and abdication of worldly greatness as marks of Jesus' followers strengthens the conclusion. As Davies and Allison note: "In Matthew the general meaning [of μικροί] is not in doubt: 'these little ones' are believers ('who believe in me'); and to harm them is to harm oneself, for one cannot cause others to stumble without causing oneself to stumble. Salvation is part of a social process" (*A Critical and Exegetical Commentary*, 2:763). The analogous use of ἐλαχίστοι in 25:40 and 45 obviously has the same secondary supporting evidence, though it is less evident from the context that Jesus' followers are specifically envisioned as the "least of these" in the parable of the Sheep and the Goats.

EXEGESIS OF THE PORTRAYAL OF THE CAUSES OF SIN AND EVIL 135

the *cause* of the stumbling in these verses is a person outside the one who sins, just as we saw in the use of πλανάω in ch. 24.

It is in the context of the message of this passage that we need to return to our examination of 17:24–27. I would argue that the chapter break between chapters 17 and 18 is quite unfortunate. The theme of not causing another to sin/stumble is the common message of both 17:24–27 and 18:5–7. In 17:27, we see Jesus modeling the kind of care that he expects of his followers: while he (and by extension Peter) are free not to pay that tax, they will do so in order not to cause anyone to stumble. Jesus sets aside privilege in order to preserve community, just as he expects his followers to exercise care for the other little ones who believe in him. If an outside force is to be the cause of the stumbling of a believer, that force should not be another from inside the community.

The next passage (18:8–9), however, introduces a twist to the scenario of sin caused by an outside entity. Here it is not an external force nor even another person that trips one up, but one's own body parts:

> But if your hand or your foot ensnares you, cut it off and throw it away! It is better for you to enter into life[60] maimed or lame than having two hands or two feet to be thrown into the eternal fire. And if your eye ensnares you, tear it out and throw it away! It is better for you to enter into life with one eye than having two eyes to be thrown into the hell of fire.

The metaphor of body parts as causes for sin will be discussed further below, but for the present we need to recognize simply that here there is a disjunction of the person from her or his own body parts such that they are on par with an outside entity or force in their ability to ensnare and trip one up, and thus to be a cause of sin. As Davies and Allison note, the hand and foot are personified, thus becoming independent agents of ensnarement.[61]

The next passage, 18:10–14, returns to the theme of the sinning of "little ones" and also returns to the use of πλανάω. Here, Jesus' followers—the μιχροί—are parabolically cast as sheep who stray and are sought by the owner of the flock. In contrast to the previous use of πλανάω in ch. 24, however, no one is leading the followers astray; it is the "sheep" themselves who stray. The lack of an explicit outside agent provoking the straying contrasts with the previous passage in which the use of σκανδαλίζω/σκάνδαλον made it clear that the stumbling of the μιχροί was attributable to some force beyond the will of the one who sins.

---

60 On "life" as equivalent to the Kingdom, see Davies and Allison, *A Critical and Exegetical Commentary*, 2:767.

61 Davies and Allison, *A Critical and Exegetical Commentary*, 2:765.

136 CHAPTER 9

Here, the straying is of more ambiguous origin, or at least the text leaves the cause undefined and open to a variety of possibilities.

2.3 *Summary*

The use of πλανάω and σκανδαλίζω/σκάνδαλον in Matthew proves to be more complex than the basic definitions of the words might initially lead one to believe. In contrast to ἁμαρτ-, we see much more ambiguity. At times it is clear that those who go astray or stumble are the victims of some outside force or (more often) that a person causes the straying or tripping, but at times the sinner strays without there being any mention of being led, and there are important passages that indicate the stumbling of a sinner may have as much to do with his or her moral or intellectual predisposition (soil type, type of tree) as it does with the presence of a snare.[62] This proves to be the case especially in the passages that depict Jesus as the cause of stumbling. In these, the stumbling appears to be much more significant than simple mental tripping or being "offended"; real sin, in the form of rejection of Jesus and his message and mission, are caused by Jesus. In this case, as opposed to the message we see in ch. 18 for example, the ones stumbled are not portrayed as victims and the one who causes the stumbling (Jesus) is guiltless. Stählin's observation that "σκάνδαλον is only an 'occasion of falling' which might lead to a fall or not" seems borne out here. Still, the overall portrayal that, in contrast to ἁμαρτ-, there are times when sin is not deliberate and the cause of sin lies outside the sinner remains dominant in the uses of πλανάω and σκανδαλίζω/σκάνδαλον. The important exception to this is Matthew's portrayal of one's own body parts as capable of σκανδαλίζιεν. These passages and others that portray the body as a cause of sin are those to which we now turn.

---

62 This parallels the use of these metaphors in the Second Temple literature where we saw in, for example, the Enochic literature, the responsibility for causing sin was dually attributed to the people and the giants/Watchers who led them astray. At points, for example in the Animal Apocalypse, some infirmity such as blindness causes the straying, yet even when the sheep are portrayed as victims of an outside force that causes the straying (sin) the people—just as in Matthew—are held responsible, and there is indication that, just as we saw with respect to some Second Temple text, the infirmity is willful. Similar use of the metaphor of straying appears in the Qumran materials, again here the straying of sinners is caused in some respects by an outside force (cf., "Angel of Darkness" in 1QS; part 1) as well as by the humans themselves.

CHAPTER 10

Metaphors for the Cause of Sin

In looking at σκάνδαλον/σκανδαλίζω as a metaphor for the cause of sin, we noted above that the basic imagery is that the cause of the sin is something external to the one who sins: it is a snare or trap or stumbling block that takes the person unawares. Sometimes, however, as we saw in looking at the Parable of the Sower and the Soils and at Jesus' opponents, a person may have something within him or her that predisposes one to be tripped up and ensnared;[1] even so, the effective cause remains an outside agent.

1   Metaphors of Body Parts as the Cause of Sin

In looking at Mt 18:8–9, however, we began exploring the logion in which Jesus points to a person's own body parts—hands, feet, and eyes—as potential causes of sin. This logion is one of the Matthean doublets, its parallel being 5:29–30. The two logia are quite similar,[2] and while the variations have significant implications for any theory of synoptic relationships,[3] the variations

---

1   Such as a lack of depth.

2   The most significant difference between the logia themselves is the inversion of the order: in the ch. 5 version, the eye as a source of sin is addressed first and the hand second, whereas ch. 18 has the hand (and feet) first and the eye second. (The choice to situate the eye verse first in ch. 5 obviously provides a thematic connection to the previous verse, the warning against looking at a woman with lust.) There are other differences as well, however. In ch. 5 both the eye and hand are designated as the "right"; ch. 18 does not designate and adds the foot as a co-subject with the hand. Other than that, the wording of the first clauses in 5:29 and 18:9 and the wording of the first clauses of 5:30 and 18:8 are nearly identical. There are more significant differences in the wording of the second clauses of the two logia, however. In ch. 5, both sentence end almost identically—συμφέρει γάρ σοι ἵνα ἀπόληται ἓν τῶν μελῶν σου καὶ μὴ ὅλον τὸ σῶμά σου βληθῇ εἰς γέενναν—except that v. 30 uses ἀπέλθῃ instead of βληθῇ. In ch. 18, the final clauses of the two sentences are also extremely similar. Verse 8 ends with "καλόν σοί ἐστιν εἰσελθεῖν εἰς τὴν ζωὴν κυλλὸν ἢ χωλόν, ἢ δύο χεῖρας ἢ δύο πόδας ἔχοντα ληθῆναι εἰς τὸ πῦρ τὸ αἰώνιον." Verse 9 ends with "καλόν σοί ἐστιν μονόφθαλμον εἰς τὴν ζωὴν εἰσελθεῖν, ἢ δύο ὀφθαλμοὺς ἔχοντα βληθῆναι εἰς τὴν γέενναν τοῦ πυρός." Aside from the changes necessitated by the change of subject from hand and foot to eye, the only notable difference is the change from τὸ αἰώνιον in v. 8 to τὴν γέενναν τοῦ πυρός in v. 9. The difference in the second half of these two verses from the version in ch. 5 is conspicuous and more substantial.

3   The lack of either form of this saying in Luke seems to make Q an unlikely source (see Hans-Dieter Betz, *The Sermon on the Mount: a Commentary on the Sermon on the Mount, Including the Sermon on the Plain* [*Matthew 5:3–7:27 and Luke 6:20–49*], Hermeneia

138　　　　　　　　　　　　　　　　　　　　　　　　　　　　　　　　　　CHAPTER 10

between the two Matthew texts themselves do not amount to a significant difference in their message.

In both passages, the overall message is that, because of the serious—indeed eternal—consequences of sin, one must do whatever can be done to avoid sin or eliminate its causes, including the most radical kinds of abrogation. The method for this is, however, expressed in metaphorical terms, just as are the causes identified and the act of "sinning" itself. The method of elimination (cutting off or plucking out) is as metaphorical as the cause of the sin (eye, foot, and hand).[4] But let us first look more closely at the use of the logion in ch. 18.

As noted in the previous section, 18:8–9 is placed within the longer exhortation regarding relations within the church (true greatness [vv. 1–5], the μιχροι, sinning [6–14], and the protocol for confronting and forgiving sin in the church [15–35]). It constitutes something of an interruption of the flow of vv. 6–14 and the theme of care for the μιχροι. The element that ties our logion to the larger context is the use of σκανδαλίζω /σκάνδαλον. The section begins with "If any of you put a σκάνδαλον before one of these little ones who believe in me, it would be better for you if a great millstone were fastened around your neck and you were drowned in the depth of the sea." Next comes the almost parenthetical "Woe": "Woe to the world because of σκάνδαλα! Σκάνδαλα are bound to come, but woe to the one by whom the σκάνδαλον comes!" Our logion begins in verse 8 and returns to the basic form of verse 6 ("If your hand.... it would be better for you ..."),[5] but here the emphasis has shifted. While in v. 6 the concern was that a μιχρός might be stumbled, vv. 8–9 constitute a warning regarding oneself being stumbled/tripped up. Verse 10 then returns to the concern for the μιχροι, with "Take care that you do not despise one of these little ones ..."

　　[Minneapolis: Augsburg Fortress, 1995], 238). In Mark the two sayings are conflated and have an expanded ending. They appear immediately after the "better to have a millstone" saying, essentially the same place as in Matthew 18, although Matthew inserts the verse "Woe to the world because of σκάνδαλα! For it is necessary that σκάνδαλα come, but woe to the man by whom the σκάνδαλον comes!"

4　I think Allison incorrectly labels the rhetorical form here. He asserts that the command to cut off or pluck out the sin-causing member is "hyperbolic" (Dale Allison, *The Sermon on the Mount: Inspiring the Moral Imagination,* Companions to the New Testament [New York: Crossroad, 1999], 76). This would only be so if a person's *actual* hand, foot, or eye were the cause of the sin. The possibility that a person's body parts are literal causes of sin is an interpretation that has not had much acceptance, though it has been held by some. See note 6 on p. 139 and note 9 on p. 140, below.

5　It is notable that v. 6 uses συμφέρει αὐτῷ as is found in the ch. 5 versions of vv. 8–9 rather than the form found in its immediate context (καλόν σοί ἐστιν). On the *tov*-saying form, see Davies and Allison, *A Critical and Exegetical Commentary,* 1:525.

METAPHORS FOR THE CAUSE OF SIN   139

Though the forms of verses 6 and 8–9 are essentially the same, the dynamics of the cause of sin in the two sayings are very different. As we saw above, in v. 6 the σκάνδαλον that threatens to ensnare or trip up the μικροί, is something external to them, something set before them by someone else, thus the cause of the sin lies wholly outside the one ensnared. When we turn to vv. 8–9, however, the cause in no longer external. Here it is the person's own body part that is the cause. The question is how far the metaphor extends. Is the metaphoricity limited to the verb, σκανδαλίζει? In that case, the hand, foot, and eye would be literal; one's literal body parts could be the cause of metaphorical stumbling moral "stumbling into" or "ensnarement in" sin. While there is nothing in the immediate context that would necessarily rule out such a reading, the historic and scholarly consensus is that the eye, hand, and foot are metaphorical as well, images representing one's thoughts, deeds, and ways. In this case, then, the solution of cutting off or plucking out and casting away the body part becomes metaphorical as well, thus precluding the possibility of actual physical self-mutilation, which would be of no real use in combating the source of the sin.[6]

Still, the dynamics of the cause of sin communicated by these metaphors is, as mentioned above, notably different than the dynamics previously explored in the use of σκανδαλίζω/σκάνδαλον. The metaphor used here introduces the idea that causes of sin can come from within oneself. The use of the metaphor of eye, hand, and foot, however, *localize* the cause. In contrast to metaphors we will explore below that indicate a more holistic internal cause, these metaphors communicate a situation in which the cause of the sin is the person herself (not something external), but it is not the *whole* person. The larger "self" is able to make a judgment against the sin-inducing "part" and essentially to

---

6 Though historically there have been some instances of taking the references to body parts literally, most have come to understand the images of body parts here as metaphorical ("In the history of interpretation the literal interpretation was for all practical purposes unanimously rejected" [Ulrich Luz, *Matthew 1–7*, Hermeneia (Minneapolis: Fortress, 1989) 247]). See also Betz, *Sermon on the Mount*, 237–239.) The metaphorical reading was particularly bolstered by interpreters putting these verses in conversation with the other version of the logion in ch. 5 where one's thoughts and intentions and not one's physical body are clearly at issue (Davies and Allison, *A Critical and Exegetical Commentary*, 2:766–767). Further cited as supporting the metaphorical understanding is Jesus' assertion in 15:18–19 that the source of "uncleanness" is not what goes into the body, but what comes from the heart. Sin then is the result of something deep within a person, something like the soul, self, or will. The fact that "the heart" is also a body part, though more obviously and traditionally used metaphorically, in the end, however, only complicates rather than resolves the problem posed by the image of the hand, foot, and eye as a source of sin (see below, regarding 15:18–19 and 12:34–35).

140 CHAPTER 10

reject it as inconsistent with the character of the whole.[7] The person has, in a sense, become estranged from a part of him- or herself.[8] This estrangement is so severe that the text can suggest metaphorical amputation. This amputation, however, does not lead to diminution but rather to wholeness[9]—a greater wholeness than one would experience if the parts were not removed and remained intact but sinful.

The idea of wholeness is a key component of the other use of this logion, the use in 5:29–30. Several aspects of the logion here, however, diverge significantly from its form and use in ch. 18.

First, in ch. 5, the logion and the context are more logically connected. In the previous passage, the use of the logion constituted an interjected shift of subject from concern about causes of sin for the μικροί to a warning against causes of sin in oneself. In ch. 5, the immediate context is the second antithesis which warns that looking at a woman πρὸς τὸ ἐπιθυμῆσαι αὐτὴν is tantamount to adultery.[10] Here, linguistically "the bridge between the antithesis and the

---

7   The idea that lack of integrity and consistency between inner and outer is the key to Matthew's understanding of the nature of sin has been explored by several scholars. A common feature of sin is the fracturing of the self or the disjunction of different parts of the self such that the integrity or wholeness of the person is compromised. Whether the lack of integrity is a cause of sin or an effect of it is not clear. See the following footnote on sin in Bultmann's *Theology of the New Testament* (2 vols. [New York: Charles Scribner's Sons, 1951]), as well as Dan O. Via, *Self-Deception and Wholeness in Matthew and Paul* (Minneapolis: Fortress Press, 1990).

8   This is similar to Bultmann's reading of Paul in his *Theology of the New Testament*. According to Bultmann, for Paul the human is not a two- or three-part being, nor do the "parts" have special faculties, but all are joined together as a unified self who has a relation to himself (1:209). One of Paul's ways of talking about the self is by the term *soma*; the *soma* is not something that one's "self" possesses but is constitutive of one's self. Yet one's *soma* can be under the sway of powers other than oneself, and there are deeds of the body (in those cases used as synonymous with *sarx*) that can put one "at odds" with oneself and God (1:192–198). But when the *soma* is ruled by the *sarx*, it becomes a nearly foreign second-self from which the "inmost self" is estranged (1:200–201).

9   Ulrich Luz notes regarding the cutting off the hand in 18:8–9 that Matthew seems closer to some instances of Hellenistic paraenesis which use the image of surgical amputation to encourage the readers to forsake the influence of bad friends or immoral practices. This is in contrast to the use of the image in Rabbinic literature where it has a more sexual overtone, one which is present in the context of the other use of this logion, 5:29–30 (*Matthew 8–20*, p. 436; see notes 35 and 36 for literature on the use of these images). See also Betz, p. 238 n. 343 and 344 for more parallels in Hellenistic and Rabbinic literature. The connection to 19:12 is also worth noting. Perhaps the two *logioi* once were more closely connected since both share the perspective of cutting off a part for the sake of the kingdom, although in 19:12 there is no implication that the removal was necessary for the eradication sin.

10 The question of whether γυνή, restricts the warning to looking lustfully at another's wife (so Luz, *Matthew 1–7*, 244) or whether it includes all women remains an open question,

added material [5:29–30] is the 'eye' in v. 28 that is understood as the instrument of seduction."[11] The historically persistent connection between the "eye" and ἔρως is underlined by Betz who notes that "the role of the eye in erotic love is a frequent theme in ancient literature."[12] Because of ancient understandings of physiology, it is not immediately clear that the eye is to be understood non-literally. Betz, in discussing the role of the eye in the development of ἔρως and thus ἐπιθυμία, cites Plato who says, "And love [ἔρως] is so called because it flows in from without, and this flowing is not inherent in him who has it, but is introduced through the eye."[13] In this conception, the literal eye becomes the pathway for the entry of ἔρως and thus the adulterous ἐπιθυμία.

The opposite "flow," however, might be the underlying conception of this passage. As will be discussed at more length regarding 6:22–23, Allison has demonstrated convincingly that most pre-modern cultures did not understand the eye to channel light (and perhaps ἔρως with it) into the person from the outside ("intromission") but from the inside of the human out into the world ("extromission").[14] Human eyes were consistently likened to torches, lamps, and the sun, and the phrase "the light of one's eye(s)" was commonly employed. The eye was a channel, but it was a channel out of which flowed the internal "fire" of life within creatures. The application that is most germane here is with the idea of *intention* communicated by the πρὸς τὸ ἐπιθυμῆσαι αὐτὴν in v. 28. If Allison is right, then the intention flows outward with the gaze. This is consistent with 6:22–23 as well with respect to the "evil eye" (ὁ ὀφθαλμός σου πονηρός). While the adjective πονηρός had a wide range of meanings from "evil" as the complete opposite of all that is good[15] to simply rotten or useless,[16] ὁ ὀφθαλμός

---

but one that does not impinge directly on our subject. The question of the meaning of πρὸς τὸ ἐπιθυμῆσαι αὐτὴν does, however, and will be addressed below.

11   Luz, *Matthew 1–7*, 242.

12   Betz, *Sermon on the Mount*, 232.

13   Betz, (*Sermon on the Mount*, 232) quoting Plato, *Crat.* 420a. "Plato explains ἔρως 'etymologically' by ἐσρέω ('flow into') which in olden times was called ἔσρος" (Betz, *Sermon on the Mount*, 232 n. 279).

14   "The Eye is the Lamp of the Body (Matthew 6.22–23 = Luke 11.34–36)," *NTS* 33 (Ja 1987): 61–83. As he points out contra Betz, most ancient philosophers and writers, including Plato and many Rabbinic texts, held the extromission view. Plato's opinion as expressed in *Cratylus* was apparently more for the sake of his etymology of ἔρως than to discuss the physics of ocular operation per se.

15   Thus, the use of πονηρός as an adjective for demons (12:43–45) and "the evil one" as a synonym for the Devil as noted above with regard to 13:38 (cf. 13:19).

16   Matthew certainly utilizes the entire semantic range of πονηρός suggesting meanings from explicit connection with ultimate evil to "sick" ("πονηρός," *DBAG* 852, citing Mt 6:23) to "worthless" (G. Harder, "πονηρός," *TDNT* 6:554; "πονηρός," *DBAG* 852, citing Mt 7:17f.) Note however that in 7:17–18, the metaphorical rottenness stands for ethical or spiritual rottenness for which there are negative apocalyptic consequences (cf. 13:48). This complicates

πονηρός had a number of specific meanings. For our text and the use in 6:22–23, the most applicable is the idea that the ὁ ὀφθαλμὸς πονηρός is a metaphor for greed or stinginess.[17] The implication of greed for the evil eye fits the context of 5:29–30 quite well. Modern commentators are on the whole agreed that the second antithesis constitutes not a new teaching on the commandment concerning adultery, but an extension of the command against coveting (Ex 20:17).[18] If the second antithesis is really a teaching that connects the two commandments and shows the fundamental link between the act of adultery and the attitude of covetousness, then the use of the metaphor of the eye which, when "evil," is the embodiment of greed, is an apt choice. It is the ὁ ὀφθαλμὸς πονηρός that is the cause of the sin because of its propensity toward lust.

Here, then, we see further evidence of how the metaphor of body parts as a cause of sin communicates that sin is a fracturing of the self. Jesus' equation of lust with adultery leaves no room for hypocrisy—a fundamental fracturing of the integrity of inner and outer, intention and act.[19] As Georg Strecker has said regarding this passage in its context within the Sermon:

> The eschatological justice that Jesus establishes is ... defined by the coming reign of God. The nearing of God's kingdom excludes all casuistry [that would condemn adultery but excuse lust] and demands the total human being. It discloses the fractured nature of human existence

---

exegesis of other passages where a person or group or thing is called πονηρός. For example, in Matt 7:11, Jesus is speaking to the crowds in general (based on 7:28, although cf. 5:1), and he says, "If, therefore, being πονηροί you know how to give good gifts to your children ..." Is Jesus really implying that the crowds are "possessed" or are they simply relatively "worthless" and "empty" compared to God? Further, when Jesus says, "Do not resist τῷ πονηρῷ, but if anyone slaps you on the right cheek, turn to him the other also" (5:39), it is obvious that he is talking about humans and not the devil, especially in the context of the previous verse: "You have heard that it was said, 'An eye for an eye and a tooth for a tooth.' But I say to you ..." The context is the limit on retribution, although given what we will see later regarding the identification of Jesus' opponents with the Devil, the situation may refer to disciples being abused by those who continue to oppose Jesus' message and those who believe in him.

17 As Keener notes, "An 'evil eye'... was a stingy, jealous, or greedy eye" (Craig Keener, *The Gospel of Matthew: a Socio-Rhetorical Commentary* [Grand Rapids; Cambridge, UK: Eerdmans, 2009], 232). Cf. Mt 20:15.

18 Some do also see this antithesis as an intensification of the command against adultery (Przybylski, *Righteousness in Matthew*, 81–82), and while I see no reason that it cannot be both, the fact that, as Keener notes, the LXX "used the same word for 'covet' that Jesus uses here for 'lust'" (Keener, 187) certainly gives force to the approach of reading this antithesis as focused more on conjunction of two commands than intensification of just one.

19 Cf. Via, *Self-Deception and Wholeness in Paul and Matthew.*

METAPHORS FOR THE CAUSE OF SIN

because it lays claim to the whole of a person's being.... It is crucial that outward action and inner direction of the will agree.[20]

The source of this sinful willing is also, it should be noted, presented by means of the metaphor of another body part: the heart. More will be said below about this metaphor and its use in several other passages, but it should be recognized that the metaphorical dynamics of both 5:28 and the use of the scandalizing eye and hand logion in 5:29–30 are the same: a body part is the cause of sin.

Beyond the much more organic connection to its context here in ch. 5, the second notable difference in the use of the logion here as compared to ch. 18 is in the form of it, namely the insertion of δεξιός to modify eye and hand. Some scholars have asserted that the right eye and right hand are specified because they are the more valuable, particularly the right hand.[21] Thus, the point is that, should even those parts most valuable for one's day-to-day life be the cause of stumbling, they ought to be sacrificed for the good of the whole body.

This introduces a final and significant difference from the version in ch. 18: here in ch. 5 the consequence of not amputating the sin-inducing member is articulated specifically in terms of the whole versus the parts. While the statement in 18:8–9 that "if your hand or your foot causes you to sin, cut it off and throw it away. It is better for you to enter life crippled or lame than with two hands or two feet to be thrown into the eternal fire" implies estrangement between one's larger self and one's members, the version in 5:29–30 makes the fracturing much more clear by use of the *topos* of parts and whole. Again, as Strecker notes:

> Even if the (more valuable) right hand gives offense, its loss weighs little vis-à-vis the threat of judgment that will affect the whole person. Σῶμα ('body') characterizes a human being comprehensively as an earthly, personal being. The parallel in 18:8–9 speaks of only two members. By contrast the totality of the individual is emphasized here.[22]

It should be recognized here that the metaphor does not point to a disjunction between, so to speak, one's inner and outer person. While Jesus will later criticize the disciples' failings using such a metaphor ("the spirit is willing, but the

---

20   *The Sermon on the Mount: an exegetical commentary*, trans. O.C. Dean, Jr. (Nashville: Abingdon, 1988), 71.

21   Davies and Allison, *A Critical and Exegetical Commentary*, 1:526. Also, Strecker, *The Sermon on the Mount*, 72; Walter Grundmann, *Das Evangelium nach Matthäus*, THKNT (Berlin: Evangelische Verlagsanstalt, 1968), 161; Betz, *Sermon on the Mount*, 237.

22   Strecker, *The Sermon on the Mount*, 72.

flesh is weak" 26:41), here the threat of judgment is levied against the human as a physical being: either the sinner must execute judgment now on the sin-inducing member or judgment will be executed finally on the whole physical person. Thus, the problem is a disjunction all on the same level—physical parts to physical whole—not a disjunction between one's physical parts and one's soul or spirit. It is not therefore a situation where some inherently good or higher part of the person (soul, spirit, inner person) repudiates the lesser and offending physical part because it is inconsistent with the desires of the higher self.[23] Rather, the metaphor communicates a situation where one finds an organically related part to no longer be consistent with the good of the whole, much as a cancerous cell turns against the good of the whole body, and regardless of how seemingly or previously helpful (a right hand) or valuable (a right eye), the person is called to repudiate and metaphorically amputate that part and cast it away (βάλε ἀπὸ σοῦ). Although βάλλω is a common Greek verb, its use in this context particularly connects this passage to the theme of judgment and eschatological punishment since Matthew uses this verb extensively in warnings and parables of judgment (3:10, 5:13, 5:25, 6:30, 7:19, 13:42, 13:48, 13:50, 18:30). It should be noted, however, that Matthew is not implying that the sin-inducing members are possessed. When Matthew talks about casting out demons, ἐκβάλλω is used; thus, there is no implication here that the sin caused by a hand, foot, or eye is ultimately caused by an external, demonic or diabolical agent which controls or animates the member.

Thus, the sinner is called to recognize the cause of sin as coming from him- or herself, but the propensity to entrap and trip up one does not spring from the whole of the person. The person cannot blame the cause of sin on some outside force (as in the previous uses of σκανδαλίζω) but neither is the cause of sin portrayed here as something springing fundamentally from the nature of the whole person. The metaphor of hands, feet, and eyes that entrap one in sin conveys a situation where the sinner cannot deny that she or he was the source, but yet can stand in judgment over a part of him or her that seems now foreign and malicious.

---

23 A number of commentators tend in this direction. For example, in commenting on vv. 28–30, Allison writes that "humans need not be the passive victims of their natural drives" and "The body need not be the master" (*Sermon on the Mount*, pp. 75 and 74, respectively). While these observations may be useful for exhortation, they obscure the force of the metaphor. Also, Betz states, "The right eye ... becomes a source of moral offense. The term σκανδαλίζω is used here in a more general sense: the eye has become a 'trap' (σκάνδαλον) entangling its owner in sin" (236); here the language of a person "owning" her or his members communicates a conception of a non-physical self that possesses the physical self, a conception that also runs counter to the metaphor of this particular passage.

METAPHORS FOR THE CAUSE OF SIN   145

Wholeness and integrity play a role in another verse of the Sermon on the Mount in which a body part is indicated as a source of sin. In 6:22–23 Jesus says that "the light (or lamp) of the body is the eye. If, therefore, your eye is single, your body will be light. But if your eye is evil (πονηρός), your whole body will be filled with darkness. If, therefore, the light that is in you is darkness, how great is the darkness!"

Darkness is obviously traditionally associated with evil and that which is opposed to God's will,[24] and in Matthew it is particularly associated with eschatological punishment for wrongdoing.[25] Also, in 4:16 the narrator's comments on the beginning of Jesus' ministry contrast light and darkness and associate darkness with death using a version of the words of Isa 9:2, and the connection of darkness to sin becomes clear in the next verse since the beginning of the activity of Jesus (the "great light" that is seen by those in darkness) consists of preaching repentance because of the coming of the kingdom.[26] Thus, although none of the most basic words for sin is used in this passage, we can see that Matthew is figuratively referring to that which is in opposition to God's will by use of the image of darkness.

In this passage, the body part in question is portrayed as potentially having either a good or bad effect. The potentially good effect (the body being

---

24 There are a variety of OT uses of מַחְשָׁךְ/חֲשֵׁכָה/חֹשֶׁךְ, but terms of the חשׁך-root are often used to signify things opposed to God's will. This is particularly true of wisdom texts (e.g., Ps 82:5: "They have neither knowledge nor understanding, they walk about in darkness"; Prov 2:13: "who forsake the paths of uprightness to walk in the ways of darkness") although אֲפֵלָה is also used in this way (Prov 4:19 "The way of the wicked is like deep darkness; they do not know over what they stumble") and these can be used in conjunction as synonyms (e.g., "And they shall look unto the earth; and behold trouble and darkness [חֲשֵׁכָה], dimness of anguish; and they shall be driven to darkness [אֲפֵלָה]" Isa 8:22). Still, walking in darkness is not always a sign of wrong-doing; the righteous can "walk in darkness [חֲשֵׁכָה]" (Isa 50:10) of oppression from which God delivers them. Further complicating the picture of darkness is the consistent portrayal of God as dwelling in darkness, particularly with the use of the word עֲרָפֶל which does not seem to have a negative moral connotation but simply to express God's hiddenness and perhaps separation from humans (Ex 20:21, Deut 4:11, Deut 5:22, 2 Sam 22:10, 1 Kgs 8:12, 2 Chr 6:1, Ps 18:9, Ps 97:2). However, חֲשֵׁכָה is also used with regard to God's dwelling in Ps 18:11, as is חֹשֶׁךְ in Deut 5:23, 2 Sam 22:29 (and arguably Gen 1:2, Ex 10:21–22, Ex 14:20, and Amos 5:18). Still, the idea of darkness as hiding or obscuring is not opposed to the tradition negative moral connotations of darkness since, as some of the texts cited above exemplify, "darkness" impairs the ability of ethical "sight" such that one can "trip" or "miss the path."

25 Τὸ σκότος τὸ ἐξώτερον is where wrong-doers are cast for weeping and gnashing of teeth (ὁ κλαυθμὸς καὶ ὁ βρυγμὸς τῶν ὀδόντων: 8:12, 22:13, 25:30).

26 The ethical seems certainly to be in view with the Isaiah text since in Isa 5:20 the prophet warns, "Woe to those who call evil good and good evil, who put darkness for light and light for darkness, who put bitter for sweet and sweet for bitter!"

filled with light) is caused by the eye being ἁπλοῦς, "single." The image here is of something unmixed or undivided, something simple and straightforward.[27] The consequence of this is that one's body will be "enlightened" or filled with light. The opposite situation—one's whole body being "endarkened"—is caused, however, not by the eye being διπλοῦς[28] but by it being πονηρός. As discussed earlier, the phrase ὀφθαλμός πονηρός was an idiom for being greedy or covetous. While it might potentially have some other meaning if this logion were in isolation,[29] Matthew has placed it (along with the parabolic saying about the inability to serve two masters [6:24]) between two warnings regarding wealth: the command against laying up treasure on earth (6:19–21) and the command not to be anxious about food, drink, or clothes (6:25–34). Given the context of these exhortations against focusing on material possessions, the most reasonable construal is that the ὀφθαλμός πονηρός is a covetous eye.

But in what way does this body part then cause sin? This saying seems at first to be a string of relatively transparent metaphors that explain how the "eye" causes sin: if one has an evil eye (attitude of greed), one's whole body (entire self, person, or perhaps life) will be filled with darkness (consumed with the sin of covetousness). This seems fairly straightforward, but let us look more closely.

This passage has a number of things in common with the verses previously examined regarding the eye as a source of sin. The first to note is that there is an emphasis on the part and the whole. The eye (one part) causes trouble (here, in the form of "darkness") for the whole body (ὅλον τὸ σῶμά), and this trouble is connected with eschatological judgment. The second commonality is pertinent especially to 5:28–30. There, as we noted above, at particular issue was the intention or attitude of the one using the eye. There, looking at a woman πρὸς τὸ ἐπιθυμῆσαι αὐτὴν is tantamount to committing adultery ἐν τῇ καρδίᾳ αὐτοῦ, an attitude that, if not amputated will lead to the whole person suffering punishment. Here, an attitude of greed leads to a similar consequence.

There are, however, at least two significant differences between the scandalizing eye, foot, and hand of chapters 18 and 5 and the "evil eye" of 6:23. The first is that in the logion about the scandalizing body parts, there was no indication that the body part itself was bad. In each case, the member has served a

---

27   ἁπλόος, *LSJ* 190–191.

28   Or διπλόος, "double," the antonym of ἁπλοῦς or ἁπλόος, sometimes with the meaning of being double-minded or doubtful (*LSJ* 436).

29   Luke places the logion (with slight differences) after the saying, "No one lighting a lamp sets it in a cellar but upon a lampstand in order that those coming in may see the light," the common thread being the image of the lamp.

METAPHORS FOR THE CAUSE OF SIN

bad purpose—causing one to be tripped up and entrapped in sin—but there is no indication that this is the inherent function of that body part. There is no indication that it might not just as well have served a righteous purpose. In contrast, in 6:23 the eye is characterized adjectivally as πονηρός. The difference in the behavior of a person might ultimately be minimal in the two situations being described, but it is significant on a metaphoric level. There is a significant difference between a good part of the body that becomes alienated from the rest of the good body because of the activity of leading it to sin and a body part that is characterized as πονηρός. While, again, the physical metaphor is used to point to the determinative character of the non-physical attitude, the word picture here communicates the idea (via the symbol of the eye) that there can be something integral to one's self that is characterized by a quality different from the whole. One can find that parts of one's self cause sin not just by misuse but by their very character. Interestingly, it is not in this case, when the body part itself is declared evil, that the remedy of plucking out is prescribed. This is the second significant difference from the use of the body part metaphor in chapters 18 and 5. There Jesus gives instructions for dealing with the offending members so that one can avoid "the Gehenna of fire." Here, no remedy is recommended. For the person who has an evil eye and thus whose σῶμά is filled with darkness, Jesus simply exclaims, "If the light in you is darkness, how great is the darkness!" This passage communicates the idea that some causes of sin may be incorrigible, the only possible response being exclamations on the direness of the situation. Although this may seemingly contradict the tenor of the previous uses of the body parts metaphor, it is, it will be seen, congruent with the message of other metaphors used by Matthew, particularly those of the familial and genetic category.[30] Still, there remains the same dynamic with this example as with the other uses of the body part metaphor: the source of sin remains localized to one part of the person, and sin is not caused by something inherent to the whole person.

2   Metaphors of Illness and Infirmity for the Cause of Sin

There is one instance in Matthew, however, where the source of sin is portrayed as both physical and generalized rather than localized. The passage comes near the beginning of the section in which Jesus' authority is questioned

---

30   Of course, in the larger context of the surrounding material in the Sermon on the Mount (6:19–33), it is clear that Jesus is calling for a change of attitude, and there is the expectation that such a change is possible.

148   CHAPTER 10

particularly on the grounds of his seeming lack of scrupulousness with regard
to Torah observance:

> And it happened that as he was reclining at the table in the house, behold
> many tax-collectors and sinners came and were dining with Jesus and his
> disciples. And seeing this, the Pharisees said to his disciples, "Why is your
> Teacher eating with the tax-gatherers and sinners?" But hearing, he said,
> "Those who are healthy do not have need of a physician, but those who
> are ill."[31]

Jesus' words are essentially the same as proverbial wisdom available in the
wider culture and recorded in a number of variations.[32] The context, however,
gives the saying its specific meaning for our study. Here, the condition of those
labeled as "sinners" is likened to that of illness.[33]

The connection of sin with actual illness was traditional. Part of the curse
that Moses articulates in Deuteronomy for disobeying the covenant is disease
(28:58–61), and there are numerous examples where sickness is portrayed as
the punishment for sin or the result of unrighteousness.[34] This was still a common perception in Jesus' day and the decades that followed, as the controversy regarding the man born blind in John 9 patently portrays.[35] While sin as
a source of illness indicates a substantive connection between the two ideas,
more germane to our study is the portrayal of sin *as* illness in the texts of the
OT and the Intertestamental period.

In the Second Temple texts examined above in ch. 1, we found that sin is
sometimes spoken of metaphorically as illness. We noted that in *1 Enoch* 10:7,

---

31   9:10–13.
32   Menander frag 591K; Dio Chrysostom 8.5; Mek. on Ex 15:26. The closest parallel seems to
      be Plutarch, *Apophth. Lacon.*, 59.2, "Pausanias,": "When, in Tegea, after he [Pausanias] had
      been exiled, he commended the Spartans, someone said, 'Why did you not stay in Sparta
      instead of going into exile?' And he said, 'Because physicians, too, are wont to spend their
      time, not among the healthy, but where the sick are.'" Here, the parallel is not limited to
      the proverb, but includes also the context of a teacher going where he feels he is needed.
33   On social dynamics of Jesus' table-fellowship with "sinners" as well as discussion of
      various scholarly understandings of the term ἁμαρτωλοί, particularly with respect to its
      potential connection to the *'am haareṣ* and later Rabbinic teaching, see Keener, *Gospel of
      Matthew*, 291–299.
34   E.g., Ex 32:35, Num 11:33, Num 14:37, Num 16:42–50, Num 25:6–9, 2 Sam 24: 10–15 and
      1 Chr 21:8–14, 2 Chr 21:12–15, Ps 38:3, Ps 41:4, Prov 20:24, Jer 14:10–12, Ezek 6:11. It is notable
      that many of these are corporate punishments of the community rather than individual
      punishments for individual transgressions.
35   Similarly, the misfortune of those killed by the tower of Siloam (Lk 13:4).

METAPHORS FOR THE CAUSE OF SIN

149

God instructs Raphael to "heal the earth which the watchers have desolated; and announce the healing of the earth, that the plague may be healed, and all the sons of men may not perish because of mystery that the watchers told and taught their sons." Images of blindness and deafness are significant in the Enochic traditions, and in *4 Ezra* sin is explicitly called a disease and its genesis linked to Adam.[36] Yet, the more extensive use of this metaphor in the OT bears additional examination.[37]

Generally in the OT, the image of sin as sickness is communicated by its opposite—that sin is dealt with by God through healing. The same verb is used for physical healing and the "healing" of sin,[38] thus communicating the analogy of sin with sickness. We see this in a number of passages. In 2 Chr 30:18–20, we read that some of the people ate the Passover in an improper manner,[39] but that "Hezekiah had prayed for them, saying, 'The good Lord pardon everyone who sets his heart to seek God, the Lord the God of his fathers, even though not according to the sanctuary's rules of cleanness.' And the Lord heard Hezekiah and healed the people."

The imagery of healing as a remedy for sin is particularly notable in the prophetic literature. In Jeremiah 3:22, The Lord declares, "Return, O faithless sons, I will heal your faithlessness."[40] The book of Hosea utilizes this imagery extensively. In Hosea 5:13, the prophet declares: "When Ephraim saw his sickness, and Judah his wound, then Ephraim went to Assyria, and sent to the great king. But he is not able to cure you or heal your wound." That this "sickness"

---

36 Cf. relevant sections on *1 Enoch* and *4 Ezra* in part 1.

37 Since, as noted above, it remains an open issue whether Matthew knew only some version of the LXX or also some precursor to the MT, both have been consulted, although in only a few of the examples (as noted below) does the imagery of the two version diverge enough to warrant differentiation.

38 In the MT רפא, in the LXX ἰάομαι.

39 "For a multitude of the people, many of them from Ephraim, Manasseh, Issachar, and Zebulun, had not cleansed themselves, yet they ate the Passover otherwise than as prescribed."

40 MT: שׁוּבוּ בָּנִים שׁוֹבָבִים אֶרְפָּה מְשׁוּבֹתֵיכֶם. LXX reads ἐπιστράφητε, υἱοὶ ἐπιστρέφοντες, καὶ ἰάσομαι τὰ συντρίμματα ὑμῶν. The use of συντρίμματα ("things that have been shattered," often translated as "bruises") obviously puts the LXX version outside the realm of our study since what is being healed here is not a sin (like faithlessness to God) or sinfulness more generally. Συντρίμματα elsewhere is often in combination with ἰάσομαι and carries connotations of moral failure or lack of faithfulness or their repercussions. Cf. the LXX of Ps 13:3 (paralleled in Isa 59:7; quoted in Rom 3:16), Ps 59:3–4, Ps 146:2–3, Isa 30:26, Jer 8:19–22, Jer 10:19, Jer 14:17–19, Jer 37:12 and 17. While these are similar metaphorically to sin as sickness especially when combined with the idea of healing, they lack the holistic, generalized character of the illness metaphor.

was sinful disobedience and unfaithfulness to the Lord is made clear in the preceding verses:

> I know Ephraim, and Israel is not hid from me; for now, O Ephraim, you have played the harlot, Israel is defiled. Their deeds do not permit them to return to their God. For the spirit of harlotry is within them, and they know not the Lord. The pride of Israel testifies to his face; Ephraim shall stumble in his guilt; Judah also shall stumble with them.[41]

Similar imagery is invoked again in 6:9–10: "In the house of Israel I have seen a horrible thing; Ephraim's harlotry is there, Israel is defiled" and again healing is mentioned as God's response: "When I would heal Israel, the corruption of Ephraim is revealed" (7:1). Finally, Hos 14:4 echoes the Jeremiah passage when God declares, "I will heal their faithlessness; I will love them freely, for my anger has turned from them."[42]

The final OT passage of significance for our exploration of this metaphor is Isa 6:9–10:

> And he said, 'Go, and say to this people, "Hearing, you shall hear, but you shall by no means understand; and seeing, you shall see, but you shall by no means perceive." For the heart of this people has become fat and their ears heavy of hearing, and they have shut their eyes; lest they should see with the eyes, and hear with the ears, and understand with the heart, and return, and I would heal them.'[43]

Isaiah's commission to prophesy comes with the Lord's prediction of failure, though the Lord says that, were the people able to turn back to him, he would heal their metaphorical deafness, blindness, and heart disease. Their

---

41 5:3–5.

42 LXX 14:5: ἰάσομαι τὰς κατοικίας αὐτῶν, ἀγαπήσω αὐτοὺς ὁμολόγως, ὅτι ἀπέστρεψεν ἡ ὀργή μου ἀπ᾿ αὐτῶν. While the "healing" or restoration of the dwellings of Israel is not the same as "healing their faithlessness," the overall sense of the larger passage (vv. 2–7) in the LXX is consonant with the message of the MT.

43 LXX, my translation. καὶ εἶπεν Πορεύθητι καὶ εἰπὸν τῷ λαῷ τούτῳ Ἀκοῇ ἀκούσετε καὶ οὐ μὴ συνῆτε καὶ βλέποντες βλέψετε καὶ οὐ μὴ ἴδητε·ἐπαχύνθη γὰρ ἡ καρδία τοῦ λαοῦ τούτου, καὶ τοῖς ὠσὶν αὐτῶν βαρέως ἤκουσαν καὶ τοὺς ὀφθαλμοὺς αὐτῶν ἐκάμμυσαν, μήποτε ἴδωσιν τοῖς ὀφθαλμοῖς καὶ τοῖς ὠσὶν ἀκούσωσιν καὶ τῇ καρδίᾳ συνῶσιν καὶ ἐπιστρέψωσιν καὶ ἰάσομαι αὐτούς. MT Isa 6:9–10: "And he said, 'Go, and say to this people: "Hear and hear, but do not understand; see and see, but do not perceive." Make the heart of this people fat, and their ears heavy, and shut their eyes; lest they see with their eyes, and hear with their ears, and understand with their hearts, and turn and be healed.'"

METAPHORS FOR THE CAUSE OF SIN
151

metaphorical physical ailment has put them in a position where they have become estranged from the Lord and are in need of healing.[44]

This passage is particularly significant since it constitutes one of Matthew's most extensive quotations of OT material. When the disciples ask Jesus why he speaks to people in parables, his response is, in part, the LXX of Isa 6:9–10. The question is whether this quote is also be classed with the other Matthew text in which the cause of sinful acts is portrayed as an illness that needs healing. As we have seen, the passage in its original context communicates this idea, but does the changed context of the Matthean text alter the message of the passage?

It is obvious that the meaning of the passage as it is used in Mt 13:14–15 remains metaphorical. Jesus is not talking about physical blindness, deafness, or heart trouble. This should not, however, lead us to jump to the assessment that Matthew consistently reads OT passages of illness and healing as metaphorical rather than literally physical. For example, in Mt 8:17, another Isaianic prophecy[45] is invoked with reference to Jesus: "This was to fulfill what was spoken by the prophet Isaiah: 'He took our infirmities and bore our diseases'." In the original context, the Hebrew of Isaiah uses terms of real illness (חֳלָיֵנוּ and מַכְאֹבֵינוּ) but uses them metaphorically. The metaphorical force of the verse in Hebrew is picked up and communicated by the translators of the LXX without the illness metaphors, translating חֳלָיֵנוּ as τὰς ἁμαρτίας and מַכְאֹבֵינוּ סְבָלָם as περὶ ἡμῶν ὀδυνᾶται. Matthew, however, apparently works from the MT, translating the Hebrew illness terms into Greek (ἀσθένεια and νόσος) and applying the verse literally to Jesus' work of healing. In this case, however, the context of the previous verses makes it clear that the prophecy is being used in reference to physical not metaphorical sickness and healing:

> And to the centurion Jesus said, 'Go; let it be done for you as you have believed.' And the servant was healed at that very moment. And when Jesus entered Peter's house, he saw his mother-in-law lying sick with a fever. He touched her hand, and the fever left her, and she rose and began to serve him. That evening they brought to him many who were oppressed by demons, and he cast out the spirits with a word and healed all who

---

44   Note also Isa 1:5–6: "Why will you still be smitten, that you continue to rebel? The whole head is sick, and the whole heart faint. From the sole of the foot even to the head, there is no soundness in it, but bruises and sores and bleeding wounds; they are not pressed out, or bound up, or softened with oil."

45   Isa 53:4.

were sick. This was to fulfill what was spoken by the prophet Isaiah: 'He took our infirmities and bore our sicknesses.'[46]

Here, an originally metaphorical use of the language of illness is applied by Matthew to the healing of physical illnesses.

In the quotation in ch. 13, however, text of Isaiah 6:9–10 is, as in the original context, applied metaphorically: the parable is about people who can or (more often) cannot receive the metaphorical seed of the word that is sown, and the explanation for why parables are used reinforces, by use of metaphors of physical limitation, the message that some people have no ability to receive the word that is given. The question then is whether this inability to receive the word is tantamount to sin. Do we have here another instance of the portrayal of sin as a physical infirmity or is the infirmity simply a limitation that is not necessarily sinful? To answer this, we need to determine what constitutes sin for Matthew. As we noted above, Matthew does not seem concerned to define explicitly within the narrative what constitutes sin, thus we must look at what is implicit in the text, what Matthew communicates indirectly about what he sees as sin, to determine whether the use of the infirmity image above is referring to sin and its metaphorical cause.

Excursus: Sin, Righteousness, the Kingdom, and the Will of God

To examine how Matthew understands the character of sin or what precisely counts as sin from his perspective, we will need to come at the problem obliquely, in part by looking at what Matthew characterizes as the opposite of sin, and also by exploring the various behaviors and attitudes that are connected with both sin (or being a sinner) and its opposite.[47] By exploring the characteristics of both, we will be able to develop a clear picture of Matthew's understanding of what constitutes sin.

We begin with the most clearly articulated juxtaposition of sin and its opposite. In 9:13, Jesus proclaims that he came "not to call the righteous

---

46 8:13–17.

47 As we examine various passages, it will become clear that there is a network of negative terms related to sin and a corresponding opposite network of related positive terms. The terms of each network are juxtaposed or contrasted in a number of texts creating a complex web of negative connections between the two networks which will be explored primarily through the footnotes. There are, however, overarching principles for each network and it will become apparent that the various element are simply examples or expressions of those principles.

METAPHORS FOR THE CAUSE OF SIN   153

but sinners." Sinners (ἁμαρτωλοί) and righteous (δίκαιοι) are juxtaposed as opposites. The question of whether those not being called by Jesus were truly righteous or only externally and superficially so can be set aside for the moment, but we will return to it. The main thing to note here is that Jesus sets up a traditional and perhaps intuitively sensible contrast between righteous and sinner.[48]

If "righteous" and "sinner" are conceived of as opposites for Matthew, then looking at the characteristics of the righteous and Matthew's understanding of righteousness—and those who lack it—should give us a good conception of his understanding of the character of sin.

Perhaps the characteristic most associated with the δίκαιοι is that they will be participants in the kingdom. In the Parable of the Net, the kingdom gathers up all the "fish," and the righteous are kept, but the πονηρός are thrown out and burned.[49] At the conclusion of the Parable of the Wheat and the Tares, Jesus says that after the angelic harvest of the cosmos, "the righteous will shine forth like the sun in the kingdom of their father." Here also, just as in 9:13, we see an instance where the righteous are contrasted with those associated with sin. As we saw above, the πάντα τὰ σκάνδαλα is one of the things that the angelic harvesters will remove from the kingdom, again reinforcing the contrast of righteous and sinners.[50]

The fact that the righteous gain the kingdom and sinners do not does not yet tell us much about what Matthew thinks constitutes sin. The parable of the Wheat and the Tares does, however, give us some further information that does help us. As we saw above, the σκάνδαλα are not the

---

48 Perhaps more intuitive is the contrast in 5:45 of the δίκαιοι and the ἄδικοι upon whom God sends rain. This, however, is Matthew's only use of ἄδικος and thus it does not move us very far along. In this same verse, however, we find another pair of contrasts that parallels the δίκαιος and the ἄδικος: the contrast of ἀγαθός and πονηρός. Ἀγαθός therefore can be added to our network of terms on the positive side with "righteous" and πονηρός can be added to the network with ἄδικοι and ἁμαρτωλοί. We find ἀγαθός and πονηρός contrasted in a number of other passages as well. In fact, the contrast is quite consistent. In 7:17–18 ἀγαθός and πονηρός trees and their fruit are contrasted; similarly, in 12:34–35 Jesus identifies ἀγαθός and πονηρός speaking as the outflow of either a good or evil heart; in the parable of the wedding banquet, the servants are to gather into the wedding hall all whom they found in the way, ἀγαθός and πονηρός; in the parable of the talents, the servants who were productive are called ἀγαθός while the unproductive servant is πονηρός.

49 13:47–50. Note also here the characterization of those not in the kingdom as πονηρός, reinforcing the identification demonstrated in the previous note, above, of the πονηροί with the ἄδικοι and thus with sinners.

50 13:41. As discussed above, πάντα τὰ σκάνδαλα are apparently people, and these are people who both cause others to sin and in so doing also become sinners themselves. Cf. 18:6–7.

only people removed; also mentioned are those ποιοῦντας τὴν ἀνομίαν (13:41). Those who do or cause lawlessness are on par with others who trip people up into sin, and both are set up as dualistic opposites of the righteous. The use here of "lawlessness" indicates that one aspect of sin for Matthew is inadequate respect for—or, in fact, outright disrespect and denial of—the Law.[51]

That lawlessness should be opposed to righteousness in this Matthean parable should not be surprising. Early in the Sermon on the Mount, Jesus claims to have come not to destroy the Law[52] but to fulfill it and stresses the ongoing validity of the Law.[53] The upholding of the Law is so important that "if anyone should loosen one of the least of these commands and should teach others to do so, that one will be called least in the Kingdom of Heaven, but the one doing and teaching the commands will be called great in the Kingdom of Heaven." Here we have another scenario of a separation or distinction being made "in" the Kingdom. The scenario here, as with the Parable of the Net and the Parable of the Wheat and the Tares, is that the Kingdom will initially encompass all—both the good and the bad—and then there will be a separating of the good from the bad.[54] Perhaps the underlying eschatology here is primarily temporal: the Kingdom is a *time* that will come (or is on the verge of coming, ἤγγικεν

---

51   The working premise of this argument—that ἀνομία carries the connotation of "lawlessness" rather than simply general "iniquity"—is not based primarily on etymology (though that is not inconsequential in this case, I think), but rather on the use ἀνομ- elsewhere in the NT and particularly the use of ἄνομος. This term is used by Paul specifically with regard to the gentiles in 1 Cor 9:21: "To those without the law (τοῖς ἀνόμοις) I became as one without the law (ἄνομος)—not being without law (ἄνομος) toward God but under the law of Christ—that I might win those without the law (τοὺς ἀνόμους)." Thus, Peter preaching to the Jews in Acts 2:23 says, "you put him to death, crucifying him by the hands of those without the law (διὰ χειρὸς ἀνόμων)." It is also clear, however, that being "lawless" is not solely the provenance of gentiles. One of Jesus' accusations against the Pharisees is that they are full of hypocrisy and lawlessness (ὑποκρίσεως καὶ ἀνομίας), the irony being, of course, that it is precisely their law*ful*ness for which they are known and in which they take pride, yet it is all hypocrisy. Similarly, Jesus says in Mt 7 that those who say to him "Lord, Lord!" but to not do the will of the Father are workers of lawlessness (οἱ ἐργαζόμενοι τὴν ἀνομίαν). As we will explore more fully below, the law and the will of the father are intertwined, and to abrogate one is to transgress the other, but it seems clear that the root sense of ἀνομ- was not a dead metaphor (like ἁμαρτ-), but its literal sense was still very much in view.

52   Cf., his prediction that the Temple will be καταλυθήσεται (24:2) and the accusations against him that he claimed he would destroy the Temple (26:61 Οὗτος ἔφη· Δύναμαι καταλῦσαι τὸν ναὸν τοῦ θεοῦ and 27:40 Ὁ καταλύων τὸν ναόν).

53   At least until "everything shall have taken place."

54   Cf. also the Parable of the Wedding Banquet, 22:1–14, esp. verses 10–13.

METAPHORS FOR THE CAUSE OF SIN

3:2, 4:17, 10:7; cf. 26:45–46), and it will come upon all, and then all will be judged.[55] Some will be judged worthy and some will not. Adherence to and promotion of the commandments of the Law (even the least of them [τῶν ἐντολῶν τούτων τῶν ἐλαχίστων]) is the criterion for who is judged most worthy (μέγας in 5:19) and who will be deemed least (ἐλάχιστος) when the kingdom comes, and all are present and subject to separation (κρίσις,[56] most often rendered "judgment"). Just as those who were ποιοῦντας τὴν ἀνομίαν will be removed from the kingdom, those who do not hold fast the commands or teach others to do so will be judged as "least." Keeping the commands of the Law is, for Matthew, a characteristic of those who remain in the Kingdom of Heaven and an integral component of righteousness;[57] not keeping the commands of the Law is sin.[58]

---

55   So in the parable of the Wheat and Tares, at the end of the age the Son of Man will send his angels to gather ἐκ τῆς βασιλείας αὐτοῦ πάντα τὰ σκάνδαλα καὶ τοὺς ποιοῦντας τὴν ἀνομίαν.

56   *LSJ* 997.

57   This in basic agreement with Przybylski that δίκαιος is descriptive of those who are "properly religious" in a Jewish sense, i.e., law observant. As should already be apparent and will become more so, I take issue, however, with Przybylski's claim that for Matthew δικαιοσύνη is neither salvific nor is it Christian since "those who followed the teaching of Jesus were designated 'disciples'" (*Righteousness in Matthew*, 111) rather than "righteous," since disciples followed "the will of God," and δικαιοσύνη is merely the proper observance of the Law (*Righteousness in Matthew*, 105–115, *passim*). As will be seen, for Matthew, although δικαιοσύνη as law-keeping is not sufficient to enter the kingdom, it is necessary, and ἀνομία will result in exclusion from the Kingdom.

58   See the helpful article by James E. Davison, "*Anomia* and the Question of an Antinomian Polemic in Matthew," *JBL* 104 (De 1985): 617–635. Though Davison's main point is to refute the idea that Matthew is engaging in polemic against an antinomian group, various points of his argument are germane to our exploration. Regarding the use of ἀνομία in the LXX, he notes that "a cursory look at the lexical information suggests that it is regularly set in opposition to *dikaiosynē* and that *anomia* and *adikia* are not infrequently found in combination" (619). This obviously accords with our observation earlier regarding Matthew that *adikia* is not the only opposite term for *dikaios*, but that there is a network of negative terms that are used, if not quite interchangeably, then certainly without great care to preserve nice distinctions among them. Further, Davison's comments on Ezekiel's use of *anomia* could very well be applied to Matthew. In commenting on Ezek 18 he says, "First, the actions designated as *anomia* are described elsewhere in the chapter by the terms *hamartia*, *adikia*, and *asebeia*. In addition, *anomia* itself translates three different Hebrew terms in this chapter: *tô'ēbâ* (18:12, 13, 24); *rāšā'* (18:20, 27); and *ḥaṭṭā't* (18:21). Finally the last of these terms is rendered not only by *anomia* but also by *hamartia* (18:14, 24). This indicates that *anomia* is understood to be interchangeable with a number of other terms, all of which refer to evil actions done in violation of God's will." Although he argues against understanding *anomia* as the "rejection of the law in principle," he grants that "the specific connotation of *anomia* among these terms, of course, has to do with violation of Torah" (621).

The righteousness needed to enter the Kingdom is not easily attained, however. In the next verse (5:20), we find that "unless your righteousness exceeds that of the scribes and the Pharisees, you shall by no means enter into the Kingdom of Heaven."[59] This compels us to look at the righteousness of the Pharisees to see the ways in which Matthew finds it to be so deficient as to be no better than ἀνομία or sin. If we look to ch. 23 as the most thorough and extensive examination of the deficiencies of the Pharisees that might keep them from the Kingdom,[60] we find several practices and attitudes at issue. The two most pervasive and thus significant are hypocrisy and the inability to discriminate between the "lighter and weightier" matters of the Law[61] and appropriately apply that discrimination.[62]

In ch. 23, the main accusation against the Pharisees is hypocrisy. Five of the six "Woes" begin by denouncing the Pharisees as hypocrites, and the introductory paragraph also condemns them because they "do all their works to be seen by people" (23:5). The denunciation of ch. 23 does not, however, deny that the Pharisees do have a level of righteousness. Jesus is thoroughly familiar with his opponents' scrupulous outward adherence to the demands of the law.[63] This he does not condemn, but, in fact, says that the law-keeping they prescribe "you ought to have done" (23:23).

---

59   Here the metaphor changes from a more temporal to a more spatial image with the language of "entering into the Kingdom of Heaven" (εἰσέλθητε εἰς τὴν βασιλείαν τῶν οὐρανῶν).

60   By "Pharisees" I mean the literary construct of the Pharisees that functions as a composite character in Matthew. Whether any actual Pharisees of either Jesus' or Matthew's day could be so characterized is beyond our present investigation, but see, for example Jacob Neusner, *From Politics to Piety: the Emergence of Pharisaic Judaism* (New York: Ktav, 1979); Albert I. Baumgarten, *The Flourishing of Jewish Sects in the Maccabean Era: an interpretation* (Leiden: Brill, 1997); Martin Hengel and Roland Deines, "E.P. Sanders' 'Common Judaism', Jesus, and the Pharisees," *JTS* 46 (April 1995): 1–70; John P. Meier, "The Quest for the Historical Pharisee: A Review Essay on Ronald Deines, *Die Pharisäer*," *CBQ* 61 (October 1999): 713–23; Anthony J. Saldarini, "Understanding Matthew's Vitriol," *BibRev* 13 (April 1997): 32–39, 45; Moshe Weinfeld, "The Jewish Roots of Matthew's Vitriol," *BibRev* 13 (October 1997): 31.

61   These are discussed elsewhere in Matthew as well, as will be seen below.

62   The scribes and Pharisees are also indicted for their pride in verses 5–12, which is certainly a count against them in the Kingdom since humility is an attribute of those who will there be the "greatest."

63   The overall enumeration of various instances of the Scribes' and Pharisees' meticulous law-keeping in 23:13–29 seems to be in tension with the tenor of Jesus opening salvo against them in 23:3–4: "They say but do not do."

METAPHORS FOR THE CAUSE OF SIN

Still, in terms of their fitness for the Kingdom, he condemns them. They will not escape being sentenced to Gehenna (23:33), are themselves sons of Gehenna, and make others so as well (23:15). They neither enter the Kingdom themselves nor allow those who would enter it to do so (23:13). They "clean the outside of the cup and the plate, but inside they are full of greed and self-indulgence" (23:25). They "are like whitewashed tombs, which outwardly appear beautiful but inwardly are full of the bones of the dead and all uncleanness" (23:27). Jesus summarizes his indictments saying, "Outwardly you appear righteous to people, but inwardly you are full of hypocrisy and lawlessness" (23:28). The righteousness of the Pharisees and scribes, since it is only outward and to be seen by others, amounts to hypocrisy and a cover for ἀνομία.

Thus, Jesus condemns the Scribes and Pharisees, but it is not for their keeping of the commands, which is upheld (even tithing mint and dill and cumin, which should not be neglected—23:23), but for their mere outward adherence to the law (hypocrisy) and their inward "lawlessness" which is shown in the second of their faults: the neglect of the principles that underlie the Law and thus whose application must take precedence over technical fulfillment.

As we noted above, five of the six "Woes" are followed by the charge of hypocrisy. The only "Woe!" that is followed by another charge is the second, and here the charge is that the Pharisees and scribes are "blind guides" (23:16). Based on the verses that follow, we see that this blindness consists of not being able to correctly apprehend how the underlying sanctity of what is greater or more general is what imparts sanctity to that which is lesser or more particular.[64] The Pharisees in particular were known for being careful, exact, and precise—ἀκριβής[65]—but their precision in hair-splitting commandment-adherence is, Jesus declares, misguided. They do not discern the deeper principles that ought to be

---

64 "Woe to you, blind guides, who say, 'If anyone swears by the temple, it is nothing, but if anyone swears by the gold of the temple, he is bound by his oath.' You blind fools! For which is greater, the gold or the temple that has made the gold sacred? And you say, 'If anyone swears by the altar, it is nothing, but if anyone swears by the gift that is on the altar, he is bound by his oath.' You blind men! For which is greater, the gift or the altar that makes the gift sacred? So, whoever swears by the altar swears by it and by everything on it. And whoever swears by the temple swears by it and by him who dwells in it. And whoever swears by heaven swears by the throne of God and by him who sits upon it."

65 See *LSJ* 55. For Paul as an ἀκριβής Pharisees, see Acts 26:5 and, using ἀκρίβεια, 22:3. On the Pharisees as ἀκριβής, see Josephus, *B.J.* 1.110 and Steve Mason, *Flavius Josephus on the Pharisees: a Composition-critical Study*, StPB 39 (Leiden; New York: E.J. Brill, 1991), ch. 1.

guiding their discrimination of what is significant and insignificant in following the Law, and thus are not reliable guides for others.

This same in ability to grasp the significant underlying principles is what is also at stake in the "Woe!" that follows this passage. Here, the Pharisees and scribes are again condemned as hypocrites, but in this case, it is because they meticulously follow certain extra-legal tithing prescription while neglecting "the weightier things of the Law" (τὰ βαρύτερα του νομοῦ). These Jesus enumerates as κρίσις, ἔλεος, and πίστις (23:23).

The initial term, κρίσις, certainly presents the most interesting options for interpretation. In fact, the various options present something of a potential difficulty, though not because of lack of use in Matthew. The most frequent use of the term in Matthew is in its sense of "judgment,"[66] particularly eschatological judgment. It is difficult to see how this might be characteristic of those desiring to be righteous in Matthean terms since Jesus explicitly forbids pronouncing judgment in 7:1–2,[67] and it also seems incongruous in the context of the "Woes" since the Scribes and Pharisees are quite willing—indeed, over-willing—elsewhere in Matthew to pass judgment.[68]

The sense of κρίσις as "justice" has some limited use in Matthew. This sense is the most likely in the Isaiah 42 quotation in 12:18–21: "I will put my spirit upon him and he will proclaim κρίσις to the Gentiles.... he will not break a bruised reed nor quench a smoldering wick until he brings κρίσις to victory." Here the sense of eschatological judgment could also be in view, but it is not patent.

While the traditional sense of κρίσις as justice could be in view in 23:23, only one of the charges against the Pharisees reflects neglect of this: the charge in 23:14 that they "devour widows' houses and for a pretense make long prayers." The immediate context of 23:23, however, opens the possibility for another valid though less common meaning of the term, and one which also accords well with its eschatological uses. If we revert to the more basic definition of κρίσις as a kind of judgment that is based on "separating," "distinguishing," or "differentiating"[69] (derived from the

---

66 5:21–22, 10:15, 11:22, 11:24, 12:36, 12:41–42, 23:33.

67 Μὴ κρίνετε, ἵνα μὴ κριθῆτε· ἐν ᾧ γὰρ κρίματι κρίνετε κριθήσεσθε, καὶ ἐν ᾧ μέτρῳ μετρεῖτε μετρηθήσεται ὑμῖν. Note also the juridical use in 5:40 and 19:28, Matthew's only other uses of κρίνω.

68 As they do on Jesus in 9:3, 9:11, and 9:34. It is notable also that in 7:5, Jesus calls those who judge the speck in a brother's eye hypocrites just as he does the Pharisees here in ch. 23 (vv. 13, 15, 23, 25, 27, 28, 29).

69 *LSJ*, 997.

basic meaning of χρίνω[70]) this accords well with the general picture of eschatological judgment as the distinguishing or separating of the good from the bad that we have already seen in the Parable of the Wheat and Tares, the Parable of the Net, the "least and greatest in the Kingdom," and which is also operative in the Sheep and the Goats.[71] If the meaning Matthew has in mind then for χρίσις is, for the most part, something like differentiation or "distinguishment," then in the context of 23:23, what is at stake is the "distinguishing" of light and weighty commandments and the use of the underlying principles of the Law as a basis for the application of the commands. This is the focus of almost every one of Jesus' indictments of the Pharisees in the "Woes" except the charge of defrauding widows. Not only would it accord with Jesus' criticism of the scribes and Pharisees here and but also with his criticisms of them elsewhere (especially their hypocrisy) and with his own χρίσις in the cases of, for example, Sabbath and purity laws.[72] Thus, to avoid sin and be righteous, one must not simply follow scrupulously and meticulously (ἀκριβῶς) the prescription and proscriptions of the Law, but more importantly distinguish (engage in χρίσις) and apply underlying principles of the Law to the enforcement of the individual commands.

What then are the weighty commands and on the basis of what underlying principles might the individual commandments be evaluated and applied? The clearest answer is to be found in the passage in ch. 22, just before Jesus begins this denunciation of the Scribes and Pharisees. In fact, the passage begins with the arrival of the Pharisees who have come with a question which seems, on the surface, innocent: "Which is the greatest commandment in the Law?" Whether the "testing" of the question was malicious and intended to trip Jesus up[73] or whether it was intended as a catalyst for debate in order to test Jesus' interpretive skill[74] is not relevant at present. What is important is that in this pericope Matthew sets out Jesus' principle for the χρίσις of the commandments before the topic is brought up in the discourse that follows. Thus, by the time readers get to Jesus' indictment in 23:23 that the Pharisees and

---

70 *LSJ*, 996; *DBAG*, 567.

71 This being the case, then perhaps the uses of χρίσις in 12:18 and 20 are actually of a piece with this meaning: proclaiming "χρίσις to the Gentiles" and bringing "χρίσις to victory" so that "in his name the Gentiles will hope" could be related to the judgment of the ἔθνη as the separation of the "sheep" from the "goats."

72 See esp. 12:1–14 and 15:1–20. Also note the Antitheses (5:21–48).

73 As is explicit in the question of whether to pay taxes to Caesar in 22:15.

74 As in the debate with the Sadducees regarding spouses at the resurrection (22:23–33).

Scribes have neglected the weightier matters of the Law, they already know what the very weightiest are: love of God and love of neighbor. On these two "hang"[75] the whole of the Law and the Prophets. Thus, the other two elements of the "weightier matters" of 23:23 can be seen to correspond to the second and first greatest commands, respectively—mercy as the expression of love toward neighbor, faith as the expression of an all-encompassing love of God.

This is, in fact, the same pattern we see in the story of the rich young man. Here, Matthew presents Jesus as upholding the following of the Law as essential for entering the kingdom. The rich young man enquires about gaining eternal life, and in 19:17 Jesus responds by saying, "If you wish to enter into eternal life, keep the commandments." Law-keeping is an essential aspect of the righteousness that characterizes the Kingdom. Yet, this is not all that Jesus prescribes. When the man claims to have kept the commands and wonders what he might still lack, Jesus does not deny that he still lacks something; thus, he indicates that, while keeping the commandments is essential for entry into the Kingdom, it is not the sole component to doing God's will. There is more the young man needs to do: first, he needs to divest himself of his wealth, but not simply for the health of his soul. He must benefit the poor by showing mercy and giving the money to them. It is notable that the term for alms given to the poor and for pity, compassion, or "mercifulness" are the same: ἐλεημοσύνη from the root ἔλεος, "mercy,"[76] thus expressly linking this to the "weightier matters" of 23:23.[77]

Finally, the young man is told he must follow Jesus as his disciple. This following as a disciple is an expression of the final of the three "weightier matters," that is "faith." Except for the use in 23:23, πίστις is used in Matthew always in the context of miracles, particularly miracles of healing, but also including miraculous answers to prayer in response to the petitioner's faith.[78] The verbal form, πιστεύω, shows more variation: it is

---

75   Though our English "depend" derives from the root "pend," it no longer (for most, anyway) conjures the image of something "hanging" that is so evocative here and which also evokes the image of scales and thus "weightiness."

76   *DBAG*, 315–316.

77   The integral role that mercy plays in the economy of the Kingdom in Matthew can be seen not only here and in the denunciation of the Scribes and Pharisees but in other of Jesus' sayings and parables as well (6:44–46, 9:10–13, 18:10–14, 18:21–35). It is an expression of adherence to the second greatest commandment and thus an underlying principle of the entire Law. Adherence to individual commands without even more strict adherence to this principle is contrary to the will of God expressed in the Law.

78   9:2, 9:22, 9:29, 15:28, 17:20, 21:21.

METAPHORS FOR THE CAUSE OF SIN

most often used to indicate giving credence to someone's sayings (21:25, 21:32, 24:23, 24:26), though almost as often to indicate general confidence in a person's ability, especially Jesus' ability to heal (8:13, 9:28, 21:22). Other uses include "believing" as a characteristic of a follower of Jesus (18:6) and the avowal of the crowd at the crucifixion that, if Jesus comes down from the cross, they will believe him (27:42). The significance of this concept, however, comes together in a passage in which both the nominal and verbal forms are used and in which the result is a declaration regarding the Kingdom—the Healing of the Centurion's Slave.

Though obviously the initial context is that of a healing, Jesus' declaration regarding the significance of the centurion's faith sets this story apart from others in which faith in Jesus leads to healing. The centurion's recognition of the authority of Jesus leads Jesus to marvel and declare: "Not even in Israel have I found faith like this! And I say to you, many will come from the east and west to sit at table with Abraham and Isaac and Jacob in the Kingdom of Heaven, but the sons of the Kingdom will be cast into outer darkness. There will be weeping and gnashing of teeth." Here, it is implied that *faith* is characteristic of those who will be in the Kingdom, and lack of it (which Jesus has found characteristic of Israel, the traditional and rightful sons of the Kingdom) is grounds for exclusion just as much as ἀνομία or any lack of righteousness ("sin").[79] However, the faith that is indicative of Kingdom participation is a faith in and acknowledgment of *Jesus* and his authority. This is supported by various other pericopes. For example, in 10:32–33 Jesus declares, "Everyone who acknowledges me before people, I also will acknowledge him before my Father who is in Heaven. But whoever should deny me before people, I also will deny him before my Father who is in Heaven." Recognition in the presence of God in Heaven (and thus in the Kingdom) is determined (at least in part) by one's acknowledgment of his Son.[80] That this vesting of authority is sanctioned and in fact initiated by the Father is asserted in 11:27 where Jesus claims, "All things have been handed over to me by my Father." Further, God himself commands those on the Mount of Transfiguration to submit to Jesus' authority by declaring "This is my

---

79 The parallels here with the first section of the Parable of the Marriage Feast are obvious (22:1–9).

80 This is correspondence between one's stance with regard to the Son being determinative for one's standing before the father is also emphasized a few verses later when Jesus says to the disciples, "He who receives you receives me, and he who receives me receives him who sent me" (10:40).

beloved son. Listen to him!"[81] Thus, Jesus' authority is an expression of the will of God and refusal to acknowledge it is opposition to God's will and thus sin.

This is congruent with the final aspect of Jesus' directive to the rich young man, and upon which we have briefly touched: the young man must demonstrate faith by recognizing Jesus' authority and responding to his call to follow—just as in the case of the centurion, where we saw that faith and acknowledgement of Jesus' authority go hand-in-hand. The "weightier matter" of *faith* turns out to have as its object Jesus quite as much as God the Father, and that faith results in obedient following of Jesus as the authoritative teacher and agent of God's will. That this following is one of the components of doing God's will and thus entering the Kingdom is seen at the conclusion of the discussion of the rich young man's question: Peter asks what those who have left all to follow Jesus will have as a result of their obedience. Jesus promises them a prominent place in the kingdom (19:27–28).

The clearest evidence for the following of Jesus as a component of the will of the Father and thus Kingdom participation is found in 12:49–50. Jesus' family wish to speak to him, but Jesus asks those who bring him this message, "Who are my mother, and who are my brothers?" In answer to his own question, "stretching out his hand toward his disciples, he said, 'Here are my mother and my brothers! For whoever does the will of my Father in Heaven is my brother and sister and mother." Jesus equates being his disciple—following him and acknowledging his authority—as doing God's will.

Thus, "the righteous" who enter the kingdom—the opposite of "sinners"—are those who follow the law, but not merely outwardly for show and with niggling scrupulousness,[82] but with discernment based on the principles of merciful love of neighbor and faith-filled love of God expressed in submission to the authority of Jesus.[83] All of these are

---

81   Mt 17:5 // Mk 9:7 // Lk 9:35; n.b., Lk changes "beloved" to "chosen" and Matthew adds "with whom I am well pleased."

82   While the composite character of "the Pharisees" in the story of Matthew's Gospel are certainly portrayed as excessively scrupulous—often to the detriment of the people around them—the accuracy of such descriptors for the historical Pharisees of Jesus' time is questionable at best. Their narrative function is as two-dimensional villains—intractable opponents of Jesus and foils for what it means to be true followers of God and lovers of the Law (i.e., disciples)—this is not the same as an attempt at an accurate historical depiction by the author of Matthew.

83   Note also the Parable of the Wise and Foolish Builders and the necessity of not only hearing Jesus teachings but doing them (7:24–27). Those who seem to acknowledge Jesus'

METAPHORS FOR THE CAUSE OF SIN

163

expressions of God's will, and any action—or indeed thought[84]—that is not in accord with God's will is sin.

As we return to Mt 13:14–15 and its context, there are a number of elements that will help us to determine, based on the exploration above, whether the blindness, deafness, and dull-heartedness referred to are metaphors for sin or mere ignorance and obtuseness. The first is Jesus' response to the disciples' initial question regarding the purpose of speaking to the crowds in parables. In 13:11 Jesus says, "To you it has been given to know the secrets of the Kingdom of Heaven, but to them it has not been given." Here Jesus makes a distinction between those with a connection to the Kingdom (the disciples) and those who do not understand and thus are disconnected. Given what we saw in the excursus above, two things stand out: first, connection to or inclusion in the kingdom was related to righteousness, and thus to lack that meant one was related to the opposite, that is, sin; second, following Jesus as a disciple was an aspect of doing God's will which was the overarching principle in opposition to sin. Thus, the dichotomy set up here between the disciples and "them"—a dichotomy utilized by both Jesus and the disciples—emphasizes that those to whom Jesus speaks in parables are not yet disciples nor are they connected to the Kingdom, thus they remain "sinners."

Further, if we look at the Isaiah quotation itself as it is used in Matthew, we see additional evidence that Matthew is utilizing the language of infirmity to indicate sin. The quotation identifies three reasons why the people see but do not perceive and hear but do not understand. First, their heart has become fat or thick (ἐπαχύνθη).[85] The use of the passive here means that the cause or source of the problem is ambiguous (it may be external or caused by the person), so whether the one with thick heart bears some guilt for its condition is not clear. The next phrase is literally "they heard heavily with [their] ears." Again, the source of the heaviness of the ears is not clear, though here the verb is active. The next phrase, however, indicates willfulness on the part of the people: "and their eyes they have shut" (τοὺς ὀφθαλμοὺς αὐτῶν ἐκάμμυσαν). This indicates that the action is purposeful; it is done in order prevent understanding.

---

authority by proclaiming "Lord, Lord!" but not doing the will of God in heaven (7:21–23)— which is apparently the words of Jesus, since the Parable of the Wise and Foolish Builders follows immediately after this—will be cast out.

84   As in the lustful thoughts of 5:28 or the unforgiveness "from the heart" of 18:35.

85   On the metaphor of the heart as an organ of understanding in the OT, NT, and wider culture, see *TDNT* 3:606–612; D.R. Goodwin, "On the Use of לֵב and Καρδία in the Old and New Testaments," *JBL* 1 (Jun 1881): 67–68 and 70; *LSJ* 877; Bultmann, *Theology of the New Testament*, 220–223.

164   CHAPTER 10

In fact, the final phrase indicates that all three metaphorical actions are to the same purpose: "... lest they see with [their] eyes and hear with [their] ears and understand with the heart."[86] This intentional lack of understanding is a rejection of Jesus' message ("the word/message of the Kingdom"—v. 19) and constitutes a rejection of his authority and thus is contrary to God's will and so is sin. The infirmities of blindness, deafness, and dull-heartedness are indeed metaphors of sin—intentional ignorance and lack of attention to God's activity.

So, what does a metaphor of sickness or infirmity communicate about the cause of sin? As with the body parts as cause, in this metaphor the cause is again located in the body. It is a problem within the individual. Here, however, the cause can be either localized (as blindness, deafness, or dull-heartedness in ch. 13) or generalized as "ill" (as in 9:12),[87] whereas with the metaphor of the body parts as cause, there was a dynamic of part over against the whole that was always present, either implicitly or explicitly. In the metaphor of the body part as cause, the sense was that the cause of sin was something that was natural and integral to the body, but that, through its functioning as a source of sin, it becomes alienated from the whole with which it ought to be congruent. This dynamic could also be present in the use of metaphors of blindness, deafness, and hard-heartedness if there was an indication that those suffering from these infirmities condemned these things—if, as with the body part metaphors, the whole stood in judgement on the part. As we have seen, however, in this case the people suffering from these infirmities do not reject the situation but rather foster it. Blindness, deafness, and hardheartedness are not the natural state of the eyes, ears, ands heart, but those experiencing them accept them and embrace them rather than reject these infirmities as contrary to what ought to be. This parallels the dynamics we saw in part 1 with regard to the use of metaphors of illness and infirmity in 1 Enoch. There as well, though the author does not overtly draw on the Isaiah passage, the people are portrayed as blind and deaf sheep, and the presence of sin in the world is likened to sickness that needs to be cured. Sin as a chronic, hereditary disease was also a significant metaphor in 4 Ezra.

As we saw in looking at how this metaphor was used in the Enochic literature and 4 Ezra, there is the underlying sense that the cause of sin is something that is causes malfunction, that it is abnormal, and contrary to God's will and intention. With the metaphor of illness, there is the sense that the cause of the sin is not a natural part of the body. The body or self is naturally good, and illness or

---

86   ... μήποτε ἴδωσιν τοῖς ὀφθαλμοῖς καὶ τοῖς ὠσὶν ἀκούσωσιν καὶ τῇ καρδίᾳ συνῶσιν.

87   The illness can even be undefined by being implied by the use of the healing metaphor as we saw in several OT texts.

METAPHORS FOR THE CAUSE OF SIN   165

infirmity is something contrary to nature that takes over the body bringing loss
of correct function, impairment of ability, and potentially death. This picture
of the source of sin portrays it as an unnatural state, one that causes the body or
self to behave in ways that are unproductive or destructive. To be healed is to
be restored to proper, natural functioning in accord with God's will.

3   The Metaphor of the Heart as a Cause of Sin

Twice in our exploration above we have touched on the heart in relation to
other body parts causing sin. In 5:28 we saw that, while Jesus identifies the
hand and eye as causes of sin and commands the (metaphorical) amputation
of them as a remedy for the sin of adultery (5:29–30), the heart is also implicated. As Betz notes, the process of committing adultery in the heart "is traced
from the outside to the inside, from eye contact to desire to the heart."[88] As
also noted above, inasmuch as the physical eye is a channel for desire to enter a
person, plucking it out would prevent the sin, but as Betz also notes the crucial
aspect is "the decision made by the heart."[89] The understanding of the "heart"
($\varkappa\alpha\rho\delta\acute{\iota}\alpha$) as the center of willing and decision-making is well attested in the
OT.[90] As a source of sin, however, the metaphorical heart's volitional capac-
ity is ambiguous. The heart can be inclined toward or will either good or evil,
toward obedience to God's will or sin.[91] Thus, in its volitional aspect the heart
is analogous to the combination of the *yetser ha-ra* and *yetser ha-tov*—it is not

---

88   Betz, *Sermon on the Mount*, 233.

89   Betz, *Sermon on the Mount*, 233.

90   LXX $\varkappa\alpha\rho\delta\acute{\iota}\alpha$: 1 Kg 8:17, Ezra 7:10, Jer 7:31, 11:20, 23:20, and 30:24; Dan 1:8; there are further
      verses which use לב/לבב in the Hebrew text but which are not rendered with $\varkappa\alpha\rho\delta\acute{\iota}\alpha$ in
      the LXX and may also be of influence (e.g., Ex 35:5, Est 7:5).

91   On the positive side, see, for example, Deut 4:29 "But from there you will seek the LORD
      your God, and you will find him, if you search after him with all your heart and with all
      your soul"; Deut 30:9–10 "The Lord will again take delight in prospering you … if you turn
      to the Lord your God with all your heart and with all your soul"; 1 Chron 22:19 "Now set
      your hearts and souls to seek after the Lord your God"; MT Ps119:36/LXX Ps118:36 "Incline
      my heart unto your witnesses/testimonies." On the negative side: Ps 58:2 "In your hearts
      you devise wrongs; your hands deal out violence on earth"; Ps 64:6 regarding the plotting
      of evil men: "'Who can search out our crimes?'.… For the inward mind and heart of a
      man are deep!"; Ps 81:12 "So I gave them over to their stubborn hearts, to follow their own
      counsels"; Eccl 11:9 "Let your heart cheer you in the days of your youth; walk in the ways
      of your heart … But know that for all these things God will bring you into judgment";
      Isa 32:6 MT "For the fool speaks folly, and his heart plots evil"; Jer 13:10 MT "This evil peo-
      ple, who refuse to hear my words, who stubbornly follow their own heart and have gone
      after other gods to serve them and worship them." So also Mt 9:4–5 "But Jesus, knowing

necessarily a source of sin but can tend in that direction when it is either not properly guarded or not instructed.

Also, as we saw above in looking at Jesus' explanation of why he uses parables, the heart can become a source of sin when it is sick and thus prevents correct understanding of the message of the Kingdom and perception of what is in accord with God's will.[92] This presumes, however, that when the heart is healthy and functioning normally, it would not be a cause of sin. Some passages in Matthew seem in tension with this, however. Two passages in particular point to the heart as a source of sin.

In 15:17–19 Jesus tells his disciples "Do you not perceive that whatever goes into the mouth passes into the stomach and is expelled? But the things that proceed out of the mouth come from the heart, and those defile a person. For out of the heart come evil thoughts, murders, adulteries, fornications, thefts, false witness, blasphemies. These are the things which defile a person; but eating with unwashed hands does not defile a person." Here, Jesus identifies the heart as the source of sin and thus defilement.[93] That these are truly sins is clear from the content of the list: murder, theft, false witness, and adultery are specifically prohibited in the Decalogue; πορνεία in the LXX is equated with unfaithfulness to God as well as sexual immorality;[94] "blasphemies" are condemned in the OT,[95] and blasphemy against the Holy Spirit is declared by Jesus to be the only unforgiveable sin (Mt 12:31); and in the first Antithesis Jesus equated evil thoughts of anger against another as tantamount to murder, and Jesus calls it thinking evil in their hearts (ἐνθυμεῖσθε πονηρὰ ἐν ταῖς καρδίαις ὑμῶν) when the Pharisees' condemn Jesus' declaration of forgiveness as

---

their thoughts, said, 'Why do you think evil in your hearts? For which is easier, to say, "Your sins are forgiven," or to say, "Rise and walk"?'"

92 Although the metaphor of sickness is not used to explain the cause of wrong ideas, Mt 9:4–5 similarly employs the understanding of the heart as an organ of thinking, perception, and understanding in Jesus' conflict with the Pharisees over the healing of the paralytic: "But Jesus, knowing their thoughts, said, 'Why do you think evil in your hearts? For which is easier—to say, "Your sins are forgiven," or to say, "Rise and walk"?'" On the heart as an organ of thought, deliberation, and understanding, see TDNT 3:606–612; Goodwin, "On the Use of לֵב and Καρδία," 67–70; LSJ 877; and Bultmann, Theology of the New Testament, 220–221.

93 Note the contrast with the perspective of Sirach (above) where κοιλία was a body part that could function as a source of sin, and the conjunction in that discussion with the mouth and heart as potential agents as well.

94 See, for example, Num 14:33, Deut 22:20–29, Deut 23:17, Ps 72:27, Isa 47:10, Isa 57:9, Jer 2:20; also note the use of ἐκπορνεύω in Num 15:39, Num 25:1, Deut 31:16.

95 Although "blasphemies" is used little in the LXX, βλασφη- is used to translate both חרף and נאץ which in the MT indicate not just impious language but defying God and despising his word or promise. See esp. 2 Kgs 19:16 and 22–23, Isa 52:5; as well as Num 14:11, Num 14:23, 1 Sam 17:36, Ps 74: 10 and 18, Isa 5:24, Isa 37:4, Isa 67:5.

METAPHORS FOR THE CAUSE OF SIN

blasphemy.[96] Here, the heart, rather than an outside agent such as the uncleanness of hands, is identified as the source of sin. The passage employs the common understanding of both the OT and NT of the heart as that which is inward over against that which is external.[97] External things are not a cause of sin and defilement, but that which is from one's inner self is the cause.

The context of the passage further emphasizes the heart as a metaphor for the internal self over against the external parts of a person. The situation that prompts Jesus' teaching on the heart as a source of sin and defilement is the Pharisees' criticism that Jesus' disciples eat with unwashed hands. In response, Jesus quotes Isa 29:13 in a version close to the LXX:[98] "You hypocrites! Well did Isaiah prophesy of you, when he said: 'This people honors me with their lips, but their heart is far from me; in vain they worship me, teaching as doctrines the commandments of men'" (15:7–9). Thus, the issue of hypocrisy with respect to the Pharisees is again brought forward, this time through the use of the metaphor of the heart. So, in conjunction with verses 17–19, the larger passage echoes Jesus' charge against the Pharisees found in 23:25–27:

> Woe to you, scribes and Pharisees, hypocrites! For you clean the outside of the cup and the plate, but inside they are full of greed and self-indulgence. You blind Pharisee! First clean the inside of the cup and the plate, that the outside also may be clean. "Woe to you, scribes and Pharisees, hypocrites! For you are like whitewashed tombs, which outwardly appear beautiful, but within are full of dead people's bones and all uncleanness. So you also outwardly appear righteous to others, but within you are full of hypocrisy and lawlessness.

Jesus' emphasis here is consistent with his proclamation in 15:17–19 that the heart, as representative of one's inner self, is the source of real sinfulness and uncleanness, regardless of external "cleanness" and righteousness.

The second passage to be considered has a similar theme—outward sins are expressions of the inner person—but the context in this case extends the implications of the use of the heart metaphor. In 12:34–36, Jesus is again in a controversy with the Pharisees. He says to them:

---

96 It is likely that the inclusion of "blasphemies" also implicates the Pharisees since previously in verses 4 and 5, Jesus quotes their citations of Ex 21:17//Lev 20:9 which says, "He who קלל his father or mother shall surely be put to death." קלל is often translated as "revile," and when used with respect to God, it is essentially synonymous with blasphemy (e.g., Ex 22:28, Lev 24:11–15, Isa 8:21).

97 *TDNT* 3:606 and 612, and Bultmann, *Theology of the New Testament* 1:222, and cited verses.

98 See Davies and Allison, *A Critical and Exegetical Commentary* 2:525–526, comparing Jesus' version of the verse, the LXX, and the MT.

168   CHAPTER 10

You offspring of vipers! How can you, being evil, speak what is good? For
out of that which fills the heart, the mouth speaks. The good person out
of her good treasure brings forth what is good; and the evil person out of
her evil treasure brings forth what is evil. And I say to you that for every
careless word people shall speak, they shall render account in the day of
judgment. For by your words you shall be justified, and by your words you
shall be condemned.

Again, it is clear that what is emanating from the heart is either sinful or righteous. The treasure that fills the heart can be either πονηρός—an adjective associated with the devil, as we have seen—or ἀγαθός—an adjective Jesus connects
with God in 19:17.[99] The importance of the treasure that defines the heart, and
indeed the person, as either good or bad is underscored by the consequences
of what issues from them: one will either be justified or condemned at the
judgment based on the words that are the expression of this treasure. Thus,
good treasure that issues in justifying words is analogous to righteousness (the
defining characteristic of those who are found worthy of the kingdom),[100] and
bad treasure that results in words by which one is condemned so is equivalent
to sin in its many forms that are in opposition to righteousness.

This passage implies more about the heart, however, than that is it simply a
neutral container for good or bad treasure, a container that expels its contents
in the form of words.[101] If we look at the first half of verse 34, we see that the
basic sense of it parallels the statement about the heart. Jesus asks, "How can
you, *being evil*, speak what is good? For out of that which fills the heart, the
mouth speaks." The next verse goes on then to make the dichotomy explicit:
"The good person out of his good treasure brings forth what is good; and the
evil person out of his evil treasure brings forth what is evil." The message here
is that the type of heart (evil or good) determines the kind of treasure that will
be brought forth—"How can you, πονηροὶ ὄντες, speak what is good?" Being
ὁ ἀγαθὸς ἄνθρωπος precedes ἐκβάλλει ἀγαθά, and being ὁ πονηρὸς ἄνθρωπος
causes ἐκβάλλει πονηρά. Apparently, the heart is not a neutral container but is
more like a fruit: just as the type of fruit determines what kind of juice can be

---

99   "And he said to him, 'Why do you ask me about what is good? There is One who is good. If
     you would enter life, keep the commandments.'"

100 Although it should be noted that the words by which one is justified are only effective
     because they are accurate expressions of the good treasure within the person. Matthew is
     consistent in his insistence that outward righteousness is only valuable inasmuch as it is
     behavior consistent with one's inner self.

101 For the discussion of the use of the heart metaphor in *Jubilees* and *4 Ezra*, see part 1.

extracted from it, so *being* a good or bad person and having the apposite heart determines the type of "treasure" that one can bring forth.

This reading is completely congruent with the context of the prior verse as well: "Either make the tree good and its fruit good, or make the tree bad and its fruit bad, for the tree is known by its fruit." The passage has as its premise that there is a fundamental, organic relationship between the type of person one is and the type of heart one has and consequently what proceeds from it—and on the basis of this one is judged.

Thus, we can see that this passage from ch. 12 both agrees with the passage from ch. 15[102] and also answers a question that was left unaddressed: what is the cause of the evil thoughts, murders, adulteries, etc. that proceed out of the heart? Here in ch. 12 we see that it is the heart itself and its evil nature.[103]

If the heart were understood as a body part like all the others, there would be little more to be observed about its use as a metaphor for the source of sin. Matthew's use of heart imagery is thus in keeping with its use in the Second Temple literature examined in part 1.[104] The heart (καρδία/לבב/לב) is, however, an unusual part of the body. Given the wide range of functions attributed to it (an organ of thought, understanding, decision, and volition, the source of courage, and the seat of the emotions and belief or unbelief), many scholars have seen it to stand for more than the sum of its functions. The "heart" becomes a metaphor for the "inner person" in general.[105] In this, it is not far from the use

---

102   "But the things that proceed out of the mouth come from the heart, and those defile a person. For out of the heart come evil thoughts, murders, adulteries, fornications, thefts, false witness, blasphemies. These are the things which defile a person; but eating with unwashed hands does not defile a person."

103   Though the conjunction of καρδία with πονηρ- is not common in the LXX, the idea that people might have an evil heart was certainly no innovation of Jesus or Matthew. The book of Jeremiah particularly uses the language of an evil (and often stubborn) heart: Jer 3:17, 5:23, 16:12, 18:12. See also Eccl 8:11 and 9:3 (note the similarity in the use of the idea of the heart being filled with evil: καί γε καρδία υἱῶν τοῦ ἀνθρώπου ἐπληρώθη πονηροῦ καὶ περιφέρεια ἐν καρδίᾳ αὐτῶν ἐν ζωῇ αὐτῶν), Dan 11:27, and Bar 2:8. The idea of the evil heart is also present in Rabbinic literature. There, while the heart tends to be associated with the *yetser ha-ra*, there are other texts that assert that a person has two hearts, an evil and a good, each directed by its respective *yetser* (Solomon Schechter, *Some Aspects of Rabbinic Theology* [New York: Macmillan, 1910], 243–244, 255–263).

104   See relevant sections above regarding the heart in *1 Enoch*, *Jubilees*, *4 Ezra*, Sirach, 1QH, CD, and 1QS.

105   "It stands for the central part in general, the inside, and so for *the interior man* as manifesting himself in all his various activities" (Goodwin, "On the Use of לב and Καρδία," 67); on לבב/לב in the OT: "Fig[uratively] the 'innermost part of man'" (*TDNT* 3:606) and in the NT: "The heart is the centre of the inner life of man and the source or seat of all the forces and functions of the souls and spirit" (*TDNT* 3:611).

of soul (נֶפֶשׁ/ψυχή)[106] or mind (νοῦς).[107] It has thus been understood to stand for one's "self."[108] If this is the case then, we are no longer really talking about a *body part* that is the source of sin—it is neither a *part* nor really an aspect of the physical *body*.[109] If the heart is representative of one's inner self (as opposed to the external) and all its faculties, then the use of this metaphor for the cause of sin points to something fundamental within a person. This certainly is consistent with the combination of tree/fruit imagery and heart imagery in 12:33–35 and perhaps also with the plant imagery used in the context of 15:17.[110] If the heart does indeed represent one's inner self as a metaphorical source of sin, then it is not far removed from our next set of images—those that are

106 "The ancients did not make the nice mental and linguistic analyses of modern thought. They used לֵב, καρδία, בִּינָה, νοῦς, &c., for the whole inner man, now with special reference to one special faculty, or state, and now to another. But καρδία, for example, is *never* in the New Testament contradistinguished from or contrasted with νοῦς, or διάνοια, &c.; and, when put side by side with them, it is by parallelism rather than distinction. Thus, when it is said thou shalt love the Lord thy God with all thy heart (καρδία) and with all thy soul (ψυχή) and with all thy mind (διάνοια), it is not meant that heart, soul, mind, are distinct parts of man; each is the whole inner man, and they are all put together to make the expression of totality the stronger" (Goodwin, "On the Use of לֵב and Καρδία," 71). It should be noted, however, that καρδία is never used to translate נֶפֶשׁ in the LXX (cf. *TDNT* 3:609), and that while perhaps not employing "the nice mental and linguistic analyses of modern thought," the translators of the LXX were notably consistent in translating לֵב וּנֶפֶשׁ as καρδία και ψυχή, thus indicating that these terms, if not quite precise, were not quite interchangeable either as one might expect them to be if they were really conceived of as each being "the whole inner man."

107 So Bultmann regarding Paul's use: "Paul uses 'heart' to a large extent synonymously with *nous*; viz. to designate the self as a willing, planning, intending self" (*Theology of the New Testament*, 220–221).

108 Many commentators make this move. For example: "In the biblical tradition, the heart (= *lēb, lēbāb*) is the real or true self, the psyche at its deepest level" (Davies and Allison, *A Critical and Exegetical Commentary*, 1:456). There is certainly evidence in the LXX that the translators took לֵב to be analogous to the self. For example, in Num 16:28 the Hebrew has "for [I have] not [done them] of mine own heart (מִלִּבִּי)" but the LXX renders that "[I have] not [done them] of myself (οὐκ ἀπ' ἐμαυτοῦ)." Similarly, Isa 57:17 has in the Hebrew "in the way of his heart" (בְּדֶרֶךְ לִבּוֹ) while the LXX has ἐν ταῖς ὁδοῖς αὐτοῦ.

109 This is not to imply, however, that there was a clear distinction between the "physical" (body) and the "spiritual" (soul) in the conception of the self among the biblical writers or ancients more generally. In fact, the opposite.

110 Luz sees Jesus declaration against the Pharisees in 15:13 that "every plant that my heavenly Father has not planted will be rooted up" as alluding back to the Parable of the Wheat and the Tares, a parable where one's fundamental nature (as determined by one's parent/planter) is certainly the cause of one's righteous or sinful deeds and subsequent judgment (*Matthew 8–20*, 333).

METAPHORS FOR THE CAUSE OF SIN

genetic and familial—and in fact acts as a bridge from the body part metaphors to the genetic metaphors.[111]

3.1   *Summary*

Matthew sometimes indicates the cause of sin to be located within the body of the one who sins. The use of the metaphor of the body parts of hand, foot, or eye as a cause of sin generally pits the part against the whole: the sin-causing part can be recognized as detrimental to the future good of the whole of the person, and thus it must be excised. Metaphors or illness and infirmity portray sin as an unnatural state that prevents the sinner from living or responding to Jesus in the way that God intends—Jesus is sent to be a physician for the sinners not the righteous (those who do God's will), the blind eyes and deaf ears cannot understand the message of the kingdom and therefore do not repent. The metaphor of the heart as a cause of sin moves in a more holistic direction for, although the literal heart is a single organ of the body, its traditional symbolic use as representing one's inner self—intellect, will, emotions, and decision-making faculties—portray sin in this case as arising from the deepest parts of the human.

---

111   This would also make sensible the interweaving of the genetic and heart metaphors that we have already just touched on above, and which will become plain in the following section.

CHAPTER 11

Genetic and Familial Metaphors for the Cause of Sin

It is not a far step from the idea that sin is caused by a part of one's physical body that represents one's "inner person" or "self" to the portrayal of certain people as inherently, genetically evil and permeated with sin. This idea is communicated in Matthew through the use of genetic[1] and familial metaphors. This type of imagery is present in four different forms: in the metaphor of a tree and its fruit, in animal metaphors, in Jesus' and John the Baptist's use of negative familial epithets for their opponents, and in the botanical metaphors of the Parable of the Wheat and the Tares.

1   Tree and Fruit Metaphors

In the passage from ch. 12 most recently examined above, we saw how the sin that flows out of a person was portrayed as the expelled contents of an evil heart and that this is analogous to a tree and its fruit. We now turn to a closer examination of this passage and its doublet in ch. 7.[2]

The passage in which the tree/fruit saying is located in ch. 12 begins with verse 31 and extends to the end of verse 37.[3] Verses 31–32 and 36–37 are both

---

1   The use of the term "genetic" is obviously anachronistic to the text. Ancient writers might have used terms like "$\phi\acute{\nu}\sigma\iota\varsigma$" (as in Jas 3:7) or "$\gamma\acute{\epsilon}\nu\sigma\varsigma$" (with the obvious connection to our term "genetic") as in Mt 13:47, Mk 9:29, 1 Cor 12:10, etc. Yet the underlying idea of a hereditary trait is not a modern discovery, and thus "genetic" will function as shorthand for that idea.

2   It could be argued that the tree/fruit logion is not a true Matthean doublet. The relationship between Mt, Lk, and Q at this point is complex. The saying is not found in Mk, and in both Mt and Lk it is included in the Sermon on the Mount/Plain. The first two verses of tree/fruit material in Luke's sermon, 6:43 and 44, are paralleled in Mt 7:18 and 16, respectively. Mt 7:17, 19 and 20 expand on the tree fruit theme with material not directly paralleled in Lk, but Luke continues in verse 45 with material paralleled in Mt 12:34–35. The fact that Mt's and Lk's sermons then continue with parallel material (Those who "call me 'Lord, Lord!'" [Lk 6:46 and Mt 7:21–23] and the Wise and Foolish Builders [Lk 6:47–49 and Mt 7:24–27]) indicate that the material was likely grouped so in Q or Matthew borrowed from Luke. In either case, the tree/fruit material in Matthew is not a true doublet since it seems that Mt took the material of Q/Lk 6:45 and moved it to the center of Mt 12:31–37.

3   "Therefore I tell you, every sin and blasphemy will be forgiven people, but the blasphemy against the Spirit will not be forgiven. And whoever speaks a word against the Son of Man

---

© KONINKLIJKE BRILL NV, LEIDEN, 2020 | DOI:10.1163/9789004419506_013

GENETIC AND FAMILIAL METAPHORS FOR THE CAUSE OF SIN   173

about words as a criterion in the Judgment, and the intervening verses give the rationale for this: words are a manifestation of the character of a person.[4] Matthew uses two metaphors here. We have already examined the use of the heart metaphor, above. In looking at the tree/fruit metaphor, we find that Matthew utilizes the adjectives καλός and σαπρός to characterize the types of tree. As we will see below, this is the same dualistic pair employed in describing the fish in the Parable of the Net (13:48) and in another use of the tree/fruit metaphor in 7:17–18 where καλός and σαπρός are paralleled with ἀγαθός and πονηρός. So here also: the tree and the fruit it produces—either καλός or σαπρός—is paralleled with the heart and the treasure brought forth—either ἀγαθός or πονηρός, and this second pair of adjectives are, we have already seen, connected to God and Satan respectively. The parallelism of the adjectives thus tends to link these terms such that καλός becomes associated with ἀγαθός and thus also with God and righteousness, and σαπρός with πονηρός and thus with Satan and sin.

In this passage, however, the tree/fruit metaphor itself and the way it is employed are in some tension. The statement "a tree is known by its fruit" fits well with the sense of the following verses: "How can you speak good, being evil" and "The good person out of his good treasure brings forth good." These statements indicate that people have a fundamental nature that will naturally become manifest in their actions. The beginning of verse 37, however, indicates otherwise. On the surface, Jesus' command to "either make the tree good and its fruit good or make the tree rotten and its fruit rotten" portrays people

---

will be forgiven, but whoever speaks against the Holy Spirit will not be forgiven, either in this age or in the age to come. Either make the tree good (καλὸν) and its fruit good (καλὸν), or make the tree rotten (σαπρὸν) and its fruit rotten (σαπρὸν), for the tree is known by its fruit. You offspring of vipers! How can you speak good (ἀγαθὰ), being evil (πονηροὶ)? For out of that which fills the heart, the mouth speaks. The good (ἀγαθὸς) person out of his good (ἀγαθοῦ) treasure brings forth good (ἀγαθά), and the evil (πονηρὸς) person out of his evil (πονηροῦ) treasure brings forth evil (πονηρά). I tell you, on the day of judgment people will give account for every careless word they speak, for by your words you will be justified, and by your words you will be condemned." Verses 31–37 are obviously all of a piece since vv. 31 and 37 introduce and conclude the section by indicating that the theme is that one will be judged by one's words (see above).

4   In this case, the determining factor of the good or evil character that will be manifest is whether the person recognizes Jesus as animated by the Holy Spirit and thus doing the will of God and with His authority (as Matthew has already informed us in his application of the Isaiah quote in 12:18: "Behold, my servant whom I have chosen, my beloved with whom my soul is well pleased. I will put my Spirit upon him") or whether one will blaspheme as the Pharisees do and not simply criticize Jesus himself ("the Son of Man," v. 32) but assert that what he is doing is at the impulse and by the authority not of God's Holy Spirit but of Beelzebul (12:24 and 28).

174   CHAPTER 11

as having some control over what their nature may be and thus the fruit they will produce. The command is in tension with the metaphor itself. If, however, we set aside the intellectual problem of a tree becoming an agent in its own change and look at the more obvious message, we see that it fits with one of Matthew's ongoing themes: the necessity of consistency between inner and outer and the rejection of hypocrisy.

The theme of hypocrisy plays a significant role in the use of the tree/fruit metaphor in the passage in ch. 7 as well. The passage begins with a different but complimentary genetic metaphor: "Beware of false prophets, who come to you in sheep's clothing but inwardly are thieving[5] wolves."[6] Jesus switches immediately from animal to botanical metaphors, however, for his instructions to his hearers on how to identify these "wolves":

> You will recognize them by their fruits. Are grapes gathered from thorn bushes, or figs from thistles? Just so, every good (ἀγαθὸν) tree produces good (καλοὺς) fruit, but the rotten (σαπρὸν) tree produces bad (πονηροὺς) fruit. A good (ἀγαθὸν) tree cannot produce bad (πονηροὺς) fruit, nor can a rotten (σαπρὸν) tree produce good (καλοὺς) fruit. Every tree that does not produce good (καλὸν) fruit is cut down and thrown into the fire. Thus, you will recognize them by their fruits.[7]

The obvious message is that one's underlying character—good or rotten—will be manifest in one's "fruit." Actions that are πονηρός are the result of an underlying rottenness of character that will result ultimately in judgment ("cut down and thrown into the fire"). Whether this rottenness is innate or can somehow be acquired (thus putting this metaphor more in the category of "illness") is

---

5   The adjective ἅρπαγες, since it is derived from ἁρπάζω (to grasp, seize, plunder, or rob [DBAG, 134]), evokes the sense of illicitly snatching away. Not surprisingly, being full of thievery or "plundering" is one of the charges against the scribes and Pharisees in ch. 23 (ἔσωθεν δὲ γέμουσιν ἐξ ἁρπαγῆς, v. 25), and plundering or "snatching away" is also what the evil one does to the word of the kingdom that is sown in the heart of one who does not understand (ἔρχεται ὁ πονηρὸς καὶ ἁρπάζει τὸ ἐσπαρμένον ἐν τῇ καρδίᾳ αὐτοῦ). "Plundering" (ἁρπάζω) is also what Jesus intends to do to the house of "the Strong Man" (12:29), and what "the violent" have been doing to the Kingdom of Heaven since the days of John the Baptist (11:12). It is possible that this last saying also refers to the Pharisees since, as we have noted, they are characterized as ἁρπαγῆς in ch. 23, and are also accused of making their proselytes children of hell and shutting the kingdom of heaven off from people (23:13–15) as well as being, like their fathers, violent in their opposition to God's chosen messengers (23:29–36). See also below on γενεὰν in 23:36.

6   7:15. The use of animal metaphors, which are also genetic, will be explored further below.

7   7:16–20.

GENETIC AND FAMILIAL METAPHORS FOR THE CAUSE OF SIN   175

not clear from the use of the metaphor itself, but when put in conjunction with the introductory verse and its use of animal metaphors, the implication is that being σαπρός is analogous to being a "wolf" and thus an inherent or genetic trait not an acquired one. Further, the second verse of the passage uses an explicitly genetic botanical metaphor in asking the question: "Are grapes gathered from thorn bushes, or figs from thistles?" The obvious answer is no, and the use of the connector οὕτως emphasizes that the same dynamics are present in the metaphor that follows: good trees produce good fruit, rotten trees produce bad fruit. The depth and pervasiveness of the "goodness" or "rottenness" is such that they are οὕτως the depth and pervasiveness of the genetic difference between grape vines and thorn bushes.

The clear connection between one's inner character and one's outer actions is, however, problematized in the following verses. 7:21–23 functions as an extended "Nevertheless ..." to the simple correspondence of character and actions indicated in vv. 16–20. The "fruit" put forward as evidence in verses 21 and 22 by those who did not do God's will certainly seems to be "good fruit": calling Jesus "Lord," prophesying in Jesus' name, exorcisms, and mighty works in Jesus' name.[8] So, seemingly in contradiction to the initial botanical metaphors of the passage, Jesus warns that this good fruit is not necessarily indicative of being "good."[9] Some who seem good—who seem to have good fruit, seem to be sheep—are not what they seem. While Jesus warns his hearers to be wary and on their guard (Προσέχετε!, 7:15), and certainly with the intention of helping them to avoid such deceivers, it is also clear that it will only be Jesus who will "on that day" be able to discern who were rotten and who produced

---

8   7:21–23: "Not everyone saying to me, 'Lord, Lord,' will enter the kingdom of heaven, but the one doing the will of my Father in heaven. Many will say to me in that day, 'Lord, Lord, did we not in your name prophesy, and in your name cast out demons, and in your name do many mighty works?' And then will I declare to them, 'I never knew you; depart from me, you workers of lawlessness.'" Note that the activities cited by these "workers of lawlessness" in their apologetic to Jesus are the same tasks Jesus set for the disciples in their missionary journey in 10:1–15, esp. vv. 7–8, so apparently the issue is not the activity, but despite outward appearances of righteous behavior (as with the Pharisees in ch. 23), the inner ἀνομία and lack of actual acceptance of Jesus as God's authoritative messenger (as opposed to the apparent lip service of those who say "Lord, lord!").

9   It is possible that the "fruit" that will result from one's inner character could be something other than outwardly observable action, but this would be then hard to identify ("by their fruit you will know them"). There is nothing particularly indicated in Matthew's use of the term καρπός that would point toward something other than outward actions as the meaning of "fruit." On the contrary, the recurring emphasis on inner and outer and the need for congruity between them would indicate that fruit is indeed outwardly righteous behavior. Cf. John the Baptist's exhortation to the Pharisees: "Produce fruit befitting repentance" (3:8), also utilizing the inner/outer theme.

good fruit—regardless of appearances[10]—and thus who is eligible to enter the Kingdom.[11] Jesus' twice repeated statement that ἀπὸ τῶν καρπῶν αὐτῶν ἐπιγνώσεσθε αὐτούς is thus not as easily applicable as it first seems. Still, the overall emphasis of the passage and of the tree/fruit metaphor is that sin (καρπός πονηρός) is the natural result of pervasive internal corruption of character so fundamental as to be analogous to a distinction among species.

The blending of two kinds of genetic images is also present in John the Baptist's exhortation and warning to the Pharisees and Sadducees:

> But when he saw many of the Pharisees and Sadducees coming for baptism, he said to them, "You offspring of vipers! Who warned you to flee from the imminent wrath? Produce fruit befitting repentance. And do not think to say to yourselves, 'We have Abraham as our father,' for I tell you, God is able from these stones to raise up children for Abraham. Already the axe is laid to the root of the trees. Every tree therefore that does not produce good fruit is cut down and thrown into the fire."[12]

Here again we see the theme of a tree and its fruit, and the tree that does not produce good fruit (καρπὸν καλόν) will be found unworthy and subject to judgment and punishment. The outward fruit that should be produced in this context is that which befits the inward experience of repentance, thus again emphasizing the necessity of congruence of inner and outer and of a lack of hypocrisy.

Botanical images are not the only genetic metaphors utilized, however. John's initial address to the Pharisees and Sadducees is to call them "offspring[13] of vipers." The phrase conjoins familial and animal images into a single metaphor. The phrase is also employed by Jesus and will be discussed further below.

---

10   Cf. the Wheat and the Tares, esp. the fact that the ζιζάνιά resemble the good wheat (*BDAG*, 429), and it is not until the "harvest" that the wheat and weeds will be distinguished (13:28–30, 40–42).

11   On the possibility that "Depart from me, you workers of lawlessness!" combined with the works pointed to by the wolves/rotten trees indicates that Matthew is engaged in polemic against antinomian charismatics, again see the refutation of this reading by Davison in "*Anomia* and the Question of an Antinomian Polemic in Matthew," 617–635. Again, also note that Jesus accuses the Pharisees of lawlessness (23:28), although it is not because they do not rigorously keep the law and thus can hardly be described as antinomian in the traditional sense, but because they do not correctly prioritize the greatest and second commandments as they should.

12   3:7–10.

13   *LSJ* 344: γέννημα = that which is produced or born, a child; and γεννηματίζω = produce offspring.

GENETIC AND FAMILIAL METAPHORS FOR THE CAUSE OF SIN 177

In this passage, however, it functions particularly to set up the contrast with the later use of familial language. John sets out the character of his hearers immediately at the start of his discourse, and his designation is that they are children of vipers.[14] As Keener notes, "'Viper' was certainly an insult ... [and] 'children of vipers' carries the insult further."[15] This is apparently in contrast with his hearers' self-perception as children of Abraham. John, however, insists that with regard to the imminent wrath, mere physical genetics will avail nothing. What will count is the production of good fruit that is the natural result of a good nature—a nature God can impart even to the most unlikely candidates, rocks—but which the hearers lack, and which invalidates any apparent authenticity in the repentance represented in their coming for baptism. The Pharisees and Sadducees have the hereditary nature of vipers, and this nature will not produce the sort of fruit that will prevent them from being cast into the fire. Thus, in this passage, the metaphors for causes of sin are mutually reinforcing: the tree/fruit metaphor used elsewhere to indicate sin as a product of one's inner nature is strengthened here by the complementary use of familial and animal metaphors that indicate an underlying nature that makes John's hearers incapable of true repentance and thus incapable of producing the fruits of it necessary to, ultimately, avoid judgment and punishment.

2   Animal Metaphors

Above we discussed briefly Jesus' use of animal metaphors in 7:15: "Beware of false prophets, who come to you in sheep's clothing but inwardly are thieving wolves." These two animal metaphors are also used in Matthew in 10:16. There, before sending them out to preach, heal, and exorcise, Jesus warns his disciples, "Behold, I am sending you out as sheep in the midst of wolves, so be wise as

---

14   On the possibility that John is connecting the Pharisees and Sadducees with the ὄφις of Gen 3, Keener points that John uses "viper" (ἔχιδνα) rather than "serpent" (ὄφις) in his denunciation, and that although by the first century Jewish writers had already connected the character of Satan with the serpent of Eden, the phrase γεννήματα ἐχιδνῶν in 3:7 does not indicate that John is calling the Pharisees and Sadducees offspring of Satan since ὄφις and ἔχιδνα are not the same (*Gospel of Matthew*, 122). Still, Jesus' application of both terms successively to the Pharisees and scribes in 23:33 ("ὄφεις γεννήματα ἐχιδνῶν!" where γεννήματα ἐχιδνῶν functions as an appositive for ὄφεις) should restrain us from over-interpreting the difference between the two. As will be seen below in our examination of the Wheat and the Tares, Matthew certainly does think that those who are οἱ ποιηταὶ τὴν ἀνομίαν are children of the devil, and as we have seen, internal ἀνομία is one of the charges against the Pharisees and scribes (23:28).

15   Keener, *Gospel of Matthew*, 122; see also cited primary and secondary literature.

178 CHAPTER 11

serpents and innocent as doves."[16] In the previous passage that employed the wolf metaphor (7:15), we were told that the people so represented were false prophets—an extremely serious charge within Judaism.[17] Here, whether Jesus is referring to precisely the same group or simply using the same metaphor, the implication is the same: these are people who are naturally and violently opposed to God's activities in the world and to those who carry them out, just as wolves are invariably, perpetually antagonistic and predatory toward sheep. Further, their behavior, as indicated in 10:17–18 and 24–25[18] is congruent with the description of the false prophets as ἅρπαγες in 7:15[19]—violent and rapacious. Thus, whether the two groups called "wolves" are the same or not, the sins associated with them are similar and are portrayed as the expected and predictable product of their nature.[20]

A somewhat different dynamic is present in the use of genetic animal metaphors in the Parable of the Net.[21] In this parable, while we have a genetic metaphor used to distinguish the bad from the good, all the creatures gathered

---

16 Since the command to "be wise as serpents and innocent as doves" is a simile, it is technically outside the purview of our study, but as was discussed in the introduction, a simile is simply a metaphor in which the tension has been reduced by the emphasis on similarity through the addition of *like* or *as*. This second pair of images also parallels and thus reinforces the wolves/sheep dichotomy since serpents like wolves were understood to be cunning but dangerous, and doves, like sheep, were thought of as weak and timid (Keener, *Gospel of Matthew*, 322). The fact that Jesus is commanding his followers to be like both—if not quite to embody both natures, at least to operate in two seemingly contrary manners—provides an interesting complication to the recurring emphasis on avoiding hypocrisy.

17 Deut 18:20: "But the prophet who presumes to speak a word in my name which I have not commanded him to speak, or who speaks in the name of other gods, that same prophet shall die."

18 Delivering Jesus' apostles before the courts, having them flogged in synagogues, and dragging them before Gentile authorities (v. 17–18) as well as maligning them as being in league with the devil (vv. 24–25).

19 And, if the use of ἅρπαγες does indeed form a verbal connection to the denunciation of the Pharisees in ch. 23 (note 5, above), the prophesied treatment of the apostles is analogous to the treatment of the prophets by the forefathers of the Pharisees, treatment which Jesus expects the Pharisees as the heirs of that nature also to engage in.

20 Note also that Jesus followers are portrayed as having the nature of sheep, not only here but also in 18:12–13 ("If a man has a hundred sheep and one of them has gone astray...."). As Keener notes, "Jesus portrays his followers as powerless in their own strength.... Sheep were notoriously defenseless against such predators as wolves.... [yet] his sheep are actually *sent* among the predators" (*Gospel of Matthew*, 321–322).

21 13:47–50: "Again, the kingdom of heaven is like a net that was thrown into the sea and gathered every kind [of fish]. When it was full, drawing it ashore and sitting down, they gathered the good into containers but threw the rotten outside. Thus, it will be at the completion of the age. The angels will come out and separate the evil from among the

GENETIC AND FAMILIAL METAPHORS FOR THE CAUSE OF SIN 179

up by the net are the same basic type—fish or at least seafood[22]—unlike the portrayal in ch. 10 of some as wolves and some as sheep (obviously antagonistic and contrary animals). Here, we have a dynamic more like that which we saw in the use of metaphors of good and bad trees. We even have the use of the same terminology: those "fish" who are eventually judged righteous are called καλός and those deemed by the angels to be evil (πονηρός) are called σαπρός. Here, of course, no mention is made of "fruit" as a criterion for judging whether the fish is καλός or σαπρός. Here the judgment is made solely on the basis of the fish's "kind" (γένος). Here, the metaphorical representation of one's nature being determinative at the judgment is most explicit. This verse is Matthew's only use of γένος.[23] The basic definition of γένος is a race or family,[24] but it also indicates more generally "class, sort, or kind" or in the case of animals, breed or species.[25] The use in the Parable of the Net is certainly in line with the basic definition, particularly in the context of separating one γένος of fish from another. So, in our present passage, the separation that is envisioned takes place not between good and rotten (καλός and σαπρός) fish within a species, but between those species of fish that are καλός and those that are σαπρός. As Keener notes, the passage draws on the common cultural occurrence of "fishermen separating the edible and kosher fish from the inedible ones." This was necessary since many species of fish in the Sea of Galilee "were unclean or inedible, and the net would not discriminate."[26] The uncleanness or inedibility of a particular fish was a function of its γένος, implying that, for people, being δίκαιος or πονηρός (with consequent outward manifestations) is a function of one's γένος.

---

righteous, and they will throw them into the furnace of fire. There will be weeping and gnashing of teeth."

22   The Greek of the passage nowhere specifies what is gathered and separated, simply that it was "every kind," and given the nature of a dragnet, it might well have gathered all sorts of aquatic animals as well as a variety of debris—debris that certainly would have been counted as σαπρός and cast away and disposed of.

23   There is broad agreement that 17:21 ("This kind [γένος]only goes out by prayer and fasting") is a later addition, although the use of γένος there does accord with its use in 13:47, with the other NT texted cited below, and with the basic definition that informs the argument.

24   Thus, its use in much of the rest of the NT (e.g., Mk 7:26; Acts 4:6, 7:13, 7:19, 13:26, 17:28–29; 2 Cor 11:26; Gal 1:14; Phil 3:5; 1 Pet 2:9); similarly, it indicates the home region or town of an individual (e.g., Acts 4:36, 18:2, 18:24).

25   LSJ 344: γένος = "race, stock, kin"; III.a: "generally, race, of beings"; III.1.e: "of animals, breed"; v.a: "class, sort, kind."

26   Keener, Gospel of Matthew, 392. Again here, the conception of the Kingdom is temporal— there will be a time when all will be gathered (as in an indiscriminate net), and then they will be separated and put in their appropriate places, the πονηρός being cast away or outside (ἔξω, cf. 5:13 and 21:39, as well as τὸ σκότος τὸ ἐξώτερον in 22:13).

180   CHAPTER 11

This conception of a correlation between one's species (γένος) and outward manifestations such as actions is also portrayed in the Parable of the Sheep and the Goats.[27] As with the Parable of the Net, the scenario begins with a gathering of those to be separated—in this case, "all the nations" (πάντα τὰ ἔθνη)[28] replaces the "every kind [of fish]" (ἐκ παντὸς γένους). In some senses, this parable combines in a much-extended form the elements of the Parable of the Net with the dynamics of the tree/fruit metaphor. Here, as with the Parable of the Net, the two kinds are gathered and then separated, but the judgment of whether each is good or bad is made on the basis of their "fruit" (actions). Unlike with the tree/fruit metaphor, however, rather than simply describing the "fruit" as καλός/ἀγαθός or σαπρός, the good or bad actions that are the result of their nature are described.[29] Also, there is a notable change in the terminology applied to the two kinds: rather than being described as either δίκαιος/ καλός or πονηρός, the sheep and goats are called "blessed of my father" and "cursed"[30] respectively.[31] In both this parable and the uses of the tree/fruit metaphor, the importance of the works/fruit is emphasized.

The action of the parable closely parallels that in the Parable of the Net. In both cases the divine and/or angelic figures separate creatures based on their outwardly visible γένος and assign them a place either in the Kingdom or in fiery torment (13:50, 25:41). Here in the Parable of the Sheep and the Goats, the fundamental connection between one's metaphorical kind or species and the actions one does is more explicit. Although one might argue that it is the *actions themselves* which make one a "sheep" or "goat," there is no indication in the text that either species had ever been at some time something other than what they ultimately are and that, through a series of choices, a transformation had taken place such that one either quickly or over time attains to a certain kind of character (sheep or goat). In fact, one could argue that the very use of

---

27   As discussed in the introduction, parables are really elaborate extended metaphors, sometimes (as in this case and, for example, the Wheat and the Tares) bordering on allegory.

28   The question of whether πάντα τὰ ἔθνη refers to all people in the world, only the Gentiles, or even only the church has been much debated. For the purposes of our study, however, the question is moot: regardless of who is envisioned as comprising πάντα τὰ ἔθνη, their genetic status as sheep or goats is made manifest in their treatment of τῶν ἀδελφῶν μου τῶν ἐλαχίστων.

29   "I was naked, and you did/did not clothe me. I was sick, and you did/did not visit me ..." etc.

30   "οἱ εὐλογημένοι τοῦ πατρός μου" (v. 34) and "οἱ κατηραμένοι" (v. 41).

31   It should be noted, however, that in v. 46 the sheep are called δίκαιος: "And these [goats] will go away into eternal punishment, but the righteous into eternal life." This obviously again reinforces the Matthean understanding of righteousness as a definitive characteristic of those who enter the kingdom.

GENETIC AND FAMILIAL METAPHORS FOR THE CAUSE OF SIN

the genetic metaphor undercuts the idea that one can choose to be a sheep or goat. Both of these positions, however, ask a question on which the text is silent—which came first: the action or the nature of the actor? The key feature is the presentation here of the Matthean theme which we have already seen in abundance: one's actions are a manifestation of one's nature, the outward will indicate the character of the inward, "by their fruits you will know them."

The final animal metaphor to note[32] is one which we have already discussed at some length above: the use of the term "serpents" or "offspring of vipers" as an epithet for Jesus' opponents. As we noted, the combined use of "serpents" and "offspring of vipers" in Jesus' address to the scribes and Pharisees in 23:33 may somewhat mitigate the difference between the terms; still, the choice to insert this term to augment the use of "offspring of vipers" in this passage points to its significance and the need to explore the various attributes associated with serpents, especially in the Septuagintal tradition that is most likely to have influenced Matthew's choice of terminology.[33] The connection

---

32 There are other uses of animal imagery with ethical connotations, though generally they do not shed much light on the question of the cause of sin and evil, and are not being considered at length. For example, in 8:31–32, we hear that the demons cast out of the Gadarenes went into a herd of pigs causing them to become suicidal. This does not tell us much about the cause of sin, though it does present the analogy of one who is possessed to the pigs (unclean and, in this case, not in control of his self-destructive tendencies). The question of possession and the influence of Satan will be explored more below. We also see the use of porcine imagery combined with canine imagery in 7:6 ("Do not give dogs [κύων] what is holy; and do not throw your pearls before swine, lest they trample them under foot and turn to attack you"). Here the patent purpose of the saying is that the hearer apply the characteristics of dog and swine to certain kinds of people, but the complete association of the nature of the animal metaphorically with particular persons seems more tenuous. Similarly, in 15:26–27 the metaphorical application of the epithet "dog" (κυνάριον) to the Syro-Phoenician woman may be holistic, but it is not necessarily indicative of a source of sin for which she will be judged unworthy of the Kingdom; rather it is indicative of her social situation vis-à-vis Palestinian Judaism. Further symbolic references to animals without distinct connotations regarding sinfulness: dove (10:16: "be ... as ἀκέραιος as doves"—simple/unmixed, innocent, lacking guile, esp. as the opposite of the φρόνιμος serpent; cf. 6:22 "If your eye is ἁπλοῦς ..."), camel (as large, 19:24 and 23:24), gnat (as small, 23:24), sparrows (as common and thus cheap/unimportant, 10:29 and 31), birds (as heedless, 6:26), sheep (as helpless and wandering when lacking a shepherd's care, 9:36, 10:6, 15:24, 26:31), vultures (as indicators of carrion, 24:28).

33 The wider cultural connotations of the serpent figure (in its various manifestations, not just ὄφις) are plural and complexly related. On this topic, see the comprehensive study *The Good and Evil Serpent: How a Universal Symbol Became Christianized* by James H. Charlesworth (ABRL [New Haven: Yale University Press, 2010]). Although some of these connotations no doubt impinged on Matthew's thinking, the attributes associated with ὄφεις in the LXX texts is very much in keeping with his critique of Jesus' opponents, as will become apparent.

182   CHAPTER 11

with the ὄφις of Gen 3 is a predictable connection. The initial characterization
of the serpent as φρονιμώτατος indicates a prudence with regard to one's own
interests that does not necessarily excluded cunning craftiness, especially in as
much as φρονιμώτατος translates the Hebrew עָרוּם.[34]

Overall, however, there are a number of consistent attributes of ὄφεις in the
LXX. The most common is their danger and the fear that it inspires. In Gen 3,
one of the consequences of the Adam and Eve's sin and expulsion from Eden
is enmity between humans and serpents, and the danger that goes along with
it ("he will strike your heel" 3:15). The primordial enmity forms the backdrop
of further passages that refer to the inherent danger of encounters with serpents. In Jacob's testamentary prophecies over his sons he declares, "Dan shall
be a serpent in the way, a viper by the path, that bites the horse's heels so that
his rider falls backward."[35] The common understanding of the danger of serpents undergirds the prophecy. Similarly, in Ex 3:4 when Moses' staff becomes
a serpent, he initially shrinks back from it in terror.[36] When the people com-
plained to Moses about the rations in the wilderness, "the Lord sent fiery serpents (ὄφεις) among the people, and they bit the people, so that many people
of Israel died."[37] Serpents are one of the dangers faced by Israel in the wilderness is mentioned in Deut 8:15,[38] and Ecclesiastes[39] uses the danger of serpents
to issue parabolic warnings in its proverbs. Other texts which emphasize the
danger of serpents include: Isa 14:28–29, Isa 65:25, LXX Jer 26:22, Amos 5:19, and
Sir 21:2 and 25:15.[40] Serpents are also portrayed as destructive and deceitful as
in 4 Macc 18:8 and PsSol 4:11.

---

34   BDB 791.

35   Gen 49:17.

36   Notably, in the actual confrontation with the Egyptian sorcerers, (Ex 7:9–12) it is Aaron
      who casts down his rod, and it becomes a δράκων rather than an ὄφις, as do also the rods
      of the Egyptian sorcerers, although in Isa 27:1, it seems that δράκων may mean the same
      thing: "In that day God shall bring his holy and great and strong sword upon the dragon,
      the serpent that flees, upon the dragon, the crooked serpent: he shall destroy the dragon."
      It is seems clear here that "serpent" functions as an appositive for δράκων, and LSJ counts
      δράκων as "interchangeable with ὄφις" (448). Cf. Wis 16:5 and 10.

37   The deadly nature of the ὄφεις may be somewhat offset by the fact that the healing of the
      people was accomplished by looking at a serpent on a stick (Num 21:6–9), an incident that
      John applies to Jesus and the cross but which Matthew does not draw upon.

38   "[The LORD] led you through the great and terrible wilderness, with its fiery serpents and
      scorpions and thirsty ground where there was no water."

39   Eccl 10:8 and 10:11.

40   It should be noted that serpents were also sometimes portrayed as instruments of God's
      punishment, as in the Numbers text above. We find this in Job 20:16 (serpent's bite as a
      punishment of the unjust), LXX Jer 8:17–18 (God will send "serpents" against his sinful
      people), and Wis 16:1–5 ("Therefore those men were deservedly punished through such

GENETIC AND FAMILIAL METAPHORS FOR THE CAUSE OF SIN 183

Perhaps most importantly, twice in the LXX Psalms people are compared to ὄφεις. In LXX Ps 57:4–6, we read that "Sinners have gone astray from the womb. They go astray from the belly. They speak lies. Their venom is like that of a serpent." The use of the genetic imagery for the source of sin here is quite apparent, sinners being depicted as going astray even before birth (from the womb). In LXX Ps 139:2–4, David pleads, "Rescue me, O Lord, from the evil man; deliver me from the unjust man. Who have devised injustice in their hearts ... They have sharpened their tongue as of a serpent; the poison of asps is under their lips." In fact, the terms David uses for his enemies in the rest of the Psalm parallel the characterization in Matthew of Jesus' opponents and those who will not enter the kingdom: πονηρός (v. 2), ἄδικος (vv. 2, 5, and 12), ἁμαρτωλοί (vv. 5 and 9), and accused of setting snares and stumbling blocks (σκάνδαλον) (v. 6).

Thus, the application of the metaphorical epithet "Serpents!" to Jesus' opponents bespeaks a nature that is manifest in the behavior they display in the Gospel and entirely fitting with Jesus' charges against them in ch. 23 and elsewhere. Their sins of deceit, destruction, and endangerment are outworkings of their serpent-like nature.

Finally, as a composite metaphor, the related characterization of Jesus' opponents as "offspring of vipers" forms a bridge between the animal and the familial genetic metaphors in Matthew, and though it could be explored under either rubric, and we will consider it under the latter category.

3 Familial Metaphors

Matthew's recurrent use of familial language with ethical connotations, especially with regard to Jesus' opponents, further expands the range of genetic metaphors used in portraying the sources of sin. As we saw above at the end of the tree/fruit subsection, when the Pharisees and Sadducees come for baptism, John the Baptist's denunciation begins with "You offspring of vipers!" This introduces the theme of lineage and its ethical connotations in the passage, a theme then developed in the issue of the efficacy of Abrahamic lineage over against bearing "fruit befitting repentance."[41]

---

creatures, and were tormented by a multitude of animals.... when the terrible rage of wild beasts came upon thy people and they were being destroyed by the bites of writhing serpents, thy wrath did not continue to the end").

41 Notice also the parallelism between "When he saw the Pharisees coming.... 'You offspring of vipers!'" and "Then Jesus came ... and behold, a voice from heaven said, 'This is my beloved Son, with whom I am well pleased'" (3:7, 13, and 17).

184   CHAPTER 11

In total, the phrase γεννήματα ἐχιδνῶν is used three times in Matthew, once by John the Baptist in the above passage and twice by Jesus. It is applied by John the Baptist, as we have seen, to the Pharisees and Sadducees, by Jesus it is applied in 12:34 only to the Pharisees,[42] but in 23:33 it is applied to both the Pharisees and scribes.[43]

We have already touched on the passage in ch. 12, but let us return to it here. This passage makes up a portion of the Beelzebul controversy between Jesus and the Pharisees. Jesus says:

> Therefore I tell you, every sin and blasphemy will be forgiven people, but the blasphemy against the Spirit will not be forgiven. And if one should speak a word against the Son of Man, it will be forgiven him, but if one should speak against the Holy Spirit, it will not be forgiven him, either in this age or in the age to come. Either make the tree good and its fruit good, or make the tree bad and its fruit bad, for the tree is known by its fruit. You offspring of vipers! How can you, being evil, speak what is good? For out of that which fills the heart, the mouth speaks. The good person out of her good treasure brings forth what is good; and the evil person out of her evil treasure brings forth what is evil. And I say to you that for every careless word people shall speak, they shall render account in the day of judgment. For by your words you shall be justified, and by your words you shall be condemned.[44]

As we noted above in our examination of the heart metaphor in this passage, the interwoven metaphors of heart and tree/fruit reinforce the idea that one's inner nature (heart or type of tree) will determine the outward manifestations (words or fruit). This is further reinforced by the use of the epithet γεννήματα ἐχιδνῶν in addressing the Pharisees. The familial metaphor particularly emphasizes the idea that the situation of having a bad heart or being a bad tree is not a condition that is acquired but is preexisting and perhaps inherent.[45] In this

---

42   Or so it appears, based on the fact that it is only they who are mentioned in 12:24 as his accusers and ensuing adversaries in the controversy. Note, however, that the scribes are included with them in the passage that follows immediately (12:38ff) which also uses familial language.

43   Based on 23:29.

44   12:31–37.

45   Interestingly, the only use in Matthew of γένημα outside the three uses of γεννήματα ἐχιδνῶν is in 26:29 when Jesus says, "I tell you I shall not drink again of this fruit (γένημα) of the vine until that day when I drink it new with you in my Father's kingdom." Here the idea of fruit (grapes, in this case) as the offspring of plants hearkens back to the use of the tree/fruit metaphor and solidifies that connection in terms of the γεννήματα ἐχιδνῶν. In

GENETIC AND FAMILIAL METAPHORS FOR THE CAUSE OF SIN

regard, it presents the same picture as Ps 58:3 referenced above: "The wicked go astray from the womb, they go astray from their birth, speaking lies."[46] Taken together with Jesus' subsequent question, "How can you, *being evil*, speak what is good?," the overall impression is that those addressed are evil in their very natures, and that this nature is so longstanding and pervasive as to be comparable to one's familial genetic inheritance, and thus they produce bad fruit.

This characterization is reinforced and extended in the next passage in ch. 12, as the scribes join the Pharisees and approach Jesus saying, "Teacher, we wish to see a sign from you." Jesus' response is in keeping with the previous characterization of his opponents:

> An evil and adulterous generation [Γενεὰ πονηρὰ καὶ μοιχαλὶς] seeks for a sign, but no sign will be given it except the sign of the prophet Jonah.... The men of Nineveh will rise up at the judgment with this generation and condemn it, for they repented at the preaching of Jonah, and behold, something greater than Jonah is here. The queen of the South will rise up at the judgment with this generation and condemn it, for she came from the ends of the earth to hear the wisdom of Solomon, and behold, something greater than Solomon is here.[47]

Jesus' characterization of his opponents as members of γενεὰ πονηρὰ καὶ μοιχαλὶς bears some investigation. While γενεά ("generation") can have the sense of a time period as it does in 24:34[48] or, in the plural, a line of descendants (as in 1:17), Matthew's usual usage draws more on the non-chronological sense of the term: a group of people of the same family, tribe, class or kind, or even of the same homeland.[49] The term γενεά does not usually mean all the people living at the time of Jesus (or Matthew) or all Jews, as can be seen by looking at Matthew's other uses of γενεά. Before looking more closely at 12:38–45, let us examine these.

---

    fact, one might argue that the best translation to make this connection clear in English would be to render γεννήματα ἐχιδνῶν as "Fruits of vipers."

46   Cf. LXX 57:4: "Sinners have gone astray from the womb: they go astray from the belly: they speak lies."

47   12:38–42.

48   "Truly, I say to you, this generation will not pass away until all these things take place." However, given the rest of the evidence, it is quite possible that this use may not refer to a chronological generation.

49   *LSJ* 342: "γενεά ... I. of the persons in a family, 1. race, family.... 4. metaph., class, kind, ... II. of Time or Place, 1. Birthplace ... 2. age, time of life."

186 CHAPTER 11

In 11:16 Jesus asks, "To what shall I compare this generation [τὴν γενεὰν ταύτην]?" and then in 16b–19 he describes analogically the opposition to and rejection of both John and Jesus by "this generation."[50] Since it is obvious from the narrative that not all the people living at that time fit this description, Matthew is not using γενεά as a chronological descriptor but as a way of referring to people who are all of a sort. Further, not only in ch. 12 but again in ch. 16, the Pharisees come, this time with the Sadducees, asking Jesus to show them a sign.[51] Jesus responds, "When it is evening, you say, 'It will be fair weather, for the sky is red.' And in the morning, 'It will be stormy today, for the sky is red and threatening.' You know how to interpret the appearance of the sky, but you cannot interpret the signs of the times. An evil and adulterous generation seeks for a sign, but no sign will be given to it except the sign of Jonah."[52] Jesus again designates those seeking signs as γενεὰ πονηρὰ καὶ μοιχαλὶς, and again it is Jesus' opponents (the Pharisees and their current associates) to whom he is speaking. The disciples and the crowds do not ask Jesus for σημεῖα to confirm his authority;[53] it is a distinguishing characteristic of those who oppose Jesus—the group called an evil and adulterous generation.

Thus, regarding γενεά, Davies and Allison find that for Matthew "the term refers firstly not to chronological duration but to character, and it is pejorative."[54] Jesus once applies the term γενεά to his disciples (and perhaps also the crowd) in 17:17 in response to their inability to exorcise a demon. While he does use the term γενεά, he does not call them "an evil and adulterous generation" as he consistently calls his opponents, but calls his followers "a generation faithless and διεστραμμένη [wandering or twisted],"[55] critiques consistent with Jesus' other

---

50 "It is like children sitting in the marketplaces and calling to their playmates, 'We played the flute for you, and you did not dance; we sang a dirge, and you did not mourn.' For John came neither eating nor drinking, and they say, 'He has a demon.' The Son of Man came eating and drinking, and they say, 'Look at him! A glutton and a drunkard, a friend of tax collectors and sinners!' and 'Wisdom is justified by her deeds.'"

51 16:1: "And the Pharisees and Sadducees came, and to test him they asked him to show them a sign from heaven."

52 16:2–4.

53 Jesus' followers do ask him, "What will be the sign of your coming and of the close of the age?" (24:3) however, this interest in signs is apparently not blameworthy since it is premised on faith in Jesus' eschatological authority and not on skepticism.

54 A Critical and Exegetical Commentary, 2:260–61.

55 From διαστρέφω, "to turn different ways, twist about ... mostly Pass., to be distorted or twisted.... 2. metaph., distort, pervert.... II. turn aside, divert" (LSJ 413). Used only here in Matthew.

criticisms of his disciples' little faith[56] and his predictions that some of them will stray (πλανάω) and fall away (σκανδαλίζω in the passive).[57]

Thus, returning to ch. 12 we see that the use of γενεά draws on the sense of the term as referring to a class or kind, a family or tribal group, rather than referring to a chronological generation. This is particularly clear given the context, for those to whom Jesus compares his hearers unfavorably in verses 41–42 are not just people of another chronological γενεά, though of the same religious and ethnic group (faithful Jews of past ages), but rather people of a different ethnic γενεά—the people of Nineveh and the "queen of the South." However, it is not their ethnic γενεά that will cause them to be in a position to condemn the Pharisees, but their γενεά of those who respond to Jesus as the messenger and representative of God. It is people of that γενεά who will condemn the γενεά of those unresponsive to Jesus, regardless of the latter's status as part of the ethnic γενεά of the Jews.[58] Thus, the terminology of "offspring of vipers" and "evil and adulterous generation" are both genetic, familial metaphors that indicate that the group's members have an underlying similarity that causes them to act contrary to God's will.

That this γενεά is called πονηρά indicates a further aspect of the depiction of those opposed to Jesus: the connection of this γενεά to God's and Jesus' archetypal opponent, Satan. As noted previously, πονηρ- is one in a web of associated terms and ideas that form a network opposite to those terms associated with righteousness, God, and the Kingdom, the most opposed being God's and Jesus' enemy, the Evil One.[59] This connection between the γενεά πονηρά καὶ μοιχαλίς and Satan is not based solely on the use of πονηρά, however. The next passage makes explicit this connection between the devil and the γενεά of Jesus' opponents. The discussion of the γενεά πονηρά does not conclude with the comparison to the Ninevites and the Queen of the South, but continues with the following passage:

---

56   6:30, 8:26, 14:31, 16:8, and 17:20.

57   18:12–13, 24:4–5, 24:10–12, 24:24, and 26:31–33.

58   Note the congruity with Jesus' declaration to the centurion: "With no one in Israel have I found such faith! I tell you, many will come from east and west and recline at table with Abraham, Isaac, and Jacob in the kingdom of heaven, while the sons of the kingdom will be thrown into the outer darkness" (8:10–12).

59   "The kingdom of heaven may be compared to a man who sowed good seed in his field, but while his men were sleeping, his enemy came and sowed weeds among the wheat and went away … The one who sows the good seed is the Son of Man. The field is the world, and the good seed is the children of the kingdom. The weeds are the sons of the Evil One and the enemy who sowed them is the devil" (13:24 and 37–39).

When the unclean spirit has gone out of a person, it travels through waterless places seeking rest but finds none. Then it says, 'I will return to my house from which I came.' And coming, it finds it unoccupied, swept, and put in order. Then it goes and brings with it seven other spirits more evil [πονηρότερα] than itself, and they enter and dwell there, and the last state of that person is worse than the first. Thus, it will also be with this evil generation [τῇ γενεᾷ ταύτῃ τῇ πονηρᾷ].[60]

The connection between the γενεά of Jesus' opponents and the Devil and his "evil spirits"[61] is here made explicit. The implications are even more clear when one considers the broader context of the passage. Coming, as it does, at the end of the Beelzebul controversy the reversal of accusation is obvious: Jesus' opponents have accused him of being animated and empowered by the Devil, but through the course of verses 31–45 Jesus turns the tables on them, such that in the end, Jesus has argued that it is they who are possessed and acting contrary to the will of God because of their unwillingness to accept Jesus as God's authoritative messenger, filled with God's spirit. Their opposition is so deep-seated and inveterate that it invites equation with a family resemblance (γενεά), and the resemblance is not just among the members of the γενεά but between them and the entity that embodies opposition to God, that is, the Devil. They have, as it were, a family resemblance of evil, a resemblance rooted in the patriarch of their γενεά, the Devil. This metaphor reflects a deep ontological dualism comparable to the use of sons of light and sons of darkness (and connected epithets) in 1QS. This makes it the most internal of the metaphors of the cause of sin. Yet it is intimately related to the activity of the Devil and the concept of possession, thus to our last set of portrayals: that of diabolical activity as a cause of sin.

---

60   12:43–45.

61   The change from describing the spirit as ἀκάθαρτον to πονηρά certainly points to a range of πονηρία in which ἀκάθαρτον is not the worst. It is also important to note, however, that this is the only point in Matthew where having an unclean spirit has moral implications. Otherwise, unclean spirits and δαιμόνια are connected only with making people sick. Note esp. that in 10:1 giving the disciples authority over πνευμάτων ἀκαθάρτων means giving them the power to heal by casting the spirit out. In 12:22–24 it is a δαιμόνιον that makes the man blind and mute, but it is not he that is ultimately implicated in sinning but Jesus' critics. See also 9:33–34, 10:8, and 17:18.

4 Summary

Matthew utilizes a number of metaphors that portray sin as caused by a person's most basic nature. These metaphors include botanical (trees, tares, thorns, thistles) and animal imagery (wolves, vipers), as well as portrayals of those who sin as being part of an unrighteous "family," the family of the Devil. These metaphors manifest an obvious underlying ontological dualism congruent with the ontological dualism seen in the Second Temple literature.[62]

---

[62] As noted, the Animal Apocalypse of *1 Enoch* utilizes animal imagery, although there even the "sheep" are eventually led into sin because of blindness. In Jubilees, we see the attribution of sinfulness to genetics in the portrayal of Esau's inherent unrighteousness and the passing on of this to his "seed" and a similar situation with the descendants of Ham. As previously noted, the use of sonship language in the Qumran documents also utilizes a genetic metaphor but the idea of sinfulness as an inherent trait of some "lots" (1QM, 1QS) or even all people (1QH) also manifests an ontological dualism that sees sin as springing up from one's inner being.

CHAPTER 12

Satanic Activity as a Cause of Sin

In Matthew there are a number of instances where the activity of Satan or the Devil is indicated as the cause of people sinning or potentially doing so. His activity in causing sin includes simple temptation but also possession, both temporary and seemingly ongoing. The most holistic indication of his activity and the closest Matthew comes to an etiology of sin is in the Parable of the Wheat and Tares where the Devil is designated as the progenitor of the tares—those that are σκάνδαλα and who are τοὺς ποιοῦντας τὴν ἀνομίαν.

Given the use of familial and genetic language noted above it might seem that there is a clear distinction between those who are inherently disposed to do the will of the Devil (Jesus' opponents) and Jesus' followers who do God's will. Jesus' opponents are not the only ones influenced by Satan, however. Even Jesus' closest followers can apparently be tempted and eventually controlled or motivated by evil spiritual forces.

That this is a concern is evident in Jesus injunction after finding his disciples asleep in the Garden of Gethsemane: "Be alert and pray lest you enter into temptation; the spirit is willing but the flesh is feeble."[1] Although Jesus does not indicate what temptation might assault his disciples, in this crucial moment they are in danger of being tempted. The disciples' potential to be tempted is not, however, limited to this situation, as Jesus' instructions for how to pray indicate: "Pray like this: 'Father in heaven.... do not lead us into temptation,[2] but save us from the Evil one'" (Mt 6:9, 13).[3] Jesus' followers, even though they are not characterized as belonging to the γενεά of the Devil, are still subject to

---

1 26:41, my translation. "Feeble" here for ἀσθενής seems better suited to Matthew's usage than "weak" since it come closer to the idea of infirmity comparable to illness, a sense captured by its usual translation as "sick" in the four uses of ἀσθεν- in the Parable of the Sheep and the Goats and the use of ἀσθενοῦντας as a description of those who need healing in 10:8. Cf. the use of ἀσθένεια in 8:17.

2 Given the identification of Jesus' opponents with the Devil, the phrase μὴ εἰσενέγκης ἡμᾶς εἰς πειρασμόν in 6:13 may be as much a prayer from deliverance from the trials set forth by those who continue to oppose Jesus and his message (as it is carried on in the Matthean community) as it is a prayer for deliverance from the temptations to sin from the Evil One. In fact, since Jesus' opponents and the Devil are so closely identified in Matthew, it is feasible both possibilities are simultaneously in view.

3 Though the request to the Father that he "not lead us into temptation" raises much the same issues as the image of Jesus as a stumbling block, the immediate indication that the opposite of this is deliverance from the Evil one certainly makes is clear that Matthew does not

---

© KONINKLIJKE BRILL NV, LEIDEN, 2020 | DOI:10.1163/9789004419506_014

SATANIC ACTIVITY AS A CAUSE OF SIN

his temptations—his efforts to cause sin—a danger for which they must keep alert and pray for God's help to combat it.[4]

Of course, not only the disciples but Jesus himself is shown to be the object of the Devil's efforts (albeit unsuccessful) to cause sin. In Jesus' temptation in the wilderness, the Devil is not only called ὁ διάβολος (vv. 1, 5, 8, and 11) and Satan (v. 10) but also called "the tempter" (ὁ πειράζων, v. 3) as well. By this, the role of the Devil (Satan, the Evil One) as a tempter and thus a cause of sin is established early in the Gospel. The sins to which Satan tempts Jesus are sins of self-gratification (4:3–4), seeking of signs from God (4:5–7), and grasping earthly power and glory (4:8–10)—all sins for which Jesus indicts the Pharisees and scribes.[5] Jesus, of course, unlike his opponents, does not succumb to these temptations.

This is not Jesus' only situation of temptation, however. Matthew's repeated use of πειράζω for the confrontations between Jesus and his opponents[6] reinforces both the identification of the opponents with the Devil and, conversely, the sense that the Devil is active in trying to cause sin through temptation by using human agents. If the Gospel did not elsewhere connect these opponents with the Devil, one might argue that the alternate meaning of "testing"— something even God can do—was more in view. Given Matthew's consistent connection of Jesus' opponents with the Devil, however, this stands as yet another instance where Matthew reinforces the idea that the animating force behind their opposition is the Devil; they stand as a proxy for the Devil who continues to exert his role as Tempter through them.[7]

We can see, however, that disciples can also be used by the Devil in this way, as discussed above in our exploration of the use of the σκάνδαλον metaphor in Peter's Confession and the subsequent rebuke (16:16–23). There, Peter is successively under the influence of the Father in the revelation of Jesus as the

---

consider God to be the author of temptation. Temptation comes from the Evil One, though God can lead Jesus' disciples to places where the Evil One is actively tempting.

4 This obviously parallels the depiction of the activity of the Watchers and giants in the Enochic literature: the people, though not inherently evil, are tempted by the agents of evil and sin in their failure to resist.

5 Self-gratification: the charge of greed and self-indulgence in 23:25; seeking of signs: 12:38; grasping earthly power and glory: 23:5–12.

6 16:1, 19:3, 22:18, 22:35.

7 In some ways this is congruent with the depiction of the Gentiles in the Second Temple literature, particularly in Jubilees but elsewhere as well (e.g. 2 Baruch;). Interestingly, in the Qumran literature, particularly the War Scroll, although the Kittim are of the lot of Belial and so oppose God, they do not function significantly as agents to ensnare God's people in sin.

Christ[8] and the agency of Satan in Peter's opposition to the cross. In Jesus' rebuke, Peter is portrayed not simply as having inadvertently become a σκάνδαλον to Jesus, but rather, in putting before Jesus the temptation to avoid the suffering and death of the cross, Peter in this moment embodies the Tempter himself.[9] In this passage, the image of the σκάνδαλον serves again to portray the cause of sin as something external with respect to Jesus, but the identification of Peter with Satan serves to portray the cause of sin as simultaneously external (Satan) and something that arises from one's being—Peter's mind is portrayed as having become so opposed to God's purposes (οὐ φρονεῖς τὰ τοῦ θεοῦ) that he is entirely identified with Satan.[10] Thus, also in this passage, with regard to the cause of sin we see the conjunction of images and statements that point in different directions—the essentially external in the image of the σκάνδαλον with the highly internal identification of Peter with Satan—but there is certainly a diabolical element to all of these causes.[11]

This incident with Peter introduces a further observation: at points, the activity of Satan in producing sin is portrayed as not just tempting people to sin or even using humans to tempt others but as actually possessing them. As we noted above in our exploration of the use of genetic and familial metaphors for the cause of sin, the Pharisees and their various allies are often the object of

---

8   "Simon Peter replied, 'You are the Christ, the Son of the living God.' And Jesus answered him, 'Blessed are you, Simon, son of Jonah, for flesh and blood has not revealed this to you, but my Father who is in heaven'" (16:16–17).

9   "From that time Jesus began to show his disciples that he must go to Jerusalem and suffer many things from the elders and chief priests and scribes, and be killed, and on the third day be raised. And taking him aside, Peter began to rebuke him, saying, 'Far be it from you, Lord! This shall by no means happen to you.' But he turned and said to Peter, 'Get behind me, Satan! You are a σκάνδαλον to me, for you do not have in mind on the things of God, but the things of humans" (16:21–23).

10   Also as noted previously, Jesus' assessment that Peter has in mind τὰ τῶν ἀνθρώπων certainly casts these things in the light of inveterate opposition to God such that human thinking or at least human opposition to the suffering and abasement of the cross, is seemingly diabolical. (Cf. 20:25–28 ["But Jesus called them to him and said, 'You know that the rulers of the Gentiles lord it over them, and their great ones exercise authority over them. It shall not be so among you. But whoever would be great among you must be your servant, and whoever would be first among you must be your slave, even as the Son of Man came not to be served but to serve, and to give his life as a ransom for many'"] and the temptation in ch. 4 both of which portray the human concern for worldly power and greatness as being opposed to God's will and esp. in ch. 4, truly diabolical.)

11   While for Jesus the cause of sin remains potential, Peter's sin in tempting Jesus is actual. This dynamic—the one who tries to "trip up" or "ensnare" another himself becomes guilty of sin—we saw above in exploring those who in "scandalizing" the little ones sin themselves (18:6–7) and thus it would better if they drown in the depths of the ocean.

SATANIC ACTIVITY AS A CAUSE OF SIN

the application of these metaphors, with the result that these Jewish leaders[12] are portrayed as people evil or sinful in their very natures[13] and thus opposed to God. We also saw that the use of the adjective πονηρός creates a verbal link to the person of Satan and implies that those so described participate in his same character. Based on the overall depiction of the leaders, many scholars have seen Jesus' opponents as completely allied with the Devil and, essentially, possessed.[14] Though it may seem an overly-fine distinction to distinguish between depicting the opponents as possessed by the Devil and depicting them as generated and animated by him through use of genetic imagery—after all, in both cases the Devil is the cause behind their opposition—the underlying dualisms are not the same. In the latter case, as noted previously, the dualism is ontological (the opponents do the devil's will because it is their nature to do so) and in the former it is cosmic (the devil is a cosmic force opposed to God and people are caught up in the battle through siding with one or the other). We will, for the time being, preserve the distinction, although, as will become apparent, there is significant overlap.

The primary locus for the idea of the leaders as possessed is the Beelzebul controversy of ch. 12. We see in this passage that, through the series of charges and counter-charges that Jesus levels against his opponents (comprising 12:27–45), the charge of being in league with and in fact motivated by the Devil is reversed, and Jesus charges the Jewish leaders with being the ones animated by the power of the evil one. Let us then look more closely at this passage.

The controversy begins in 12:24 with the Pharisees' response to Jesus' exorcism of a demon causing blindness and muteness: "They said, 'It is only by

---

12   Many commentators using narrative critical approaches have noted that the Jewish leaders are a "composite character," that is, the religious leaders—including the Pharisees, scribes, chief priests, elders, etc.—can be considered a single character since Matthew does not discriminate among them very carefully. They are seen as essentially homogenous in their fundamental opposition to Jesus and in their "evilness." See, for example, Jack Dean Kingsbury, *Matthew as Story*, 17–18, 115; *idem*, "The Developing Conflict between Jesus and the Jewish Leaders in Matthew's Gospel: a Literary-Critical Study," CBQ 49 (1987): 57–73; Warren Carter, *Matthew: Storyteller, Interpreter, Evangelist* (Peabody, Mass.: Hendrickson Publishers, 1996), 202; Mark Allan Powell, "The Religious Leaders in Matthew: a Literary Critical Approach."

13   On "evilness" as the root trait of the leaders, see Kingsbury, *Matthew*, 19–24 and 115; Kingsbury, "Developing," 59–60; and Sjef van Tilborg, *The Jewish Leaders in Matthew*, especially Chapter Two, "PONHROI," pp. 26–45, and especially its section A: "Ponhroi as a Qualification of the Jewish Leaders," pp. 28–38.

14   Kingsbury, *Matthew*, 117: "Jesus' encounter with Satan likewise anticipates Jesus' later encounters with the leaders because Satan is the Evil One with whom they have affinity"; Graham Stanton, *A Gospel for a New People: Studies in Matthew* (Louisville: Westminster/John Knox Press, 1993): "The Pharisees and scribes are demon possessed."

Beelzebul, the prince of demons, that this man casts out demons.'" The situation is set up, however, in 11:17–21 by the narrator's use of Isaiah 42 to comment on Jesus' healing of multitudes. The quoted passage begins with "This was to fulfill what was spoken by the prophet Isaiah: 'Behold, my servant whom I have chosen, my beloved with whom my soul is well pleased. I will put my Spirit upon him, and he will proclaim justice to the Gentiles ...'" Matthew thus indicates what spirit is animating and empowering Jesus' healing ministry even before the controversy fully arises.[15] When Jesus perceives the charge against him, he first shows the illogic of it ("If Satan casts out Satan, he is divided against himself. How then will his kingdom stand?")[16] and then goes on to indict the Pharisees for opposing God through their opposition to him.[17] Then, as discussed previously, Jesus predicts the condemnation of his accusers on basis of their blasphemous assertion that the activity of the Holy Spirit in Jesus is actually the work of Satan.[18]

In 12:38–42,[19] the scribes join the Pharisees in asking for a sign from Jesus. Jesus' response further indicates condemnation for his opponents because of

---

15   The charge that Jesus heals by the power of Satan had already been leveled by the Pharisees in 9:32–34 in response to Jesus' healing exorcism of another mute man ("And the crowds marveled, saying, 'Never was anything like this seen in Israel.' But the Pharisees said, 'He casts out demons by the prince of demons'"), however, this situation does not develop into a controversy and thus seems simply to foreshadow the controversy to come and demonstrate that the issue was ongoing, not momentary.

16   12:26.

17   "If it is by the Spirit of God that I cast out demons, then the kingdom of God has come upon you.... Whoever is not with me is against me, and whoever does not gather with me scatters" (12:28–30).

18   "Therefore I tell you, every sin and blasphemy will be forgiven people, but the blasphemy against the Spirit will not be forgiven. And if one should speak a word against the Son of Man, it will be forgiven him, but if one should speak against the Holy Spirit, it will not be forgiven him, either in this age or in the age to come. Either make the tree good and its fruit good, or make the tree bad and its fruit bad, for the tree is known by its fruit. You offspring of vipers! How can you, being evil, speak what is good? For out of that which fills the heart, the mouth speaks. The good person out of her good treasure brings forth what is good; and the evil person out of her evil treasure brings forth what is evil. And I say to you that for every careless word people shall speak, they shall render account in the day of judgment. For by your words you shall be justified, and by your words you shall be condemned" (12:31–37).

19   "Then some of the scribes and Pharisees answered him, saying, 'Teacher, we wish to see a sign from you.' But he answered them, 'An evil and adulterous generation seeks for a sign, but no sign will be given to it except the sign of the prophet Jonah. For just as Jonah was three days and three nights in the belly of the great fish, so will the Son of Man be three days and three nights in the heart of the earth. The men of Nineveh will rise up at the judgment with this generation and condemn it, for they repented at the preaching of Jonah, and behold, something greater than Jonah is here. The queen of the South will rise up at the judgment with this generation and condemn it, for she came from the ends of

SATANIC ACTIVITY AS A CAUSE OF SIN   195

their obduracy; they are unwilling to accept Jesus and his message and thus to repent. Such a γενεά is evil and adulterous, as shown by their sign-seeking. Furthermore, Jesus then goes on to equate this γενεά to a person that is possessed:

> When the unclean spirit has gone out of a person, it travels through wa-
> terless places seeking rest but finds none. Then it says, 'I will return to my
> house from which I came.' And coming, it finds it unoccupied, swept, and
> put in order. Then it goes and brings with it seven other spirits more evil
> [πονηρότερα] than itself, and they enter and dwell there, and the last state
> of that person is worse than the first. Thus, it will also be with this evil
> generation [τῇ γενεᾷ ταύτῃ τῇ πονηρᾷ].

Here again, the connection between Jesus' opponents and evil spiritual forces is reinforced by the use of a form of πονηρός to describe both. And with this passage, Jesus completes the reversal of charge of possession: by their blasphemous charge that the Holy Spirit is not the agent in Jesus' ministry, by their seeking of signs, and by their refusal to accept Jesus and his message of the Kingdom and thus repent, his opponents demonstrate that it is they, and not Jesus, who are operating under the power of evil spiritual forces opposed to God.

To return to our primary issue then: if the Jewish leaders are in fact possessed, their sinning "does not come from man, but from the Evil One himself."[20] Jesus' opponents are not the actual agents of their own sin; the true agents are the malevolent spiritual forces that control them. This is certainly in line with the genetic and familial metaphors of for the cause of sin, particularly the idea that those who sin and cause do others to do so (σκάνδαλα and τοὺς ποιοῦντας τὴν ἀνομίαν, 13:41) are children of the evil one (13:39).

This, however, raises the question that was also relevant to our discussion of the use of the metaphors of blindness and deafness as applied to those who do not understand the parables[21] in 13:13–16; that is, to what extent are those who are seeming victims of this malady (blindness/deafness or possession) cooperative with or even actively pursuing the malady? In the passage in ch. 13, it became apparent that those who do not understand have

---

the earth to hear the wisdom of Solomon, and behold, something greater than Solomon is here'."

20   Van Tilborg, *The Jewish Leaders in Matthew*, 45.

21   While it is not clear that these are the same groups as Jesus' opponents, the two groups share enough similarities (rejection of Jesus' message of the Kingdom—and thus rejection of him in his role as God ordained messenger—and condemnation for it) that the analogy can be drawn between the passages.

willingly and purposefully "closed their eyes, lest they should see with their eyes and hear with their ears and understand with their heart and turn, and I would heal them."[22] It may be possible to apply the principle of this passage to the charge of possession in ch. 12: while it might seem that a condition like metaphorical spiritual blindness or possession would be something over which one would not have control,[23] Matthew indicates some level of consent or willingness for (even perhaps active participation in) acquiring the malady. In any case, Matthew is not disposed to split hairs regarding the relationship of agency to culpability. Those who oppose God and God's work in Jesus will be judged and condemned, whatever the ultimate source of their opposition.[24] For Matthew, the evil spirit that is animating and empowering Jesus' opponents is so deeply entwined with the character of the sinners as to be fundamental to their nature and thus not possible to disentangle from it. Yet, it is a force outside themselves, and in this sense the portrayal of sin as caused by possession bridges the two ends of the spectrum: as with the metaphor of the σκάνδαλον, the sin is caused by something outside the sinner (Satan or the evil spirit), yet as with genetic metaphors, this outside element has become so fused with the person as to be comparable to his nature and indistinguishable from his own will.

The clearest portrayal of the Devil as the progenitor of evil people is the Parable of the Wheat and the Tares in which the Devil is portrayed as causing sin is through his activity of "planting" his children in the cosmos. There are several key elements that bear investigation, some of which we have already touched upon. First, while this is, of course, a parable about the Kingdom (it begins, "Ὡμοιώθη ἡ βασιλεία τῶν οὐρανῶν ..."), it is also a parable about the source of sinners in the field of the κόσμος.[25] The initial question of the parable

---

22   13:15.

23   Note that in the interpretation of Parable of the Sower, the one whose heart is too hard to accept the word is portrayed simply as a victim of the work of Satan: "When anyone hears the word of the kingdom and does not understand it, the evil one comes and snatches away what has been sown in his heart. This is what was sown along the path."

24   Note 16:27: "For the Son of Man is going to come with his angels in the glory of his Father, and then he will repay each person according to what he has done." For Matthew, actions demonstrate character and are thus a criterion for judgment.

25   The use of this term certainly militates against understanding the theme of the parable to be the problem of the church as a *corpus mixtum*. The "field" is expressly identified as the world (κόσμος) in 13:38. The *corpus mixtum* interpretation can only arise if one equates the church with the Kingdom. As we have seen, however, Matthew often parabolically portrays the Kingdom as an eschatological in-gathering of all, after which the unrighteous are removed (cast into outer darkness, cast into the fire) while the righteous enter eternal life. Such a conception seems to be behind this parable as well, a situation that is hard to apply to the church prior to the eschaton, though Matthew certainly recognizes that there are issues with sin (Ch. 18) and pseudo-believers (7:21–23) in the church.

itself is that asked by the servants: "Master, did you not sow good seed in your field? How then does it have weeds?" (13:27). As with our previous examination of texts in the genetic category, the metaphor here is of types of organisms (in this case, plants) that either bear the appropriate fruit (ἐβλάστησεν ὁ χόρτος καὶ καρπὸν ἐποίησεν, v. 26) or do not. In this case, the "weeds," by not doing so, make manifest their nature.[26] Here, however, the source of the genetically bad organism (and the source of the καλὸν σπέρμα as well [v. 24]) is made clear, whereas in our previous passages the source was at most implied by the use of πονηρ-. Here, both the narrator (in v. 25) and the master of the house who sowed the good seeds (in v. 28) say explicitly that the presence of "weeds" is the work of an enemy, an enemy who is identified in vv. 38–39 as ὁ πονηρος and ὁ διάβολος. Furthermore, it is apparent that these "weeds" are not merely unfruitful, but are, in fact, perpetrators of sinful and unrighteous acts, as can be seen from the interpretation of the parable in 13:40–42: "Therefore, just as the weeds are gathered and burned with fire, so will it be at the completion of the age. The Son of Man will send his angels, and they will gather out of his kingdom all σκάνδαλα and τοὺς ποιοῦντας τὴν ἀνομίαν, and throw them into the furnace of fire." The σκάνδαλα and τοὺς ποιοῦντας τὴν ἀνομίαν are destined from the start for removal from the Kingdom because of their nature as "weeds," though it is only eventually manifest, and this nature is based on the one who planted them: "the weeds are the children of the evil one" (13:38). Conversely, "the good seed is the children of the Kingdom" (13:38), and these are also called "the righteous" who will "will shine like the sun in the kingdom of their Father" (13:43).[27] The genetic metaphors for the cause of sin here become melded with those of diabolical activity. Those who sin do so because it is their nature to do, but their nature, and indeed their very existence, is portrayed as the result of Satanic activity.

This parable then is Matthew's most straightforward statement regarding not only the cause of sin (genetic metaphor) but its ultimate source: Satan. In this respect, Matthew's parable bears some connection to the etiologies for sin that placed the blame for sin ultimately upon the angelic Watchers and their offspring the Giants. There are a number of parallels, in fact between the activity of the Watchers/Giants in the Enochic literature and the activity of Satan

---

26   "But when the plants sprouted and produced fruit, then the weeds became manifest" (ὅτε δὲ ἐβλάστησεν ὁ χόρτος καὶ καρπὸν ἐποίησεν, τότε ἐφάνη καὶ τὰ ζιζάνια, 13:26). The injunction not to uproot communicates two things: first that it is not the job of the servants to try to distinguish who is wheat and who are tares ("lest you gather up the tares, you pull up the wheat also with them"), and second that the servants must be patient, assured that God will judge and punish evil at the coming of the kingdom.

27   Interestingly, even though it seems from v. 43 that God is their father, it is not God who is depicted as sowing them into the world, but "the Son of Man" (v. 37).

in Matthew: both tempt humanity to sin, both utilize human thinking to cause sin (the Watchers by teaching illicit knowledge, the Devil by inspiring thoughts that are opposed to God), and both indicate that malevolent spiritual forces have generated offspring in the world who oppose God, do evil, and cause humans to sin.[28]

Still, the metaphorical character of the parable remains. In fact, it is in Jesus' interpretation of the parable that the parabolically metaphorical language of the initial parable becomes explicit metaphors. So, for example, at the beginning of the explanation we are told that the Son of Man sows the good seed, the field is the world, and the good seeds are the children of the kingdom. To arrange that into one complete statement, "The children of the kingdom are good seeds sown by the Son of Man into the field of the world." Even the explicit explanation remains metaphorical. To continue with the explanation, the statement that "the weeds are the children of the evil one, and the enemy that sowed them is the Devil," though it is certainly etiological, continues to be metaphorical: the "children" are metaphorical children not physical offspring, and they come into the world by being "sown" but obviously are not literally planted in the soil of the earth. This corroborates Ricoeur's observation that whenever we undertake to talk about an idea or give an explanation, especially for something theological or philosophical, we are immediately compelled to use metaphors. There is no non-metaphorical way to talk about things like sin and salvation, evil and the kingdom of God (itself a metaphor). Even in Matthew's clearest statement about the source of sin and evil in the world, there will be the yes/no tension of all metaphorical statements.

1   **Summary**

The activity of Satan through temptation, possession, and planting his children in the world forms a significant part of Matthew's depiction of the causes of sin. Given that the Parable of the Wheat and Tares offers the clearest etiology of sin in Matthew, it provides a significant key to understanding his other depictions, yet its parabolic character, even in its more allegorical interpreted form, contains metaphorical elements that resist literal reductionism.

---

28   There is certainly also, as noted before, a similarity of thinking between Matthew's perspective here and that found in the Qumran sectarian documents, most notably 1QS and its use of "sons of" language and the combination of ontological and metaphysical dualisms.

CHAPTER 13

Conclusion on Causes of Sin and Evil in the Gospel of Matthew

Matthew utilizes a wide range of metaphors in portraying the causes of sin and evil in human beings. Though it would seem a logical starting point, words of the ἁμαρτ- root prove surprisingly unhelpful in investigating Matthew's view of the causes of sin; the word seems to have lost the metaphorical force of its etymology of "missing the mark" and to have become a dead metaphor. In fact, if missing the mark carries some sense of inadvertence, Matthew's usage of ἁμαρτ- points in the opposite direction: words of this root are used in situations where sin is portrayed as intentional. Still, this does not necessarily tell us anything about the cause of sin. For portrayals of the cause, it was necessary to look to other, more metaphorical, statements.

In looking at the metaphors Matthew uses to portray the causes of sin, we saw that these metaphorical causes can be arranged on a spectrum from external to internal. One of the metaphors Matthew uses with regard to sin is the language of "straying" (πλανάω). Here, unlike with ἁμαρτ-, there is a definite sense that the sinning was unintentional. Oftentimes, however, there is no indication of the cause of straying. The exception is when a person is "led astray." In this case, the cause is external: the person does not intend to sin but another leads her or him in that direction. There is a dual dynamic here, however: it is not only the one who strays who is guilty of sin, but also the one who led her or him astray. A similar dynamic is present in Matthew's use of σκάνδαλ- words. The σκάνδαλον as a snare or stumbling block that trips one up certainly communicates a sense of external causation, yet in the verbal form to "scandalize" someone—to cause him or her to be tripped up or ensnared by sin—or to become a σκάνδαλον oneself is itself a sin with grave consequences (Mt 13: 41–42, 18:6–7).

The passages in which a body part is indicated as cause of sin represent a step toward depicting a more internal cause of sin. The portrayal of one's hand, eye, or foot as a cause of sin pits the sinning member over against the whole person; the cause of sin is internal, part of person him- or herself, but it is localized rather than pervasive, and the greater part of the person can recognize the part as sin-causing. Sin is thus depicted as that which splits the self and makes parts of us (those that cause sin) foreign objects to be repudiated and excised by the larger self.

© KONINKLIJKE BRILL NV, LEIDEN, 2020 | DOI:10.1163/9789004419506_015

A similar dynamic is present in the depiction of sin being caused by infirmity or illness. In the case of infirmity, metaphorical blindness and deafness cause people to reject Jesus' message of the kingdom and thus sin by pitting themselves against God and God's will. This infirmity, however, is depicted as willed by those who have it, thus, their sin is caused as much by their stubborn resistance to God's will as by any lack of ability. Such resistance is often related to the final body part metaphor, that of the heart. The heart is referred to several times as a cause of sin (12:34–37, 15:17–19), and while not inherently a cause of sin, it can tend in that direction. Because of the traditional use of the metaphor of the heart to represent one's will, emotions, intellect, and volition—indeed, one's whole "inner person"—the metaphor of the heart as a cause of sin forms a bridge between the body-part metaphors (the members that cause sin are part of the person but not his whole being) and metaphors that present sin as being caused by one's essential nature. These metaphors indicate the most internal cause. This cause is a person's essential nature, a nature portrayed through genetic and familial metaphors such as botanical and animal metaphors that point to a creature's species as the cause of its behavior or "fruit" and familial metaphors that indicate a likeness of kind within a particular "generation."

These metaphors of family likeness also form a bridge—this time from these metaphors of sin being caused by one's essential nature to Matthew's portrayal of sin as caused by the activity of the Devil. Matthew portrays the devil as tempting and using others to temp, such that they become σκάνδαλα, as possessing people, and ultimately, in the Parable of the Wheat and the Tares, portrays Satan as the one who "plants" his children in the world among the children of the kingdom. As the progenitor of those who sin and cause others to sin, Satan becomes ultimately the source of all sin. All other causes are perceived causes; the metaphors give expression to the experience of the cause of sin, whether it be one's hand or eye or a person who leads you astray. Yet while the perceived causes expressed metaphorically have their source in the activity of the devil, even his activity is expressed metaphorically within the parable, and thus the "yes-no/is-is not" dynamic resists resolution and makes a simplistic attribution of sin to diabolical agency untenable.

CHAPTER 14

Summary

The causes of sin and evil depicted in the Gospel of Matthew manifest several notable characteristics. First, in all the passages in Matthew that indicate a cause of human sin or evil, the cause is depicted by way of metaphor. Second, these metaphors exhibit a significant diversity, a diversity that spans a spectrum from those that indicate essentially external causes to those that indicate causes that are so internal to the human as to be portrayed as inherent to who the person is. Third, the closest Matthew comes to a clear etiology of sin is in identifying the Evil One as the ultimate source of sin in the Parable of the Wheat and the Tares, although in this depiction the metaphorical language militates against reduction to literal correspondence. Fourth, the spectrum of diversity of metaphors used to portray the cause of sin in Matthew is congruent with the diversity of images we saw used in the Second Temple literature examined in part 1 such that the overall depiction in Matthew is consonant with the depictions in his milieu.

© KONINKLIJKE BRILL NV, LEIDEN, 2020 | DOI:10.1163/9789004419506_016

Conclusion
The Significance of Metaphorical Dynamics in Portraying the Causes of Sin and Evil for the Theology of Matthew's Gospel

The significance of the previous goes beyond simply establishing that all the causes of sin and evil are portrayed metaphorically in the Gospel of Matthew and that the use of these metaphors did not differ significantly from the use and perspectives of the texts of its immediate milieu. While this is certainly true and not an unimportant point to establish, the significance of the study, when viewed in the context of the theological use of metaphor, has further implications.

The ubiquity of metaphor in portrayals of the cause of sin and evil in Matthew and the other texts discussed exemplifies an aspect of metaphor in theological discourse that metaphor theorists have already claimed to be fundamental: metaphors function both descriptively and heuristically and yet remain resistant to reduction or simplification to "literal" language.

Both Ricoeur and Soskice posit that for thinking theologically, metaphors are essential. As discussed in the introduction, Soskice delineates the difference between theory-constitutive metaphors and paramorphic models (which can be physical or linguistic, and if linguistic then metaphors). Matthew's metaphors for sin and evil function as both.[1] In both the sciences and in philosophy and theology, paramorphic models are heuristic rather than simply representative and comparative:

> The task of theory construction itself [through paramorphic models] is customarily the task of constructing models to explain better what we do not fully understand, rather than that of building models of states of affairs whose nature is clear to us. Rather than demonstrating clear parallels, the paramorphic model suggests candidates for similarity and gives form to deliberation on unfamiliar subject matters.... In science, social science, ethics, theology, indeed the whole realm of abstract theorising, it is the paramorphic models which are used in attempts to speak about the 'mysterious overplus'.[2]

Metaphors are how we conceptualize and communicate what we want to say about, for example, the cause of sin, and though each metaphor attempts to

---

1　Their significance as theory-constitutive metaphors will be discussed below.
2　Soskice, *Metaphor and Religious Language*, 103.

CONCLUSION

203

express some conception or existential experience of the cause of sin, all are approximations.[3] If one needed an explanation for the multiplicity of metaphors portraying the cause of sin in Matthew, this is where it lies: multiple experiences of sin and reflection upon these experiences yields multiple models (metaphors) to articulate that experience.[4] As noted above, however, the use of these metaphors functions not just descriptively but also heuristically: something is discovered in the use of the metaphor, both something positive and something negative. There is the positive experience of recognizing similarity—perhaps even similarity that was previously only vaguely grasped—and the negative experience of recognizing the inadequacies or limitations of the metaphor. This is the yes-and-no of metaphor. In the introduction we noted that all metaphors embody an "is" and an "is not," a "yes" and a "no"—this yes-and-no tension makes metaphors lively and evocative, pushing the reader to think about how the metaphor communicates something true but not altogether unproblematic. This yes-and-no tension of the metaphor also prevents any ultimate settling on one metaphor for definition.[5] Matthew's range and diversity of metaphors for the cause of sin reflects this indeterminate situation.

The portrayal of the devil as the ultimate source of sin seems on some levels to give determination to this undetermined state: though there may be many metaphorical expressions of the "causes" of sin, their ultimate source is simple and not ambivalent—the spiritual force that opposes God in all things. On the one hand we may see it as Matthew's assertion of the identity of the "no" of the other metaphors. That is (for example), does one's hand cause one to sin? Yes ... but also no: it is ultimately the Devil. Does one sin because it is one's basic nature? Yes ... but no, that nature comes ultimately from the Devil. Yet, this is not, in the end, enough to resolve the tension of the metaphorical statements. The assertion of the work of the Devil as the ultimate source is itself put forth in a parable, and parables are metaphors writ large, as Kelber explains:

---

3 As noted in the introduction (n. 11), the field of cognitive linguistics related to metaphor—particularly in the conceptualization and articulation of the experience of sin and its source(s) as we see them portrayed in Matthew—would be a welcome next step or expansion of the conversation. Hopefully this current work will catalyze such further investigation.

4 On experience and the role of community in articulating theological models, see Soskice, *Metaphor and Religious Language*, 149–151 and 158–159.

5 As Soskice notes, religious models are always qualified and "lead to absurdity if pushed too far," that is, if taken to be utterly representative of the thing of which they speak, since "*all* paramorphic models are qualified; if they were not, they would be, not models, but replicas of the modeled subject" (Soskice, *Metaphor and Religious Language*, 116).

> The message [of the parable] to be delivered in each case can barely be offered at all, and never in straightforward language. This is symptomatic for speaking in parables. Something is left unsaid, and it is this unsaid that matters most. Parables are more important for what they do not say than for what they say. There is an understanding, whether conscious or not, shared by parabolists that all does not submit to language. It is through the vehicle of the parabolic story that one seeks to gain a hearing for the as yet unexpressed and to break ground for the unheard-of. Transposition of parabolic meaning into propositional language, a congenital defect of much of parable scholarship in the past, is the last thing parables are capable of tolerating. The parabolic commitment is to emancipation from general principles and conventional wisdom into the hearing of a new voice. Parables as metaphors may arouse the sense of mystery over the unfathomable reservoir of language, or despair over the inadequacy of spoken words. But hard definitions and set formulations have long lost their purpose in parabolic talk. To give voice to what has yet not come to expression—that is paradoxical task fallen upon the speakers of parables.[6]

The Parable of the Wheat and Tares, far from solving the problem or answering the question of the cause or source of sin, invites the reader to wonder what it would mean for the Devil to "plant" *skandala* and "doers of lawlessness" in the cosmos, how a part of one's own body could be a "child of the evil one." While it may go too far to assert that the Evil One is metaphorical in the parable, the activity of the Evil One is portrayed metaphorically, and put in conjunction with the various causes indicated elsewhere in Matthew, the portrayal is both richly complex and perplexingly multifaceted. Attempts to simplify the picture in order to arrive at a single, non-metaphorical answer to the theological question of the cause (singular) of sin according to Matthew will be unrepresentative of the diversity of the text and untrue to the vital dynamics inherent in the original metaphors.

Further, for future work in Matthean theology, the portrayal of the causes of sin as pluriform and diverse has significant consequences. To return to the original motivating question of this study, the salvific work of Jesus (including the resurrection) will need to deal with these multiple manifestations of the cause of sin. If Jesus "will save his people from their sins," what sort of salvation will deal with all the various causes of sin and also the source, the Devil? Any proposed Matthean soteriology will need to be both multifaceted and holistic.

---

6 Kelber, *The Oral and Written Gospel*, 64.

CONCLUSION

Further, the recognition of these metaphors as theory-constitutive as well as paramorphic must also be explored. As was discussed briefly in the introduction, metaphors do not simply operate descriptively, they also organize our thinking about the subject of the metaphor. That is to say, as soon as a metaphor moves from an internal thought (potentially descriptive of an experience or impression) to an articulated utterance, it has the potential to act as a "lens" or "filter" or paradigm for how we understand that experience or impression.[7] The importance of this function vis-à-vis a canonical religious text should be quickly apparent: serious consideration needs to be taken of the impact of Matthew's metaphors on the way readers (especially those who take the text as holy scripture) understand their own experiences of sin. For practical theologians, pastors, and counselors, recognizing the theory-constitutive function of these metaphors—and recognizing the variety of metaphors available from the Gospel—presents an area for reflection and research into how these metaphors should best be incorporated into the preaching and pastoral practice of the community in order to engender both faithful and life-giving teaching and practice.

---

7   Indeed, one could argue that the moment one thinks a metaphor, it begins to organize our thoughts. If it does so well, we may hold on to it, if not, discard it in favor of a more adequate metaphor.

Bibliography

Allison, Dale. "The Eye is the Lamp of the Body (Matthew 6.22–23 = Luke 11.34–36)." *New Testament Studies* 33, no. 1 (Ja 1987): 61–83.

Allison, Dale. *The Sermon on the Mount: Inspiring the Moral Imagination.* Companions to the New Testament. New York: Crossroad, 1999.

Anderson, Gary A. *Sin: a History.* New Haven: Yale University Press, 2009.

Aristotle. *Poetics.* Loeb Classic Library 199. Cambridge: Harvard University Press, 1932.

Aristotle. *Rhetoric.* Loeb Classic Library 193. Cambridge: Harvard University Press, 1926.

Bacon, B.W. *Studies in Matthew.* New York: H. Holt and Company, 1930.

Barclay, John and Simon Gathercole, eds. *Divine and Human Agency in Paul and his Cultural Environment.* New York: T & T Clark, 2008.

Barclay, John M.G. *Jews in the Mediterranean Diaspora: From Alexander to Trajan (323 BCE–117 CE).* Edinburgh: T&T Clark, 1996.

Baumgarten, Albert I. *The Flourishing of Jewish Sects in the Maccabean Era: an Interpretation.* Leiden: Brill, 1997.

Beardsley, Monroe. "The Metaphorical Twist." *Philosophy and Phenomenological Research* 22, no. 3 (Mr 1962): 293–307.

Betz, Hans-Dieter. *The Sermon on the Mount: a Commentary on the Sermon on the Mount, Including the Sermon on the Plain (Matthew 5:3–7:27 and Luke 6:20–49).* Edited by Adela Yarbro Collins. Hermeneia. Minneapolis: Augsburg Fortress, 1995.

Bianchi, Ugo. "Dualism." Pages 506–507 of volume 4 in *The Encyclopedia of Religion.* Mircea Eliade, editor. 16 vols. New York: Macmillan Publishing, 1987.

Black, Max. *Models and Metaphors.* Ithaca: Cornell University Press, 1962.

Boccaccini, Gabriele. *Middle Judaism: Jewish Thought, 300 B.C.E. to 200 C.E.* Minneapolis: Fortress Press, 1991.

Brown, Raymond E. Introduction to 2 Esdras in volume 2 of *The Jerome Biblical Commentary.* Englewood Cliffs, N.J.: Prentice Hall, 1968.

Büchler, Adolf. *Studies in Sin and Atonement in the Rabbinic Literature of the First Century.* London, Oxford University Press, 1928.

Bultmann, Rudolph. *Theology of the New Testament.* 2 vols. New York: Charles Scribner's Sons, 1951.

Carter, Warren. *Matthew: Storyteller, Interpreter, Evangelist.* Peabody, Mass.: Hendrickson Publishers, 1996.

Charles R.H., editor. *The Apocrypha and Pseudepigrapha of the Old Testament in English: with Introduction and Critical and Explanatory Notes to the Several Books.* Oxford: Clarendon Press, 1913.

Charlesworth, James H. "A Critical Comparison of the Dualism in 1QS 3:13–4:26 and the 'Dualism' Contained in the Gospel of John." Pages 76–106 in *John and Qumran.* Edited by James Charlesworth. London: Geoffrey Chapman, 1972.

Charlesworth, James H. "Can We Discern the Composition Date of the Parables of Enoch?" Pages 450–468 in *Enoch and the Messiah Son of Man: Revisiting the Book of Parables*. Gabriele Boccaccini, editor. Grand Rapids/Cambridge, U.K.: Eerdmans, 2007.

Charlesworth, James H. "Forgiveness (Early Judaism)." *Anchor Bible Dictionary*. David Noel Freedman, editor-in-chief. 5 Vols. New York, N.Y.: Doubleday and Co., 1992.

Charlesworth, James H. ed. *Old Testament Pseudepigrapha*. 2 Vols. Garden City, N.Y.: Doubleday and Co., 1983–1985.

Charlesworth, James H. *The Good and Evil Serpent: How a Universal Symbol Became Christianized*. The Anchor Bible Reference Library. New Haven: Yale University Press, 2010.

Charlesworth, James H. *The Old Testament Pseudepigrapha and the New Testament*. Society for New Testament Studies Monograph Series 54 Cambridge; New York: Cambridge University Press, 1985.

Charlesworth, James H., ed., with F.M. Cross. *The Dead Sea Scrolls: Hebrew, Aramaic, and Greek texts with English Translations*. Princeton Theological Seminary Dead Sea Scrolls Project. 7 vols. Tübingen: J.C.B. Mohr (Paul Siebeck); Louisville: Westminster John Knox Press, 1994–2013.

Childs, Brevard S. *Memory and Tradition in Israel*. Studies in Biblical Theology. Second series 37. Naperville, Ill.,: A.R. Allenson /s.c.m. Press, 1962.

Coggins, Richard J. *Sirach*. Guides to Apocrypha and Pseudepigrapha. Sheffield, U.K.: Sheffield Academic Press, 1998.

Cohon, Samuel S. "Original Sin." *Hebrew Union College Annual*. 21 (1948): 275–330.

Collins, John J. "Wisdom, Apocalypticism, and Generic Compatibility." Pages 385–404 in *Seers, Sybils, and Sages in Hellenistic-Roman Judaism*. Leiden: Brill, 1997.

Collins, John J. "Wisdom, Apocalypticism, and the Dead Sea Scrolls." Pages 385–404 in *Seers, Sybils, and Sages in Hellenistic-Roman Judaism*. Leiden: Brill, 1997.

Collins, John J. *Between Athens and Jerusalem: Jewish Identity in the Hellenistic Diaspora*. Biblical Resources Series. Grand Rapids: Eerdmans, 2000.

Cook, Johann. "The Origin of the Tradition of the YSR HTWB and YSR HR." *Journal for the Study of Judaism in the Persian, Hellenistic, and Roman Periods*. 38 (2007): 86–87.

Cope, O. Lamar "'To the Close of the Age': the Role of Apocalyptic Thought in the Gospel of Matthew." Pages 113–124 in *Apocalyptic and the New Testament*. Sheffield, Eng: Journal for the Study of the Old Testament Press, 1989.

Cover, Robin. "Sin, Sinners (OT)." Pages 31–40 in vol. 4 of *Anchor Bible Dictionary*. David Noel Freedman, editor-in-chief. 6 vols. New York, N.Y.: Doubleday, 1992.

Crenshaw, James L. "Problem of Theodicy in Sirach: On Human Bondage." *Journal of Biblical Literature* 94, no. 1 (Mr 1975): 47–64.

Culpepper, R. Alan. *Anatomy of the Fourth Gospel: a Study in Literary Design*. Foundations and Facets: New Testament. Minneapolis: Fortress Press, 1983.

BIBLIOGRAPHY

Davies, Phillip R. "Dualism and Eschatology in the Qumran War Scroll." *Vetus Testamentum* 28, no. 1 (Ja 1978): 28–36.

Davies, Phillip R. "The Origin of Evil in Ancient Judaism," *Australian Biblical Review* 50 (2002): 43–54.

Davies, W.D. and Dale C. Allison. *A Critical and Exegetical Commentary on the Gospel According to Saint Matthew.* International Critical Commentary. 3 volumes. Edinburgh: T. & T. Clark, 1988–1997.

Davies, W.D. *Paul and Rabbinic Judaism: Some Rabbinic Elements in Pauline Theology.* London: S. P. C. K., 1958.

Davison, James E. "*Anomia* and the Question of an Antinomian Polemic in Matthew." *Journal of Biblical Literature* 104, no. 4 (De 1985): 617–635.

Derrida, Jacques. "White Mythology." F.C.T. Moore, translator. *New Literary History* 6, no. 1 (1974): 5–74.

Dodd, C.H. *The Parables of the Kingdom.* New York: Scribner, 1961.

Donaldson, Terence L. *Jesus on the Mountain: a study in Matthean theology.* Journal for the Study of the New Testament: Supplement Series 8. Sheffield: JSOT Press, 1985.

Donfried, Karl P. and Peter Richardson, editors. *Judaism and Christianity in Rome in the First Century.* Grand Rapids: Eerdmans, 1998.

Engberg-Pedersen, Troels, editor. *Paul Beyond the Judaism/Hellenism Divide.* Louisville: Westminster John Knox Press, 2001.

Gammie, John G. "Spatial and Ethical Dualism in Jewish Wisdom and Apocalyptic Literature." *Journal of Biblical Literature* 93, no. 3 (Sep 1974): 356–385.

Garland, David. *Reading Matthew: a Literary and Theological Commentary on the First Gospel.* New York: Crossroad, 1993.

Goatly, Andrew. *The Language of Metaphors.* London and New York: Routledge, 1997.

Goodwin, D.R. "On the Use of לֵב and Καρδία in the Old and New Testaments." *Journal of Biblical Literature* 1, no. 1 (Jun 1881): 67–68 and 70.

Gruen, Erich S. *Heritage and Hellenism: The Reinvention of Jewish Tradition.* Berkeley: University of California Press, 1998.

Grundmann, Walter. *Das Evangelium nach Matthäus.* Theologischer Handkommentar zum Neuen Testament. Berlin: Evangelische Verlagsanstalt, 1968.

Hagner, Donald A. "Apocalyptic Motifs in the Gospel of Matthew: Continuity and Discontinuity." *Horizons in Biblical Theology* 7, no. 2 (Dec. 1985): 53–82.

Hausman, Carl R. *Metaphor and Art: Interactionism and Reference in the Verbal and Non-Verbal Arts.* Cambridge, U.K.: Cambridge University Press, 1989.

Hengel, Martin and Roland Deines. "E.P. Sanders' 'Common Judaism', Jesus, and the Pharisees." *Journal of Theological Studies* 46 (April 1995): 1–70.

Johnson, Sherman E. "Biblical Quotations in Matthew." *Harvard Theological Review* 36, no. 2 (Ap 1943): 135–153.

Kaegi, Adolf. *A Short Grammar of Classical Greek.* London: Herder, 1936.

Keener, Craig. *The Gospel of Matthew: a Socio-Rhetorical Commentary.* Grand Rapids; Cambridge, UK: Eerdmans, 2009.

Kelber, Werner. *The Oral and the Written Gospel: the Hermeneutics of Speaking and Writing in the Synoptic Tradition, Mark, Paul, and Q.* Bloomington and Indianapolis: Indiana University Press, 1997.

Kingsbury, Jack Dean. "The Developing Conflict between Jesus and the Jewish Leaders in Matthew's Gospel: a Literary-Critical Study," *Catholic Biblical Quarterly* 49, no. 1 (1987): 57–73.

Kingsbury, Jack Dean. *Matthew as Story.* Philadelphia: Fortress Press, 1988.

Kingsbury, Jack Dean. *Matthew: Structure, Christology, Kingdom.* Philadelphia: Fortress Press, 1975.

Kittel, Gerhard, ed. *Theological Dictionary of the New Testament.* Geoffrey W. Bromiley, translator and editor. 10 volumes. Grand Rapids: Eerdmans, 1964–1976.

Klawans, Jonathan. "Josephus on Fate, Free Will, and Ancient Jewish Types of Compatibilism." *Numen* 56, no. 1 (2009): 44–90.

Klijn, A.F.J. Introduction to 2 Baruch in vol. 1 of *Old Testament Pseudepigrapha.* 2 vols. Garden City, N.Y.: Doubleday and Co., 1983–1985.

Knowles, Murray and Rosamund Moon. *Introducing Metaphor.* London: Routledge, 2006.

Kuhn, Karl Georg. "New Light on Temptation, Sin, and Flesh in the New Testament." Pages 94–113 in *The Scrolls and the New Testament.* Edited by Krister Stendahl with James H. Charlesworth. Christian Origins Library. New York: Crossroad, 1992.

Kupp, David D. *Matthew's Emmanuel: Divine Presence and God's People in the First Gospel.* Society for New Testament Studies Monograph Series 90. Cambridge; New York: Cambridge University Press, 1996.

Levison, John. "Is Eve to Blame? A Contextual Analysis of Sirach 24:25." *Catholic Biblical Quarterly* 47 (1985): 617–23.

Levison, John. *Portraits of Adam in Early Judaism: From Sirach to 2 Baruch.* Journal for the Study of the Pseudepigrapha: Supplement Series 1. Sheffield, U.K.: Sheffield academic Press, 1988.

Liddell, H.G., with Robert Scott, H. Stuart Jones, Roderick McKenzie, P.G.W. Glare, and A.A. Thompson. *Greek-English Lexicon.* New 9th edition, revised with supplement. Oxford: Clarendon Press, 1983.

Lieu, Judith, John North, and Tessa Rajak, eds. *The Jews among Pagans and Christian in the Roman Empire.* New York: Routledge, 1992.

Longenecker, Bruce. *2 Esdras.* Sheffield: Sheffield Academic Press, 1995.

Luomanen, Petri. *Entering the Kingdom of Heaven.* Wissenschaftliche Untersuchungen zum Neuen Testament. Second series 101. Tübingen: Mohr Siebeck, 1998.

Luz, Ulrich. *Matthew 1–7: a Commentary.* Hermeneia. Translated by James E. Crouch. Edited by Helmut Koester. Minneapolis: Fortress, 1989.

BIBLIOGRAPHY

Luz, Ulrich. *Matthew 21–28: a Commentary.* Hermeneia. Translated by James E. Crouch. Edited by Helmut Koester. Minneapolis: Fortress, 2005.

Luz, Ulrich. *Matthew 8–20: a Commentary.* Hermeneia. Translated by James E. Crouch. Edited by Helmut Koester. Minneapolis: Fortress, 2001.

Malina, Bruce J. "Some Observations on the Origin of Sin in Judaism and St. Paul." *Catholic Biblical Quarterly* 31, no. 1 (Ja 1969): 18–34.

Marshall, I. Howard. "'Sins' and 'Sin.'" *Bibliotheca Sacra* 159 (Ja-Mr 2002): 3–20.

Mason, Steve. *Flavius Josephus on the Pharisees: a Composition-critical Study.* Studia Post-Biblica 39. Leiden; New York: E.J. Brill, 1991.

Maston, Jason. *Divine and Human Agency in Second Temple Judaism and Paul.* Wissenschaftliche Untersuchungen zum Neuen Testament. Second series 297. Tübingen: Mohr Siebeck, 2010.

McFague, Sallie. *Metaphorical Theology: Models of God in Religious Language.* Philadelphia: Fortress Press, 1982.

McFague, Sallie. *Speaking in Parables: a Study in Metaphor and Theology.* London: SCM, 2002.

Meier, John P. "The Quest for the Historical Pharisee: A Review Essay on Ronald Deines, *Die Pharisäer.*" *Catholic Biblical Quarterly* 61, no. 4 (Oct. 1999): 713–23.

Mohrlang, Roger. *Matthew and Paul: a Comparison of Ethical Perspectives.* Society for New Testament Studies Monograph Series 48. Cambridge; London: Cambridge University Press, 1984.

Murphy, Fredrick James. *The Structure and Meaning of Second Baruch.* Society of Biblical Literature Dissertation Series 78. Atlanta, Ga.: Scholars Press, 1985.

Myers, Jacob M. *I and II Esdras.* Anchor Bible 42. Garden City, N.Y.: Doubleday, 1974.

Neuser, Jacob. *From Politics to Piety: the Emergence of Pharisaic Judaism.* New York: Ktav, 1979.

Newsom, Carol. "Apocalyptic Subjects: Social Construction of the Self in the Qumran Hodayot." *Journal for the Study of the Pseudepigrapha.* 12, no. 1 (Ap 2001): 3–33.

Nickelsburg George, and James VanderKam. *1 Enoch: a New Translation.* Minneapolis: Fortress Press, 2004.

Nickelsburg, George and Robert Kraft, eds. *Early Judaism and Its Modern Interpreters.* Second edition. The Bible and Its Modern Interpreters. Atlanta: Scholars Press, 1986.

Nickelsburg, George. "Enochic Wisdom and Its Relationship to the Mosaic Torah." Pages 81–94 in *The Early Enoch Literature.* Edited by Gabriele Boccaccini and John J. Collins. Supplements to the Journal for the Study of Judaism 121. Leiden; Boston: Brill, 2007.

Novakovic, Lidija. *Messiah, the healer of the sick: a study of Jesus as the Son of David in the Gospel of Matthew.* Wissenschaftliche Untersuchungen zum Neuen Testament. Second series 170. Tübingen: Mohr Siebeck, 2003.

Otzen, Benedikt. "Old Testament Wisdom Literature and Dualistic Thinking in Late Judaism." Pages 146–157 in *Congress Volume: Edinburgh 1974.* Supplements to Vetus Testmentum. Leiden: Brill, 1975.

Parry, Donald W. and Emmanuel Tov, eds. *The Dead Sea Scrolls Reader: Part 5: Poetical and Liturgical Texts.* Boston; Leiden: Koninklijke Brill, 2005.

Pennington, Jonathan T. "Dualism in Old Testament Cosmology: Weltbild and Weltanschauung." *Scandinavian Journal of the Old Testament* 18, no. 2 (2004): 260–277.

Perrin, Norman. *Jesus and the Language of the Kingdom: Symbol and Metaphor in New Testament Interpretation.* Philadelphia: Fortress Press, 1976.

Porúbčan, Štefan. *Sin in the Old Testament: a Soteriological Study.* Rome: Herder, 1963.

Powell, Mark Alan. "The Religious Leaders in Matthew: a Literary Critical Approach." Ph.D. dissertation: Union Theological Seminary in Virginia, 1988.

Przybylski, Benno. *Righteousness in Matthew and His World of Thought.* Society for New Testament Studies Monograph Series 41. Cambridge, U.K.: Cambridge University Press, 1980.

Reed, Annette Yoshiko. *Fallen Angels and the History of Judaism and Christianity: the Reception of Enochic Literature.* Cambridge, UK; Cambridge University Press, 2005.

Ricoeur, Paul. *The Rule of Metaphor: Multi-disciplinary Studies of the Creation and Meaning in Language.* Translated by R. Czerny. Toronto: University of Toronto Press, 1975.

Ricoeur, Paul. *The Symbolism of Evil.* New York: Harper & Row, 1967.

Röhser, Günter. *Metaphorik und Personifikation der Sünde: Antike Sündevorstellungen und Paulinische Hamartia.* Tübingen: J.C.B. Mohr, 1987.

Rosen-Zvi, Ishay. "Two Rabbinic Inclinations? Rethinking a Scholarly Dogma." *Journal for the Study of Judaism* 39, no. 4–5 (Nov 2008): 513–539.

Russell, Bertrand. *The Philosophy of Logical Atomism.* David Pears, editor. La Salle, Ill.: Open Court, 1985.

Saldarini, Anthony J. "Understanding Matthew's Vitriol." *Bible Review* 13, no. 2 (April 1997): 32–39, 45.

Sanders, E.P. *Paul and Palestinian Judaism: A Comparison of Patterns of Religion.* Philadelphia: Fortress Press, 1977.

Sanders, Jack T. "Wisdom, Theodicy, Death, and the Evolution of Intellectual Traditions." *Journal for the Study of Judaism* 36, no. 3 (2005): 263–277.

Sayers, Gwendolyn. *Have the Promises Failed?: a Literary Analysis of 2 Baruch.* Society of Biblical Literature Dissertation Series 72. Chico, Calif.: Scholars Press, 1984.

Schechter, Solomon. *Some Aspects of Rabbinic Theology.* New York: Macmillan, 1910.

Schnackenburg, Rudolph. *The Gospel of Matthew.* Translated by Robert R. Barr. Grand Rapids, Mich.: Eerdmans, 2002.

Segal, Michael. *The Book of Jubilees: Rewritten Bible, Redaction, Ideology, and Theology.* Supplements to the Journal for the Study of Judaism 117. Leiden, Boston: Brill, 2007.

BIBLIOGRAPHY

Sim, David C. *Apocalyptic Eschatology in the Gospel of Matthew*. Society for New Testament Studies Monograph Series 88. Cambridge: Cambridge University Press, 1996.

Skehan, Patrick W. and Alexander A. Di Lella. *The Wisdom of Ben Sira*. Anchor Bible 39. New York: Doubleday, 1987.

Skelton, David A. "Ben Sira's Imaginative Theodicy: Reflections on the Aaronide Priesthood Under Gentile Rule." *Restoration Quarterly* 51, no. 1 (2009): 1–12.

Smend, Rudolph. *Die Weisheit des Jesus Sirach erklärt*. Berlin: Reimer, 1906.

Smyth, H.W. *Greek Grammar*. Revised by Gordon M. Messing. Cambridge, Mass.: Harvard University Press, 1956.

Stanton, Graham. *A Gospel for a New People: Studies in Matthew*. Louisville: Westminster/ John Knox Press, 1993.

Steudel, Annette. "God and Belial." Pages 332–340 in *The Dead Sea Scrolls, Fifty Years After Their Discovery: Proceeding of the Jerusalem Congress, July 20–25, 1997*. Edited by Lawrence H. Schiffman, Emanuel Tov, and James VanderKam. Jerusalem: Israel Exploration Society, 2000.

Strecker, Georg. *The Sermon on the Mount: an Exegetical Commentary*. O.C. Dean, Jr., translator. Nashville: Abingdon, 1988.

Stuckenbruck, Loren T. "Giant Mythology and Demonology: from the Ancient Near East to the Dead Sea Scrolls." Pages 318–338 in *Die Dämonen/Demons: the Demonology of Israelite-Jewish and Early Christian Literature in Context of their Environment*. Tübingen: Mohr Siebeck, 2003.

Stuckenbruck, Loren T. "The Origin of Evil in Jewish Apocalyptic Tradition: the Interpretation of Genesis 6:1–4 in the Second and Third Centuries B.C.E." Pages 87–118 in *The Fall of Angels*. Edited by Christoph Auffarth and Loren T. Stuckenbruck. Themes in Biblical Narrative 6. Leiden; Boston: Brill, 2004.

Stuckenbruck, Loren T. *1 Enoch 91–108*. Commentaries on Early Jewish Literature. Berlin; New York: Walter de Gruyter, 2007.

Turbayne, Colin Murray. *The Myth of Metaphor*. New Haven: Yale University Press, 1962.

van Aarde, Andries. *God-With-Us: the Dominant Perspective in Matthew's Story, and Other Essays*. Pretoria: Periodical Section of the Nederduitsch Hervormde Kerk van Afrika, 1994.

van Tilborg, Sjef. *The Jewish Leaders in Matthew*. Leiden: Brill, 1972.

VanderKam, James C. "The Demons in the Book of Jubilees." Pages 339–364 in *Die Dämonen/Demons: the Demonology of Israelite-Jewish and Early Christian Literature in Context of their Environment*. Tübingen: Mohr Siebeck, 2003.

VanderKam, James C. *The Book of Jubilees*. Guides to Apocrypha and Pseudepigrapha. Sheffield: Sheffield Academic Press, 2001.

VanderKam, James C., ed. and trans. *The Book of Jubilees: a critical text*. Corpus scriptorum christianorum orientalium 511/*Scriptores Aethiopici* 88. Lovanii: Peeters, 1989.

VanGemeren, Willem A., general editor. *New International Dictionary of Old Testament Theology and Exegesis.* 5 vols. Grand Rapids, Mich.: Zondervan Pub. House, 1997.

Via, Dan Otto. *Self-Deception and Wholeness in Matthew and Paul.* Minneapolis: Fortress Press, 1990.

Watson, Wilfred, translator. *The Dead Sea Scrolls Translated: the Qumran Texts in English.* Florentino García Martínez, editor. Leiden; New York: E.J. Brill; Grand Rapids: Eerdmans, 1996.

Weinfeld, Moshe. "The Jewish Roots of Matthew's Vitriol." *Bible Review* 13, no. 5 (October 1997): 31.

West, David. Review of Murray Knowles and Rosamund Moon, *Introducing Metaphor. Language and Literature* 17, no. 2 (2008): 167–169.

Westerholm, Stephen. "Paul's Anthropological 'Pessimism' in its Jewish Context." Pages 71–98 in *Divine and Human Agency in Paul and his Cultural Environment.* Library of Early Christianity /Library of New Testament Studies 335. London; New York: T & T Clark, 2006.

Wheelwright, Philip. *Metaphor and Reality.* Bloomington: Indiana University Press, 1962.

Wheelwright, Philip. *The Burning Fountain.* Bloomington: Indiana University Press, 1968.

Wimsatt, W.K. and M. Beardsley. *The Verbal Icon: Studies in the Meaning of Poetry.* Lexington, Ky.: University of Kentucky Press, 1954.

Wright, Benjamin G. "*1 Enoch* and Ben Sira: Wisdom and Apocalypticism in Relationship." Pages 159–176 in *The Early Enochic Literature.* Journal for the Study of Judaism Supplement Series 121. Leiden; Boston: Brill, 2007.

Index of Ancient Texts

Bible and Apocrypha

Gen 2:7	78
Gen 3	182
Gen 3:15	182
Gen 49:17	182
Ex 3:4	182
Deut 8:15	182
Deut 28:58–61	148
2 Chr 30:18–20	149
Ps 57:4–6 (LXX)	183
Ps 58:3	185
Ps 139 (LXX)	183
Eccl 10:8	182
Eccl 10:11	182
Isa 1:5–6	151
Isa 6:9–10	150–152
Isa 7:14	115
Isa 9:2	145
Isa 14:28–29	182
Isa 29:13	167
Isa 42	158
Isa 53:4	151
Isa 65:25	182
Jer 3:22	149
Jer 26:22 (LXX)	182
Ezek 18	155n58
Hos 5:3–5	150
Hos 5:13	149
Hos 6:9–10	150
Hos 7:1	150
Hos 14:4	150
Amos 5:19	182
Sir 21:2	182
Sir 25:15	182

Gospel of Matthew

1:17	185
1:21	115, 116
3:5–6	114
3:10	130n52
4:1–11 (Temptation in the Wilderness)	127, 191
4:8–9	128
4:16	145
5:19	155
5:20	109, 115, 156
5:17–19	110
5:21–48	159n72
5:27	143
5:28	163n84, 165
5:29–30	137, 140–143, 146–147, 165
5:40	158n67
5:45	121n30, 153n48
6:9	190
6:13	190
6:19–33	147n30
6:19–21	146
6:22–23	145–147
6:24	146
6:25–34	146
6:25	33n17
7:1–2	158
7:5	158n68
7:15–20	123n34, 130n52
7:15	178
7:16–20	174–175
7:17–18	153n48
7:21–23	123n34, 175–176, 196n25
7:24–27	123n34, 162n83
8:5–13	160–161
8:10–12	187
8:12	145n25
8:13–17	152
8:17	151, 190n1
9:2–3	114
9:3	158n68
9:4–5	165n91, 166n92
9:10–13	114, 121n31, 148

Gospel of Matthew (cont.)

9:12	164
9:13	152
9:32–34	194n15
9:34	158n68, 188n61
10:1	188n61
10:8	188n61, 190n1
10:17–18	178
10:24–25	178
10:28	33n17
10:32–33	161
10:40	161n80
11:5–6	128, 128
11:12	174n5
11:16–19	186
11:27	161
12:1–14	110, 159n72
12:18–21	158
12:18	130n52, 159n71, 173n4
12:22–45 (Beelzebul Controversy)	193–194
12:22–32	130n52, 173n4
12:22–24	188n61
12:28–30	194
12:29	174n5
12:31–45	188
12:31–37	172–174, 184, 194
12:31–32	114, 130n52
12:31	166
12:33–37	130n52
12:38–42	185
12:33	169
12:34	184
12:34–36	167–169, 170
12:34–35	153n48
12:38	191n5
12:41–42	187
12:43–45	
12:49–50	162
13:3–23 (Parable of the Sower)	125
13:13–16	129n50, 195–196
13:14–15	163–163
13:19	164
13:37–43 (Parable of the Wheat and the Tares)	125, 127, 159, 176n10, 196–198, 204

13:39	195
13:41	153–154, 195
13:47–50 (Parable of the Net)	153, 159, 178–179
13:50	180
13:53–58	128
15:1–20	110, 159n72
15:4–5	167n96
15:7–9	167
15:10–14	129
15:13	170n110
15:17–19	166–167
15:17	170
15:27–29	118
16:2–4	186
16:16–23	191–192
16:16–17	192
16:17	126
16:21–22	128
16:23	126, 127
16:27	196n24
17:17	186
17:18	188n61
17:24–27	135
17:27	131
18:5–7	135
18:6–22	134
18:6–7	192n11
18:6	124
18:8–9	135, 137, 143, 146–147
18:10–14	135
18:12–13	178n20
18:15–17	121
18:21	121
18:35	163n84
19:3–9	110
19:16–22	160
19:17	160, 168
19:27–28	162
19:28	158n67
20:13	121n30, 145n25
22:1–9	161n79
22:15	159n73
22:23–33	159n74
22:34–40	110, 159–160
22:37	33n17

INDEX OF ANCIENT TEXTS

23 (Woes against the Scribes and Pharisees)	156–160, 183	Jn 9	148
23:3–4	156n63	Acts 2:23	154n51
23:5–12	156n62, 191n5		
23:5	156	1 Cor 9:21	154n51
23:13–29	156n63		
23:13–15	174n5	1 Th 5:23	33n17
23:13	157, 158n68		
23:15	157, 158n68		
23:16	157	**Non-Canonical Texts**	
23:23	156, 157, 158, 159, 160	1 Enoch	35–44, 60, 164, 189n62
23:25–27	167		
23:25	157, 158n68, 174n5, 191n5	1QM (War Scroll)	84–87, 189n62, 191n7
23:27	157	1QH (The Hodayot)	87–94, 189n62
23:28	176n11, 177n14	1QS (The Rule of the Community)	97–101, 188, 189n62, 198n28
23:29–36	174n5		
23:33	157, 177n14, 181, 184	2 Baruch	66–70, 191n7
24:2	154n52		
24:4–5	132	4 Ezra	60–65, 164
24:10	133		
24:11	132	Aristotle	
24:12	133	Poetics	6, 7
24:24	132	Rhetoric	6
24:34	185		
25:30	145n25		
25:31–46 (The Sheep and the Goats)	159, 180–181, 190n1	CD (The Damascus Document)	94–97
25:41	180		
26:28	114, 116	Enochic literature	35–59, 191n4
26:31–33	131		
26:41	144, 190	Jubilees	44–59, 60, 191n7
26:45	121n31		
26:61	154n52	Plato, *Republic*	33n17
27:4	122		
27:40	154n52	Qumran Texts	84–102
Lk 2:34	129	Sirach	71–83

Index of Subjects and Terms

Adam   62–65, 67–70, 72–3, 101

Blindness/deafness, sin as   *see* illness, infection, disability, or infirmity, sin as

Body parts as cause of sin   5, 80–83, 94, 100, 135, 137–147, 170

Devil/Evil One/Satan/Belial   1, 49n34, 85–87, 93–94, 95–97, 98–99, 126, 127–128, 168, 173, 174n5, 177n14, 187–188, 190–198, 204

Dualism   31–35, 74–77, 84–87, 88–89, 98–99, 112, 127n48

Evil/πονηρός/πονηρία   141–142, 153, 168, 173–174, 176, 179n26, 180, 183–188

Eye, Evil   141–142, 145–147

Faith   160–162

Forgiveness   114–115, 117, 122n33

Free will, human   41–42, 52–53, 64–65, 68–69, 77, 79–80, 96, 99–100, 122, 123n34

Genetic, sin as (*see also* "Sons/Children of" metaphor)   42–43, 57–58, 88–91, 97–101, 177–189

God's will   110, 112, 123, 123n34, 129, 130, 132, 145, 154n51, 162–163, 166, 190, 192, 196

Hamartia/ἁμαρτία/ἁμαρτάνω (Greek term)   113–123

Heart   42, 54–56, 58, 61–62, 67, 80–81, 94–96, 99–101, 112, 143, 165–171

Hypocrisy   142–143, 156–159, 167–168, 174, 178n16

Illness, infection, disability, or infirmity, sin as   40–44, 45–46, 62–63, 147–152, 195–196

Iniquity/ἀδικία/ἀδίκημα   117n15, 183

Integrity   140n7, 140n8, 142–146

Judgement, eschatological   61, 64, 111, 112, 125n41, 129, 143, 144, 145, 146, 154–159, 173, 174, 176–177, 179–180, 184, 196

Kingdom of God/Kingdom of Heaven   34, 110, 112, 153–163, 166, 168, 174n5, 176, 180, 183, 187, 196, 197, 198

Law/Torah   62–65, 109, 110–112, 154–160

Lawlessness/ανομία   110, 117n15, 125, 133, 154, 190, 197, 204

Love   111, 112

Lust   82, 140–142

Metaphor
   As mental event   4–5, 4n11
   As yes/no, "tensive"   13–18, 198, 200, 203
   Versus symbols   5

Parables, relation to metaphor (for specific parables, see Index of Ancient Texts)   21–22

Paul the Apostle   55n50, 107, 111

Pharisees   110, 112, 129–130, 156–159, 167–168, 174n5, 176–177, 178n19, 183–188

Righteous/Righteousness (including related Greek and Hebrew terms)   40, 92, 107–112, 153–163, 168, 179–180, 187, 197

Sermon on the Mount   111,

Septuagint   116, 116n11, 117, 118, 119, 124, 132

Sin
   definition of   113n1, 152–162
   personified   43–44

"Sons/Children of" metaphor (*see also* Genetic, sin as)   84–87, 89–91, 97–101, 190, 204

Soteriology/salvation   1, 61, 64, 107, 108, 115–116, 198, 204

Straying/πλανάω   40–44, 46–47, 94–96, 119–120, 121, 121n30, 132–136, 187

INDEX OF SUBJECTS AND TERMS

Stumbling block/σκάνδαλα/σκάνδαλον/
  σκανδαλίζω   82n40, 83, 93, 117, 123–136,
    146–147, 153, 183, 187, 190–192, 196, 204
  Gentiles as   50
  Jesus as   124n39, 128–132

Watchers and Giants   35, 36–41, 44–49,
    71–72, 94–95, 136n62, 191n4
  having power over humans   46–51, 53,
    197–198

yetser hara and *yetser hatov*   56, 78–79, 94,
    99

Printed in the United States
By Bookmasters